Prentice Hall
LITERATURE
Timeless Voices, Timeless Themes

Reader's Companion

SILVER LEVEL

Prentice
Hall

Upper Saddle River, New Jersey
Glenview, Illinois
Needham, Massachusetts

ISBN 0-13-062378-4

6 7 8 9 10   07 06 05 04 03

Acknowledgments

Grateful acknowledgment is made to the following for permission to reprint copyrighted material:

Arte Público Press
"Old Man" by Ricardo Sánchez from *Selected Poems* (Houston: Arte Publico Press-University of Houston, 1985). Reproduced by permission of the publisher, Arte Publico Press. "Baseball" by Lionel Garcia from *I Can Hear the Cowbells Ring* (Houston: Arte Publico Press - University of Houston, 1994).

Brandt & Hochman Literary Agents, Inc.
From *John Brown's Body* (originally titled "Invocation") by Stephen Vincent Benét from *John Brown's Body*. Copyright © 1927, 1928 by Stephen Vincent Benét. Copyright renewed 1954, 1955 by Rosemary Carr Benét.

Jonathan Clowes Ltd. on behalf of Andrea Plunket, Administrator of the Sir Arthur Conan Doyle Copyrights
The Adventure of the Speckled Band by Sir Arthur Conan Doyle. Copyright © 1996 Sir Arthur Conan Doyle Copyright Holders.

Don Congdon Associates, Inc., Literary Agents
"The Drummer Boy of Shiloh" by Ray Bradbury from *The Machineries of Joy*. Copyright © 1960 by Curtis Publishing Co., renewed 1988 by Ray Bradbury.

Farrar, Straus & Giroux, Inc.
"Charles" from *The Lottery* by Shirley Jackson. Copyright © 1948, 1949 by Shirley Jackson, and copyright renewed © 1976, 1977 by Laurence Hyman, Barry Hyman, Mrs. Sarah Webster and Mrs. Joanne Schnurer.

Farrar, Straus & Giroux, Inc.
"Animal Craftsmen" by Bruce Brooks from *Nature by Design*. © 1992 by the Educational Broadcasting Corporation and Bruce Brooks.

Gish Jen c/o Maxine Groffsky, Literary Agency
"The White Umbrella" by Gish Jen. Copyright © 1984 by Gish Jen. All rights reserved. First published in *The Yale Review*.

Harcourt, Inc.
Excerpts from *The People, Yes* by Carl Sandburg, copyright 1936 by Harcourt Brace & Company and renewed 1964 by Carl Sandburg. "Forest Fire" from *The Diary of Anais Nin 1947-1955*, Volume V, copyright © 1974 by Anais Nin.

HarperCollins Publishers, Inc.,
"Brown vs. Board of Education" from *Now Is Your Time: The African-American Struggle for Freedom* by Walter Dean Myers. Copyright © 1991 by Walter Dean Myers. "Why the Waves Have Whitecaps" from *Mules and Men* by Zora Neale Hurston. Copyright © 1935 by Zora Neale Hurston. Copyright renewed 1963 by John C. Hurston and Joel Hurston.

Harvard University Press
From "The Tell-Tale Heart" in *Collected Works of Edgar Allan Poe: Tales and Sketches 1843-1849*, edited by Thomas Olive Mabbott, pp. 789-798, Cambridge, Mass.: Harvard University Press. Copyright © 1978 by the President and Fellows of Harvard College.

Hill and Wang, a division of Farrar, Straus & Giroux
"Thank You M'am" from *Short Stories* by Langston Hughes, edited by Akiba Sullivan. Copyright © 1996 by Romana Bass and Arnold Rampersad.

Alfred A. Knopf Children's Books, a division of Random House, Inc.
"Pecos Bill: The Cyclone" from *Pecos Bill: Texas Cowpuncher* by Harold W. Felton, copyright © 1949 by Alfred A. Knopf, a division of Random House, Inc. Copyright renewed 1976 by Harold W. Felton.

Robert MacNeil
"The Trouble with Television" by Robert MacNeil, condensed from a speech, November 1984 at President Leadership Forum, SUNY. Copyright © 1985 Reader's Digest and Robert MacNeil.

Naomi Shihab Nye
"Hamadi" by Naomi Shihab Nye, copyright © 1993 by Naomi Shihab Nye. First published in *American Street*.

Pantheon Books, a division of Random House, Inc.
"Coyote Steals the Sun and Moon" from *American Indian Myths and Legends* edited by Richard Erdoes and Alfonso Ortiz, copyright © 1984 by Richard Erdoes and Alfonso Ortiz.

(Acknowledgments continue on page 272)

© Pearson Education, Inc.

Contents

Part 2: Selection Summaries With Alternative Reading Strategies

Unit 2: Meeting Challenges

Unit 3: Quest for Justice

Unit 4: From Sea to Shining Sea

Unit 5: Extraordinary Occurrences

Unit 6: Short Stories

Unit 7: Nonfiction

Unit 8: Drama

Unit 9: Poetry

Unit 10: The American Folk Tradition

Part 1

Selections With Interactive Reading Support and Practice

Part 1 is a companion for *Prentice Hall Literature: Timeless Voices, Timeless Themes*. It will guide and support you as you interact with the literature from *Prentice Hall Literature: Timeless Voices, Timeless Themes*.

- Start by looking at the **Prepare to Read** pages for the literature selection in *Prentice Hall Literature: Timeless Voices, Timeless Themes*.

- Review the **Literary Analysis** and **Reading Strategy** skills taught on those **Prepare to Read** pages. You will apply those skills as you use the *Reader's Companion*.

- Look at the art for the selection in *Prentice Hall Literature: Timeless Voices, Timeless Themes*.

- Now go to the Preview page in the *Reader's Companion*. Use the written and visual summaries of the selection to direct your reading.

- Then read the selection in the *Reader's Companion*.

- Respond to all the questions as you read. Write in the *Reader's Companion*—really! Circle things that interest you—underline things that puzzle you. Number ideas or events to help you keep track of them. Look for the **Mark the Text** logo for special help with active reading.

- Use the Reader's Response and Thinking About the Skill questions at the end of each selection to relate your reading to your own life.

Interacting With the Text

As you read, use the information and notes to guide you in interacting with the selection. The examples on these pages show you how to use the notes as a companion when you read. They will guide you in applying reading and literary skills and in thinking about the selection. When you read other texts, you can practice the thinking skills and strategies found here.

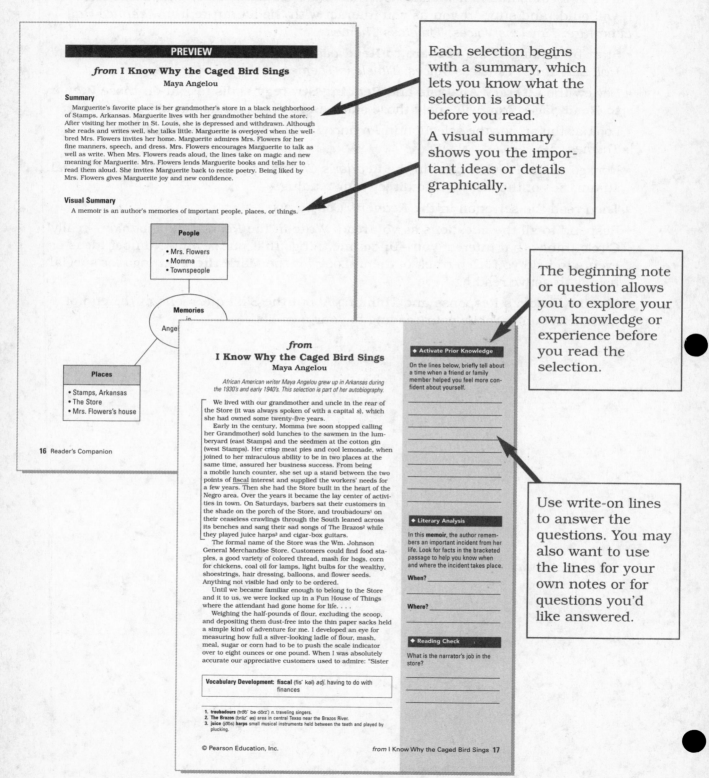

PREVIEW

from I Know Why the Caged Bird Sings
Maya Angelou

Summary

Marguerite's favorite place is her grandmother's store in a black neighborhood of Stamps, Arkansas. Marguerite lives with her grandmother behind the store. After visiting her mother in St. Louis, she is depressed and withdrawn. Although she reads and writes well, she talks little. Marguerite is overjoyed when the well-bred Mrs. Flowers invites her home. Marguerite admires Mrs. Flowers for her fine manners, speech, and dress. Mrs. Flowers encourages Marguerite to talk as well as write. When Mrs. Flowers reads aloud, the lines take on magic and new meaning for Marguerite. Mrs. Flowers lends Marguerite books and tells her to read them aloud. She invites Marguerite back to recite poetry. Being liked by Mrs. Flowers gives Marguerite joy and new confidence.

Visual Summary

A memoir is an author's memories of important people, places, or things.

People
- Mrs. Flowers
- Momma
- Townspeople

Memories
in
Angel

Places
- Stamps, Arkansas
- The Store
- Mrs. Flowers's house

16 Reader's Companion

Each selection begins with a summary, which lets you know what the selection is about before you read.

A visual summary shows you the important ideas or details graphically.

---

from I Know Why the Caged Bird Sings
Maya Angelou

African American writer Maya Angelou grew up in Arkansas during the 1930's and early 1940's. This selection is part of her autobiography.

We lived with our grandmother and uncle in the rear of the Store (it was always spoken of with a capital s), which she had owned some twenty-five years.

Early in the century, Momma (we soon stopped calling her Grandmother) sold lunches to the sawmen in the lumberyard (east Stamps) and the seedmen at the cotton gin (west Stamps). Her crisp meat pies and cool lemonade, when joined to her miraculous ability to be in two places at the same time, assured her business success. From being a mobile lunch counter, she set up a stand between the two points of <u>fiscal</u> interest and supplied the workers' needs for a few years. Then she had the Store built in the heart of the Negro area. Over the years it became the lay center of activities in town. On Saturdays, barbers sat their customers in the shade on the porch of the Store, and troubadours[1] on their ceaseless crawlings through the South leaned across its benches and sang their sad songs of The Brazos[2] while they played juice harps[3] and cigar-box guitars.

The formal name of the Store was the Wm. Johnson General Merchandise Store. Customers could find food staples, a good variety of colored thread, mash for hogs, corn for chickens, coal oil for lamps, light bulbs for the wealthy, shoestrings, hair dressing, balloons, and flower seeds. Anything not visible had only to be ordered.

Until we became familiar enough to belong to the Store and it to us, we were locked up in a Fun House of Things where the attendant had gone home for life. . . .

Weighing the half-pounds of flour, excluding the scoop, and depositing them dust-free into the thin paper sacks held a simple kind of adventure for me. I developed an eye for measuring how full a silver-looking ladle of flour, mash, meal, sugar or corn had to be to push the scale indicator over to eight ounces or one pound. When I was absolutely accurate our appreciative customers used to admire: "Sister

Vocabulary Development: fiscal (fis´ kəl) *adj.* having to do with finances

1. **troubadours** (trōō´ be dôrz´) *n.* traveling singers.
2. **The Brazos** (bräz´ əs) area in central Texas near the Brazos River.
3. **juice** (jōōs) **harps** small musical instruments held between the teeth and played by plucking.

© Pearson Education, Inc.   *from* I Know Why the Caged Bird Sings 17

◆ Activate Prior Knowledge

On the lines below, briefly tell about a time when a friend or family member helped you feel more confident about yourself.

_____

_____

_____

_____

_____

◆ Literary Analysis

In this **memoir**, the author remembers an important incident from her life. Look for facts in the bracketed passage to help you know when and where the incident takes place.

When? _____

_____

Where? _____

_____

◆ Reading Check

What is the narrator's job in the store?

_____

_____

_____

The beginning note or question allows you to explore your own knowledge or experience before you read the selection.

Use write-on lines to answer the questions. You may also want to use the lines for your own notes or for questions you'd like answered.

When you see this symbol, you should underline, circle, or mark the text as indicated.

◆ Literary Analysis

This **memoir** includes several **descriptive details** showing how Marguerite reacts to Mrs. Flowers. As you read the page, draw a box around details that indicate Marguerite's reactions. Then, based on these details, write a sentence below that tells how she feels about Mrs. Flowers.

_____

_____

_____

◆ Stop to Reflect

In what way does Angelou's use of **figurative language** "infuse" the descriptions in the memoir with "shades of deeper meaning"?

_____

_____

_____

◆ Reading Strategy

"Come and walk along with me, Marguerite." I couldn't have refused even if I wanted to. She pronounced my name so nicely. Or more correctly, she spoke each word with such clarity that I was certain a foreigner who didn't understand English could have understood her.

"Now no one is going to make you talk—possibly no one can. But bear in mind, language is man's way of communicating with his fellow man and it is language alone which separates him from the lower animals." That was a totally new idea to me, and I would need time to think about it.

"Your grandmother says you read a lot. Every chance you get. That's good, but not good enough. Words mean more than what is set down on paper. It takes the human voice to <u>infuse</u> them with the shades of deeper meaning."

I memorized the part about the human voice infusing words. It seemed so valid and poetic.

She said she was going to give me some books and that I not only must read them, I must read them aloud. She suggested that I try to make a sentence sound in as many different ways as possible.

"I'll accept no excuse if you return a book to me that has been badly handled." My imagination boggled at the punishment I would deserve if in fact I did abuse a book of Mrs. Flowers's. Death would be too kind and brief.

The odors in the house surprised me. Somehow I had never connected Mrs. Flowers with food or eating or any other common experience of common people. There must have been an outhouse, too, but my mind never recorded it. The sweet scent of vanilla had met us as she opened the door.

"I made tea cookies this morning. You see, I had planned to invite you for cookies and lemonade so we could have this little chat. The lemonade is in the icebox."

It followed that Mrs. Flowers would have ice on an ordinary day, when most families in our town bought ice late on Saturdays only a few times during the summer to be used in the wooden ice cream freezers.

She took the bags from me and disappeared through the kitchen door. I looked around the room that I had never in my wildest fantasies imagined I would see. Browned photographs leered or threatened from the walls and the white, freshly done curtains pushed against themselves and against the wind. I wanted to gobble up the room entire and take it to Bailey, who would help me analyze and enjoy it.

"Have a seat, Marguerite. Over there by the table." She carried a platter covered with a tea towel. Although she warned that she hadn't tried her hand at baking sweets for

Vocabulary Development: infuse (in fyoo̅z´) v. put into

◆ Literary Analysis

Based on the personal reactions the writer includes in this **memoir**, why do you think she ran, rather than walked, down the hill? Write your answer on the lines below.

_____

_____

_____

◆ Reading Check

Mrs. Flowers makes cookies for Marguerite and reads to her. What do these actions prove to Marguerite?

_____

_____

_____

years for the enchantment I so easily found in those gifts. The essence escapes but its aura[6] remains. To be allowed, no, invited, into the private lives of strangers, and to share their joys and fears, was a chance to exchange the Southern bitter wormwood[7] for a cup of mead with Beowulf[8] or a hot cup of tea and milk with Oliver Twist. When I said aloud, "It is a far far better thing that I do, than I have ever done . . ."[9] tears of love filled my eyes at my selflessness.

On that first day, I ran down the hill and into the road (few cars ever came along it) and had the good sense to stop running before I reached the Store.

I was liked, and what a difference it made. I was respected not as Mrs. Henderson's grandchild or Bailey's sister but for just being Marguerite Johnson.

Childhood's logic never asks to be proved (all conclusions are absolute). I didn't question why Mrs. Flowers had singled me out for attention, nor did it occur to me that Momma might have asked her to give me a little talking to. All I cared about was that she had made tea cookies for _me_ and read to _me_ from her favorite book. It was enough to prove that she liked me.

6. **aura** (ôr´ ə) n. atmosphere or quality.
7. **wormwood** (wʉrm´ wood´) n. plant that produces a bitter oil.
8. **Beowulf** (bā´ ə wool̇f) hero of an old Anglo-Saxon epic. People in this poem drink mead (mēd), a drink made with honey and water.
9. **"It is . . . than I have ever done"** speech from _A Tale of Two Cities_ by Charles Dickens.

Reader's Response: Does Mrs. Flowers remind you of anyone you know? Explain.

_____

_____

Thinking About the Skill: Explain how figurative language can make a story or memoir more interesting to read.

_____

_____

After reading, you can write your thoughts and reactions to the selection.

You can also comment on how certain skills and strategies were helpful to you. Thinking about a skill will help you apply it to other reading situations.

The Drummer Boy of Shiloh

Ray Bradbury

Summary

   During the Civil War, an army sleeps. The next day, a few thousand young boys will fight the battle of Shiloh. Except for Joby, age fourteen, all the soldiers have guns. Without even a shield to protect himself, Joby will carry only his drum. He is so worried about the danger that he breaks down in tears. Just then the general walks by and sees him weeping. The general stops beside Joby and tells him the soldiers are young and untrained. He explains that the drummer helps soldiers pull together as one army. The beat drives the soldiers forward, gives them courage. If the drum beats slowly, the soldiers move slowly. A steady, fast beat moves them faster. Now that he knows that his job is important, Joby waits with confidence and pride for morning.

Visual Summary

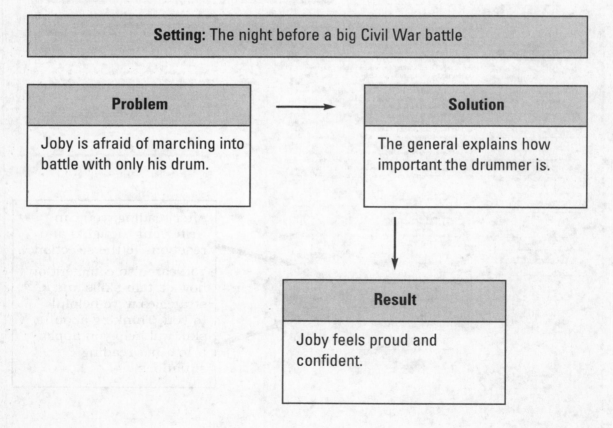

Setting: The night before a big Civil War battle

Problem	Solution
Joby is afraid of marching into battle with only his drum.	The general explains how important the drummer is.

Result

Joby feels proud and confident.

The Drummer Boy of Shiloh
Ray Bradbury

Imagine that you are preparing to fight in your first Civil War battle. What thoughts might go through your mind?

In the April night, more than once, blossoms fell from the orchard trees and lit with rustling taps on the drumskin. At midnight a peach stone left miraculously on a branch through winter, flicked by a bird, fell swift and unseen, struck once, like panic, which jerked the boy upright. In silence he listened to his own heart ruffle away, away—at last gone from his ears and back in his chest again.

After that, he turned the drum on its side, where its great lunar face peered at him whenever he opened his eyes.

His face, alert or at rest, was solemn. It was indeed a solemn time and a solemn night for a boy just turned fourteen in the peach field near the Owl Creek not far from the church at Shiloh.[1]

". . . thirty-one, thirty-two, thirty-three . . ."

Unable to see, he stopped counting.

Beyond the thirty-three familiar shadows, forty thousand men, exhausted by nervous expectation, unable to sleep for romantic dreams of battles yet unfought, lay crazily askew in their uniforms. A mile yet farther on, another army was strewn helter-skelter, turning slow, basting themselves[2] with the thought of what they would do when the time came: a leap, a yell, a blind plunge their strategy, raw youth their protection and benediction.

Now and again the boy heard a vast wind come up, that gently stirred the air. But he knew what it was—the army here, the army there, whispering to itself in the dark. Some men talking to others, others murmuring to themselves, and all so quiet it was like a natural element arisen from South or North with the motion of the earth toward dawn.

What the men whispered the boy could only guess, and he guessed that it was: "Me, I'm the one, I'm the one of all the rest who won't die. I'll live through it. I'll go home. The band will play. And I'll be there to hear it."

Yes, thought the boy, that's all very well for them, they can give as good as they get!

For with the careless bones of the young men harvested by

Vocabulary Development: benediction (ben´ ə dik´ shən) *n.*
blessing

---

1. **Shiloh** (shĭ´ lō) *n.* site of a Civil War battle in 1862; now a national military park in southwest Tennessee.
2. **basting themselves** here, letting their thoughts pour over them as they turn in their sleep.

◆ **Activate Prior Knowledge**

Write at least three things you know about the Civil War.

_____

_____

_____

_____

_____

_____

_____

_____

◆ **Reading Strategy**

Circle words in the bracketed paragraph that are **context clues** that suggest that *askew* means "lying in a crooked way."

◆ **Reading Check**

What are the boy and all of the other soldiers thinking about?

_____

_____

_____

_____

night and bindled[3] around campfires were the similarly strewn steel bones of their rifles, with bayonets fixed like eternal lightning lost in the orchard grass.

Me, thought the boy, I got only a drum, two sticks to beat it, and no shield.

There wasn't a man-boy on this ground tonight who did not have a shield he cast, <u>riveted</u> or carved himself on his way to his first attack, <u>compounded</u> of remote but nonetheless firm and fiery family devotion, flag-blown patriotism and cocksure immortality strengthened by the touchstone of very real gunpowder, ramrod, Minié ball[4] and flint. But without these last, the boy felt his family move yet farther off away in the dark, as if one of those great prairie-burning trains had chanted them away never to return—leaving him with this drum which was worse than a toy in the game to be played tomorrow or some day much too soon.

The boy turned on his side. A moth brushed his face, but it was peach blossom. A peach blossom flicked him, but it was a moth. Nothing stayed put. Nothing had a name. Nothing was as it once was.

If he lay very still, when the dawn came up and the soldiers put on their bravery with their caps, perhaps they might go away, the war with them, and not notice him lying small here, no more than a toy himself.

"Well, . . . now," said a voice.

The boy shut up his eyes, to hide inside himself, but it was too late. Someone, walking by in the night, stood over him.

"Well," said the voice quietly, "here's a soldier crying *before* the fight. Good. Get it over. Won't be time once it all starts."

And the voice was about to move on when the boy, startled, touched the drum at his elbow. The man above, hearing this, stopped. The boy could feel his eyes, sense him slowly bending near. A hand must have come down out of the night, for there was a little *rat-tat* as the fingernails brushed and the man's breath fanned his face.

"Why, it's the drummer boy, isn't it?"

The boy nodded, not knowing if his nod was seen. "Sir, is that *you*?" he said.

"I assume it is." The man's knees cracked as he bent still closer.

He smelled as all fathers should smell, of salt sweat,

Predict who the man standing above the boy is. Then, read ahead to see if you are right.

_____

_____

_____

Vocabulary Development: riveted (riv′ it əd) *adj.* fastened or made firm
compounded (käm pound′ ed) *adj.* mixed or combined

---

3. **bindled** (bin′ dəld) *adj.* bedded.
4. **Minié** (min′ ē) **ball** cone-shaped rifle bullet that expands when fired.

ginger tobacco, horse and boot leather, and the earth he walked upon. He had many eyes. No, not eyes—brass buttons that watched the boy.

He could only be, and was, the general.

"What's your name, boy?" he asked.

"Joby," whispered the boy, starting to sit up.

"All right, Joby, don't stir." A hand pressed his chest gently, and the boy relaxed. "How long you been with us, Joby?"

"Three weeks, sir."

"Run off from home or joined legitimately, boy?"

Silence.

". . . Fool question," said the general. "Do you shave yet, boy? Even more of a . . . fool. There's your cheek, fell right off the tree overhead. And the others here not much older. Raw, raw, the lot of you. You ready for tomorrow or the next day, Joby?"

"I think so, sir."

"You want to cry some more, go on ahead. I did the same last night."

"You, sir?"

"It's the truth. Thinking of everything ahead. Both sides figuring the other side will just give up, and soon, and the war done in weeks, and us all home. Well, that's not how it's going to be. And maybe that's why I cried."

"Yes, sir," said Joby.

The general must have taken out a cigar now, for the dark was suddenly filled with the smell of tobacco unlit as yet, but chewed as the man thought what next to say.

"It's going to be a crazy time," said the general. "Counting both sides, there's a hundred thousand men, give or take a few thousand out there tonight, not one as can spit a sparrow off a tree, or knows a horse clod from a Minié ball. Stand up, bare the breast, ask to be a target, thank them and sit down, that's us, that's them. We should turn tail and train four months, they should do the same. But here we are, taken with spring fever and thinking it blood lust, taking our sulfur with cannons instead of with molasses, as it should be, going to be a hero, going to live forever. And I can see all of them over there nodding agreement, save the other way around. It's wrong, boy, it's wrong as a head put on hindside front and a man marching backward through life. . . . More innocents will get shot out of pure . . . enthusiasm than ever got shot before. Owl Creek was full of boys splashing around in the noonday sun just a few hours ago. I fear it will be full of boys again, just floating, at sundown tomorrow, not caring where the tide takes them."

The general stopped and made a little pile of winter leaves and twigs in the darkness, as if he might at any moment strike fire to them to see his way through the coming days when the sun might not show its face because of what was happening here and just beyond.

◆ **Reading Strategy**

If, according to the **context** in the underlined sentence, the boy ran off from home instead of joining the army legitimately, what does *legitimately* probably mean? Write your guess, and then check the meaning with a dictionary.

_____

_____

_____

◆ **Reading Check**

Why did the general cry?

_____

_____

_____

_____

_____

◆ **Literary Analysis**

Underline details or expressions in the bracketed paragraph that show that the story is set in the past.

Mark the Text

◆ **Reading Check**

What does the general think may happen at Owl Creek tomorrow?

_____

_____

_____

_____

◆ **Reading Check**

What does the general know that
the rest of the soldiers don't know?

_____

_____

_____

_____

◆ **Reading Strategy**

Circle any words in the bracketed
passage that help you know that *lag*
means "move slowly"
or "dawdle."

◆ **Stop to Reflect**

In what way does thinking about
the **historical setting** of the story
help you understand what is going
on?

_____

_____

_____

_____

_____

_____

_____

_____

_____

The boy watched the hand stirring the leaves and opened
his lips to say something, but did not say it. The general
heard the boy's breath and spoke himself.

"Why am I telling you this? That's what you wanted to
ask, eh? Well, when you got a bunch of wild horses on a
loose rein somewhere, somehow you got to bring order, rein
them in. These lads, fresh out of the milkshed, don't know
what I know, and I can't tell them: men actually die, in war.
So each is his own army. I got to make *one* army of them.
And for that, boy, I need you."

"Me!" The boy's lips barely twitched.

"Now, boy," said the general quietly, "you are the heart of
the army. Think of that. You're the heart of the army. Listen,
now."

And, lying there, Joby listened. And the general spoke on.

If he, Joby, beat slow tomorrow, the heart would beat slow
in the men. They would <u>lag</u> by the wayside. They would
drowse in the fields on their muskets. They would sleep forever, after that, in those same fields—their hearts slowed by a
drummer boy and stopped by enemy lead.

But if he beat a sure, steady, ever faster rhythm, then,
then their knees would come up in a long line down over that
hill, one knee after the other, like a wave on the ocean shore!
Had he seen the ocean ever? Seen the waves rolling in like a
well-ordered cavalry charge to the sand? Well, that was it,
that's what he wanted, that's what was needed! Joby was his
right hand and his left. He gave the orders, but Joby set the
pace!

So bring the right knee up and the right foot out and the
left knee up and the left foot out. One following the other in
good time, in brisk time. Move the blood up the body and
make the head proud and the spine stiff and the jaw
<u>resolute</u>. Focus the eye and set the teeth, flare the nostrils
and tighten the hands, put steel armor all over the men, for
blood moving fast in them does indeed make men feel as if
they'd put on steel. He must keep at it, at it! Long and
steady, steady and long! Then, even though shot or torn,
those wounds got in hot blood—in blood he'd helped stir—
would feel less pain. If their blood was cold, it would be more
than slaughter, it would be murderous nightmare and pain
best not told and no one to guess.

The general spoke and stopped, letting his breath slack
off. Then, after a moment, he said, "So there you are, that's
it. Will you do that, boy? Do you know now you're general of
the army when the general's left behind?"

The boy nodded mutely.

"You'll run them through for me then, boy?"

Vocabulary Development: resolute (rez´ ə lo͞ot) *adj.* showing a firm
purpose; determined

"Yes, sir."

"Good. And, maybe, many nights from tonight, many years from now, when you're as old or far much older than me, when they ask you what you did in this awful time, you will tell them—one part humble and one part proud—'I was the drummer boy at the battle of Owl Creek,' or the Tennessee River, or maybe they'll just name it after the church there. 'I was the drummer boy at Shiloh.' Good grief, that has a beat and sound to it fitting for Mr. Longfellow. 'I was the drummer boy at Shiloh.' Who will ever hear those words and not know you, boy, or what you thought this night, or what you'll think tomorrow or the next day when we must get up on our legs and *move*!"

The general stood up. "Well, then. . . . Bless you, boy. Good night."

"Good night, sir." And tobacco, brass, boot polish, salt sweat and leather, the man moved away through the grass.

Joby lay for a moment, staring but unable to see where the man had gone. He swallowed. He wiped his eyes. He cleared his throat. He settled himself. Then, at last, very slowly and firmly, he turned the drum so that it faced up toward the sky.

He lay next to it, his arm around it, feeling the tremor, the touch, the muted thunder as, all the rest of the April night in the year 1862, near the Tennessee River, not far from the Owl Creek, very close to the church named Shiloh, the peach blossoms fell on the drum.

Charles

Shirley Jackson

Summary

After Laurie's first day of kindergarten, he is rude to his parents. He spills milk and uses bad language. Then he tells his parents the teacher spanked a classmate named Charles for being fresh. Each day, Laurie has a story about Charles. Charles hits, kicks, and uses bad language. He does not obey. When Charles must stay after school, Laurie stays with him and comes home late. After a few weeks, Laurie reports that Charles is behaving well and helping the teacher. When Laurie's mother goes to a parent-teacher meeting, she meets his teacher. The teacher says Laurie made trouble at first, but now he is a helper. Laurie's mother learns there is no Charles in the class.

Visual Summary

A surprise ending can provide a pleasant shock: like the A that you weren't expecting on a test or the birthday present you never thought you would get.

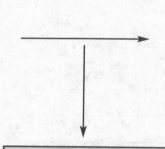

Set-up
Laurie gives daily reports to his parents on the strange doings of his classmate Charles.

What We Expect
Laurie's mother will go to meet with Laurie's teacher. She will learn more about Charles.

What Happens
The teacher tells Laurie's mother that there is no Charles in her class.

Charles
Shirley Jackson

The first days of kindergarten can pose surprises and worries for both a young child and his or her parents.

The day my son Laurie started kindergarten he renounced corduroy overalls with bibs and began wearing blue jeans with a belt; I watched him go off the first morning with the older girl next door, seeing clearly that an era of my life was ended, my sweet-voiced nursery-school tot replaced by a long-trousered, swaggering[1] character who forgot to stop at the corner and wave good-bye to me.

He came home the same way, the front door slamming open, his cap on the floor, and the voice suddenly become raucous[2] shouting, "Isn't anybody here?"

At lunch he spoke insolently to his father, spilled his baby sister's milk, and remarked that his teacher said we were not to take the name of the Lord in vain.

"How *was* school today?" I asked, elaborately casual.

"All right," he said.

"Did you learn anything?" his father asked.

Laurie regarded his father coldly. "I didn't learn nothing," he said.

"Anything," I said. "Didn't learn anything."

"The teacher spanked a boy, though," Laurie said, addressing his bread and butter. "For being fresh," he added, with his mouth full.

"What did he do?" I asked. "Who was it?"

Laurie thought. "It was Charles," he said. "He was fresh. The teacher spanked him and made him stand in a corner. He was awfully fresh."

"What did he do?" I asked again, but Laurie slid off his chair, took a cookie, and left, while his father was still saying, "See here, young man."

The next day Laurie remarked at lunch, as soon as he sat down, "Well, Charles was bad again today." He grinned enormously and said, "Today Charles hit the teacher."

"Good heavens," I said, mindful of the Lord's name, "I suppose he got spanked again?"

"He sure did," Laurie said. "Look up," he said to his father.

"What?" his father said, looking up.

> **Vocabulary Development: renounced** (ri nounst´) *v.* gave up
> **insolently** (in´ sə lənt lē) *adv.* boldly disrespectful in speech or behavior

---

1. **swaggering** (swag´ ər iŋ) *v.* strutting; walking with a bold step.
2. **raucous** (rô´ kəs) *adj.* harsh, rough-sounding.

◆ **Activate Prior Knowledge**

Briefly describe how you felt or acted on your first day of kindergarten or elementary school.

_____

_____

_____

_____

◆ **Literary Analysis**

Who is the narrator who is telling the story from a first-person ("I") **point of view?**

_____

_____

_____

◆ **Reading Check**

List two ways that Charles was bad during the first days of school.

1. _____

_____

_____

2. _____

_____

_____

Circle the two words in the under-lined sentence that contain the same **word origin**—the Latin root *priv*, which means "separate" or "special."

Mark the Text

How do Laurie's parents react to his stories about Charles?

_____

_____

_____

_____

_____

_____

Does the person telling the story from a first-person **point of view** know all of the facts about Charles? Why or why not?

_____

_____

_____

_____

_____

_____

_____

"Look down," Laurie said. "Look at my thumb. Gee, you're dumb." He began to laugh insanely.

"Why did Charles hit the teacher?" I asked quickly.

"Because she tried to make him color with red crayons," Laurie said. "Charles wanted to color with green crayons so he hit the teacher and she spanked him and said nobody play with Charles but everybody did."

The third day—it was Wednesday of the first week—Charles bounced a see-saw on to the head of a little girl and made her bleed, and the teacher made him stay inside all during recess. Thursday Charles had to stand in a corner during story-time because he kept pounding his feet on the floor. Friday Charles was deprived of blackboard privileges because he threw chalk.

On Saturday I remarked to my husband, "Do you think kindergarten is too unsettling for Laurie? All this toughness, and bad grammar, and this Charles boy sounds like such a bad influence."

"It'll be all right," my husband said reassuringly. "Bound to be people like Charles in the world. Might as well meet them now as later."

On Monday Laurie came home late, full of news. "Charles," he shouted as he came up the hill; I was waiting anxiously on the front steps. "Charles," Laurie yelled all the way up the hill, "Charles was bad again."

"Come right in," I said, as soon as he came close enough. "Lunch is waiting."

"You know what Charles did?" he demanded, following me through the door. "Charles yelled so in school they sent a boy in from first grade to tell the teacher she had to make Charles keep quiet, and so Charles had to stay after school. And so all the children stayed to watch him."

"What did he do?" I asked.

"He just sat there," Laurie said, climbing into his chair at the table. "Hi, Pop, y'old dust mop."

"Charles had to stay after school today," I told my husband. "Everyone stayed with him."

"What does this Charles look like?" my husband asked Laurie. "What's his other name?"

"He's bigger than me," Laurie said. "And he doesn't have any rubbers and he doesn't ever wear a jacket."

Monday night was the first Parent-Teachers meeting, and only the fact that the baby had a cold kept me from going; I wanted passionately to meet Charles's mother. On Tuesday Laurie remarked suddenly, "Our teacher had a friend come to see her in school today."

"Charles's mother?" my husband and I asked simultaneously.

Vocabulary Development: simultaneously (sī′ məl tā′ nē əs lē) *adv.*
at the same time

"Naaah," Laurie said scornfully. "It was a man who came and made us do exercises, we had to touch our toes. Look." He climbed down from his chair and squatted down and touched his toes. "Like this," he said. He got solemnly back into his chair and said, picking up his fork, "Charles didn't even *do* exercises."

"That's fine," I said heartily. "Didn't Charles want to do exercises?"

"Naaah," Laurie said. "Charles was so fresh to the teacher's friend he wasn't *let* do exercises."

"Fresh again?" I said.

"He kicked the teacher's friend," Laurie said. "The teacher's friend told Charles to touch his toes like I just did and Charles kicked him."

"What are they going to do about Charles, do you suppose?" Laurie's father asked him.

Laurie shrugged elaborately. "Throw him out of school, I guess," he said.

Wednesday and Thursday were routine; Charles yelled during story hour and hit a boy in the stomach and made him cry. On Friday Charles stayed after school again and so did all the other children.

With the third week of kindergarten Charles was an institution in our family; the baby was being a Charles when she cried all afternoon; Laurie did a Charles when he filled his wagon full of mud and pulled it through the kitchen; even my husband, when he caught his elbow in the telephone cord and pulled the telephone, ashtray, and a bowl of flowers off the table, said, after the first minute, "Looks like Charles."

During the third and fourth weeks it looked like a reformation in Charles; Laurie reported grimly at lunch on Thursday of the third week, "Charles was so good today the teacher gave him an apple."

"What?" I said, and my husband added warily, "You mean Charles?"

"Charles," Laurie said. "He gave the crayons around and he picked up the books afterward and the teacher said he was her helper."

"What happened?" I asked incredulously.

"He was her helper, that's all," Laurie said, and shrugged.

"Can this be true, about Charles?" I asked my husband that night. "Can something like this happen?"

"Wait and see," my husband said cynically.[3] "When you've got a Charles to deal with, this may mean he's only plotting."

Vocabulary Development: incredulously (in krej´ ᴏᴏ ləs lē) *adv.* with doubt or disbelief

3. **cynically** (sin´ i klē) *adv.* with disbelief as to the sincerity of people's intentions or actions.

◆ **Reading Strategy**

What word can you see inside *elaborately* that helps you know that it means "with great effort"?

_____

_____

_____

◆ **Literary Analysis**

Mark the Text

In the bracketed passage, circle the first-person pronouns and underline the third-person pronouns. Then, answer the questions below:

1. Who is the "I" narrating the passage?

_____

2. Who is the "he" being spoken about in the passage?

_____

3. Who else's words are related by the narrator?

_____

◆ **Reading Check**

How does Laurie seem to feel about Charles's "reformation"? How do you know?

_____

_____

_____

_____

_____

_____

_____

_____

_____

_____

_____

_____

_____

_____

_____

He seemed to be wrong. For over a week Charles was the teacher's helper; each day he handed things out and he picked things up; no one had to stay after school.

"The PTA meeting's next week again," I told my husband one evening. "I'm going to find Charles's mother there."

"Ask her what happened to Charles," my husband said. "I'd like to know."

"I'd like to know myself," I said.

On Friday of that week things were back to normal. "You know what Charles did today?" Laurie demanded at the lunch table, in a voice slightly awed. "He told a little girl to say a word and she said it and the teacher washed her mouth out with soap and Charles laughed."

"What word?" his father asked unwisely, and Laurie said, "I'll have to whisper it to you, it's so bad." He got down off his chair and went around to his father. His father bent his head down and Laurie whispered joyfully. His father's eyes widened.

"Did Charles tell the little girl to say *that*?" he asked respectfully.

"She said it *twice*," Laurie said. "Charles told her to say it *twice*."

"What happened to Charles?" my husband asked.

"Nothing," Laurie said. "He was passing out the crayons."

Monday morning Charles abandoned the little girl and said the evil word himself three or four times, getting his mouth washed out with soap each time. He also threw chalk.

My husband came to the door with me that evening as I set out for the PTA meeting. "Invite her over for a cup of tea after the meeting," he said. "I want to get a look at her."

"If only she's there," I said prayerfully.

"She'll be there," my husband said. I don't see how they could hold a PTA meeting without Charles's mother."

At the meeting I sat restlessly, scanning each comfortable matronly face, trying to determine which one hid the secret of Charles. None of them looked to me haggard enough. No one stood up in the meeting and apologized for the way her son had been acting. No one mentioned Charles.

After the meeting I identified and sought out Laurie's kindergarten teacher. She had a plate with a cup of tea and a piece of chocolate cake; I had a plate with a cup of tea and a piece of marshmallow cake. We maneuvered[4] up to one another cautiously, and smiled.

---

4. **maneuvered** (mə nōō´ vərd) *v.* moved in a planned way.

"I've been so anxious to meet you," I said. "I'm Laurie's mother."

"We're all so interested in Laurie," she said.

"Well, he certainly likes kindergarten," I said. "He talks about it all the time."

"We had a little trouble adjusting, the first week or so," she said primly, "but now he's a fine little helper. With occasional lapses, of course."

"Laurie usually adjusts very quickly," I said. "I suppose this time it's Charles's influence."

"Charles?"

"Yes," I said, laughing, "you must have your hands full in that kindergarten, with Charles."

"Charles?" she said. "We don't have any Charles in the kindergarten."

Reader's Response: Did it surprise you to learn that Laurie and Charles were the same person? Why or why not?

_____

_____

_____

_____

Thinking About the Skill: How can looking for a root word inside an unfamiliar word help you figure out its meaning?

_____

_____

_____

© Pearson Education, Inc.

◆ **Stop to Reflect**

Do you think the ending would be different if the story were told in first person through Laurie's eyes? Explain.

_____

_____

_____

_____

_____

_____

_____

from I Know Why the Caged Bird Sings

Maya Angelou

Summary

Marguerite's favorite place is her grandmother's store in a black neighborhood of Stamps, Arkansas. Marguerite lives with her grandmother behind the store. After visiting her mother in St. Louis, she is depressed and withdrawn. Although she reads and writes well, she talks little. Marguerite is overjoyed when the well-bred Mrs. Flowers invites her home. Marguerite admires Mrs. Flowers for her fine manners, speech, and dress. Mrs. Flowers encourages Marguerite to talk as well as write. When Mrs. Flowers reads aloud, the lines take on magic and new meaning for Marguerite. Mrs. Flowers lends Marguerite books and tells her to read them aloud. She invites Marguerite back to recite poetry. Being liked by Mrs. Flowers gives Marguerite joy and new confidence.

Visual Summary

A memoir is an author's memories of important people, places, or things.

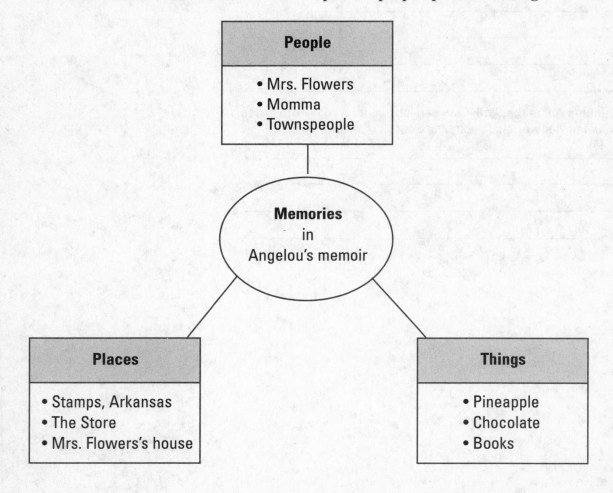

from
I Know Why the Caged Bird Sings
Maya Angelou

African American writer Maya Angelou grew up in Arkansas during the 1930's and early 1940's. This selection is part of her autobiography.

We lived with our grandmother and uncle in the rear of the Store (it was always spoken of with a capital *s*), which she had owned some twenty-five years.

Early in the century, Momma (we soon stopped calling her Grandmother) sold lunches to the sawmen in the lumberyard (east Stamps) and the seedmen at the cotton gin (west Stamps). Her crisp meat pies and cool lemonade, when joined to her miraculous ability to be in two places at the same time, assured her business success. From being a mobile lunch counter, she set up a stand between the two points of <u>fiscal</u> interest and supplied the workers' needs for a few years. Then she had the Store built in the heart of the Negro area. Over the years it became the lay center of activities in town. On Saturdays, barbers sat their customers in the shade on the porch of the Store, and troubadours[1] on their ceaseless crawlings through the South leaned across its benches and sang their sad songs of The Brazos[2] while they played juice harps[3] and cigar-box guitars.

The formal name of the Store was the Wm. Johnson General Merchandise Store. Customers could find food staples, a good variety of colored thread, mash for hogs, corn for chickens, coal oil for lamps, light bulbs for the wealthy, shoestrings, hair dressing, balloons, and flower seeds. Anything not visible had only to be ordered.

Until we became familiar enough to belong to the Store and it to us, we were locked up in a Fun House of Things where the attendant had gone home for life. . . .

Weighing the half-pounds of flour, excluding the scoop, and depositing them dust-free into the thin paper sacks held a simple kind of adventure for me. I developed an eye for measuring how full a silver-looking ladle of flour, mash, meal, sugar or corn had to be to push the scale indicator over to eight ounces or one pound. When I was absolutely accurate our appreciative customers used to admire: "Sister

---

Vocabulary Development: fiscal (fis´ kəl) *adj.* having to do with finances

---

1. **troubadours** (trōō´ bə dôrz´) *n.* traveling singers.
2. **The Brazos** (bräz´ əs) area in central Texas near the Brazos River.
3. **juice** (jōōs) **harps** small musical instruments held between the teeth and played by plucking.

◆ **Activate Prior Knowledge**

On the lines below, briefly tell about a time when a friend or family member helped you feel more confident about yourself.

_____

_____

_____

_____

_____

_____

_____

◆ **Literary Analysis**

In this **memoir**, the author remembers an important incident from her life. Look for facts in the bracketed passage to help you know when and where the incident takes place.

When? _____

_____

Where? _____

_____

◆ **Reading Check**

What is the narrator's job in the store?

_____

_____

_____

_____

_____

_____

_____

In the bracketed passage, the narrator describes the Store by using **figurative language**—expressions in which words are used out of their ordinary way to express vivid or imaginative ideas. Underline a phrase in the paragraph that compares the Store to something else. Underline another phrase that gives the Store a human quality.

Mark the Text!

In the underlined sentence below, the narrator says she met a lady who threw her a "lifeline." What is a lifeline?

_____

_____

What idea is Angelou trying to communicate with this expression?

_____

_____

_____

Henderson sure got some smart grandchildrens." If I was off in the Store's favor, the eagle-eyed women would say, "Put some more in that sack, child. Don't you try to make your profit offa me."

Then I would quietly but persistently punish myself. For every bad judgment, the fine was no silver-wrapped kisses, the sweet chocolate drops that I loved more than anything in the world, except Bailey. And maybe canned pineapples. My obsession with pineapples nearly drove me mad. I dreamt of the days when I would be grown and able to buy a whole carton for myself alone.

Although the syrupy golden rings sat in their exotic cans on our shelves year round, we only tasted them during Christmas. Momma used the juice to make almost-black fruit cakes. Then she lined heavy soot-encrusted iron skillets with the pineapple rings for rich upside-down cakes. Bailey and I received one slice each, and I carried mine around for hours, shredding off the fruit until nothing was left except the perfume on my fingers. I'd like to think that my desire for pineapples was so sacred that I wouldn't allow myself to steal a can (which was possible) and eat it alone out in the garden, but I'm certain that I must have weighed the possibility of the scent exposing me and didn't have the nerve to attempt it.

Until I was thirteen and left Arkansas for good, the Store was my favorite place to be. Alone and empty in the mornings, it looked like an unopened present from a stranger. Opening the front doors was pulling the ribbon off the unexpected gift. The light would come in softly (we faced north), easing itself over the shelves of mackerel, salmon, tobacco, thread. It fell flat on the big vat of lard and by noontime during the summer the grease had softened to a thick soup. Whenever I walked into the Store in the afternoon, I sensed that it was tired. I alone could hear the slow pulse of its job half done. But just before bedtime, after numerous people had walked in and out, had argued over their bills, or joked about their neighbors, or just dropped in "to give Sister Henderson a 'Hi y'all,'" the promise of magic mornings returned to the Store and spread itself over the family in washed life waves. . . .

When Maya was about ten years old, she returned to Stamps from a visit to St. Louis with her mother. She had become depressed and withdrawn.

For nearly a year, I sopped around the house, the Store, the school and the church, like an old biscuit, dirty and inedible. Then I met, or rather got to know, the lady who threw me my first lifeline.

Mrs. Bertha Flowers was the aristocrat[4] of Black Stamps. She had the grace of control to appear warm in the coldest weather, and on the Arkansas summer days it seemed she had a private breeze which swirled around, cooling her. She was thin without the <u>taut</u> look of wiry people, and her printed voile[5] dresses and flowered hats were as right for her as denim overalls for a farmer. She was our side's answer to the richest white woman in town.

Her skin was a rich black that would have peeled like a plum if snagged, but then no one would have thought of getting close enough to Mrs. Flowers to ruffle her dress, let alone snag her skin. She didn't encourage familiarity. She wore gloves too.

I don't think I ever saw Mrs. Flowers laugh, but she smiled often. A slow widening of her thin black lips to show even, small white teeth, then the slow effortless closing. When she chose to smile on me, I always wanted to thank her. The action was so graceful and inclusively <u>benign</u>.

She was one of the few gentlewomen I have ever known, and has remained throughout my life the measure of what a human being can be. . . .

One summer afternoon, sweet-milk fresh in my memory, she stopped at the Store to buy provisions. Another Negro woman of her health and age would have been expected to carry the paper sacks home in one hand, but Momma said, "Sister Flowers, I'll send Bailey up to your house with these things."

She smiled that slow dragging smile, "Thank you, Mrs. Henderson. I'd prefer Marguerite, though." My name was beautiful when she said it. "I've been meaning to talk to her, anyway." They gave each other age-group looks.

Momma said, "Well, that's all right then. Sister, go and change your dress. You going to Sister Flowers's." . . .

There was a little path beside the rocky road, and Mrs. Flowers walked in front swinging her arms and picking her way over the stones.

She said, without turning her head, to me, "I hear you're doing very good school work, Marguerite, but that it's all written. The teachers report that they have trouble getting you to talk in class." We passed the triangular farm on our left and the path widened to allow us to walk together. I hung back in the separate unasked and unanswerable questions.

Vocabulary Development: taut (tôt) *adj.* tightly stretched
benign (bi nīn´) *adj.* kindly

---

4. **aristocrat** (ə ris´ tə krat) *n.* person belonging to the upper class.
5. **voile** (voil) *n.* light cotton fabric.

◆ **Reading Check**

How do the people of Black Stamps view Mrs. Flowers?

_____

_____

_____

What about her makes them feel that way?

_____

_____

_____

_____

◆ **Reading Strategy**

What does the narrator mean when she says the afternoon was "sweet-milk fresh" in her memory?

_____

_____

_____

_____

◆ **Reading Check**

Why are Marguerite and Mrs. Flowers walking together?

_____

_____

_____

_____

_____

_____

This **memoir** includes several **descriptive details** showing how Marguerite reacts to Mrs. Flowers. As you read the page, draw a box around details that indicate Marguerite's reactions. Then, based on these details, write a sentence below that tells how she feels about Mrs. Flowers.

_____

_____

_____

_____

In what way does Angelou's use of **figurative language** "infuse" the descriptions in the memoir with "shades of deeper meaning"?

_____

_____

_____

_____

Underline a sentence in the bracketed paragraph in which the author gives a human quality to something that is not human.

"Come and walk along with me, Marguerite." I couldn't have refused even if I wanted to. She pronounced my name so nicely. Or more correctly, she spoke each word with such clarity that I was certain a foreigner who didn't understand English could have understood her.

"Now no one is going to make you talk—possibly no one can. But bear in mind, language is man's way of communicating with his fellow man and it is language alone which separates him from the lower animals." That was a totally new idea to me, and I would need time to think about it.

"Your grandmother says you read a lot. Every chance you get. That's good, but not good enough. Words mean more than what is set down on paper. It takes the human voice to <u>infuse</u> them with the shades of deeper meaning."

I memorized the part about the human voice infusing words. It seemed so valid and poetic.

She said she was going to give me some books and that I not only must read them, I must read them aloud. She suggested that I try to make a sentence sound in as many different ways as possible.

"I'll accept no excuse if you return a book to me that has been badly handled." My imagination boggled at the punishment I would deserve if in fact I did abuse a book of Mrs. Flowers's. Death would be too kind and brief.

The odors in the house surprised me. Somehow I had never connected Mrs. Flowers with food or eating or any other common experience of common people. There must have been an outhouse, too, but my mind never recorded it.

The sweet scent of vanilla had met us as she opened the door.

"I made tea cookies this morning. You see, I had planned to invite you for cookies and lemonade so we could have this little chat. The lemonade is in the icebox."

It followed that Mrs. Flowers would have ice on an ordinary day, when most families in our town bought ice late on Saturdays only a few times during the summer to be used in the wooden ice cream freezers.

She took the bags from me and disappeared through the kitchen door. I looked around the room that I had never in my wildest fantasies imagined I would see. Browned photographs leered or threatened from the walls and the white, freshly done curtains pushed against themselves and against the wind. I wanted to gobble up the room entire and take it to Bailey, who would help me analyze and enjoy it.

"Have a seat, Marguerite. Over there by the table." She carried a platter covered with a tea towel. Although she warned that she hadn't tried her hand at baking sweets for

Vocabulary Development: infuse (in fyo͞oz´) *v.* put into

some time, I was certain that like everything else about her the cookies would be perfect.

They were flat round wafers, slightly browned on the edges and butter-yellow in the center. With the cold lemonade they were sufficient for childhood's lifelong diet. Remembering my manners, I took nice little ladylike bites off the edges. She said she had made them expressly for me and that she had a few in the kitchen that I could take home to my brother. So I jammed one whole cake in my mouth and the rough crumbs scratched the insides of my jaws, and if I hadn't had to swallow, it would have been a dream come true.

As I ate she began the first of what we later called "my lessons in living." She said that I must always be <u>intolerant</u> of ignorance but understanding of illiteracy. That some people, unable to go to school, were more educated and even more intelligent than college professors. She encouraged me to listen carefully to what country people called mother wit. That in those homely sayings was <u>couched</u> the collective wisdom of generations.

When I finished the cookies she brushed off the table and brought a thick, small book from the bookcase. I had read *A Tale of Two Cities* and found it up to my standards as a romantic novel. She opened the first page and I heard poetry for the first time in my life.

"It was the best of times and the worst of times . . ." Her voice slid in and curved down through and over the words. She was nearly singing. I wanted to look at the pages. Were they the same that I had read? Or were there notes, music, lined on the pages, as in a hymn book? Her sounds began cascading gently. I knew from listening to a thousand preachers that she was nearing the end of her reading, and I hadn't really heard, heard to understand, a single word.

"How do you like that?"

It occurred to me that she expected a response. The sweet vanilla flavor was still on my tongue and her reading was a wonder in my ears. I had to speak.

I said, "Yes, ma'am." It was the least I could do, but it was the most also.

"There's one more thing. Take this book of poems and memorize one for me. Next time you pay me a visit, I want you to recite."

I have tried often to search behind the sophistication of

Vocabulary Development: intolerant (in täl′ ər ənt) *adj.* not able or willing to accept
couched (koucht) *v.* put into words; expressed

◆ **Reading Check**

What does Mrs. Flowers tell Marguerite in the first of her "lessons in living"?

_____

_____

_____

_____

◆ **Reading Strategy**

Underline a sentence in the bracketed paragraph in which Angelou describes Mrs. Flowers's reading as being like flowing water.

Mark the Text

◆ **Reading Check**

What are some ways that Mrs. Flowers hopes to change Marguerite?

_____

_____

_____

_____

_____

_____

◆ Literary Analysis

Based on the personal reactions the writer includes in this **memoir**, why do you think she ran, rather than walked, down the hill? Write your answer on the lines below.

_____

_____

_____

_____

◆ Reading Check

Mrs. Flowers makes cookies for Marguerite and reads to her. What do these actions prove to Marguerite?

_____

_____

_____

_____

_____

_____

years for the enchantment I so easily found in those gifts. The essence escapes but its aura[6] remains. To be allowed, no, invited, into the private lives of strangers, and to share their joys and fears, was a chance to exchange the Southern bitter wormwood[7] for a cup of mead with Beowulf[8] or a hot cup of tea and milk with Oliver Twist. When I said aloud, "It is a far far better thing that I do, than I have ever done . . ."[9] tears of love filled my eyes at my selflessness.

On that first day, I ran down the hill and into the road (few cars ever came along it) and had the good sense to stop running before I reached the Store.

I was liked, and what a difference it made. I was respected not as Mrs. Henderson's grandchild or Bailey's sister but for just being Marguerite Johnson.

Childhood's logic never asks to be proved (all conclusions are absolute). I didn't question why Mrs. Flowers had singled me out for attention, nor did it occur to me that Momma might have asked her to give me a little talking to. All I cared about was that she had made tea cookies for _me_ and read to _me_ from her favorite book. It was enough to prove that she liked me.

6. **aura** (ôr´ ə) *n.* atmosphere or quality.
7. **wormwood** (wurm´ wood´) *n.* plant that produces a bitter oil.
8. **Beowulf** (bā´ ə woolf´) hero of an old Anglo-Saxon epic. People in this poem drink mead (mēd), a drink made with honey and water.
9. **"It is . . . than I have ever done"** speech from *A Tale of Two Cities* by Charles Dickens.

Reader's Response: Does Mrs. Flowers remind you of anyone you know? Explain.

_____

_____

_____

Thinking About the Skill: Explain how figurative language can make a story or memoir more interesting to read.

_____

_____

_____

Old Man
Ricardo Sánchez

Summary

The speaker addresses this poem to this grandfather. He describes old age as a treasure of memory and experience. For the poet the lines on his grandfather's face are not just a sign of age—they are traces of wisdom. In the poet's love and respect for his grandfather's past, the reader feels the fullness of a long life. We understand that old age is not a loss of youth but a gain of wisdom.

Visual Summary

Poetry often helps us to see new truths about the world. It often helps us rethink our old ideas. "Old Man" asks its readers to rethink their ideas of old age.

How a Poem Can Change Our Usual Ideas

Usual Idea	Fresh Idea in "Old Man"
Family histories are dull.	Family histories are rich and fascinating.
I have nothing in common with older people in my family.	I have an important connection to older people in my family.
Old age is bad and ugly.	Old age is wonderful and beautiful.
Poems have to rhyme and have a regular rhythm.	Poems do not always have to rhyme or have a regular rhythm.

List three details you can recall about the oldest relative whom you ever met.

Relative: _____

1. _____

2. _____

3. _____

Circle any words or phrases in the bracketed passage you can **use as context clues** to show that *legacy* means "something handed down from an ancestor."

What two cultures are mixed in the blood of the old man and the grand-child?

_____

_____

_____

_____

_____

_____

Old Man
Ricardo Sánchez

remembrance (smiles/hurts sweetly)
October 8, 1972

Important memories and feelings are often passed along from grandfather to grandchild.

old man
with brown skin
talking of past
    when being shepherd
5   in utah, nevada, colorado and
        new mexico
was life lived freely;

old man,
    grandfather,
wise with time
10   running <u>rivulets</u> on face,
deep, rich <u>furrows</u>,
    each one a legacy,
deep, rich memories
of life . . .
15   "you are indio,[1]
       among other things,"
    he would tell me
       during nights spent
       so long ago
20   amidst familial gatherings
    in albuquerque . . .

old man, loved and respected,
he would speak sometimes
of pueblos,[2]
25   san juan, santa clara,
    and even santo domingo,
and his family, he would say,
came from there:
    some of our blood was here,
30   he would say,

Vocabulary Development: rivulets (riv´ yo͞o lits) *n.* little streams
furrows (fur´ ōz) *n.* deep wrinkles

---

1. **indio** (ēn´ dyō) *n.* Indian; Native American.
2. **pueblos** (pweb´ lōz) *n.* here, Native American towns in central and northern New Mexico.

before the coming of coronado,[3]
other of our blood
    came with los españoles,[4]
and the mixture
35   was rich,
    though often painful . . .
old man,
who knew earth
    by its awesome aromas
40   and who felt
the heated sweetness
    of chile verde[5]
by his <u>supple</u> touch,
gone into dust is your body
45   with its <u>stoic</u> look and resolution,
but your reality, old man, lives on
in a mindsoul touched by you . . .

Old Man . . .

Vocabulary Development: supple (sup´ əl) *adj.* flexible and pliant
                    stoic (stō´ ik) *adj.* calm and unbothered
                    in spite of suffering

---

3. coronado (kô rô nä´ dô) Coronado explored what is today the American Southwest.
4. los españoles (lōs es pä nyōl´ es) *n.* the Spaniards.
5. chile verde (chē´ le vehr´ dē) *n.* green pepper.

Reader's Response: How can remembrances make you smile and hurt at the same time?

_____

_____

Thinking About the Skill: Explain how being aware of sensory language helps you appreciate this poem more.

_____

_____

◆ **Literary Analysis**

On the lines below, list a **sensory image or detail** from the poem that appeals to each of your senses.

Sight: _____

_____

Sound: _____

_____

_____

Smell: _____

_____

_____

Taste: _____

_____

_____

Touch: _____

_____

_____

Cub Pilot on the Mississippi
Mark Twain

Summary

When Mark Twain, the author, was a riverboat cub pilot, he worked under a terribly mean and bossy master pilot named Brown. In his memoir, Twain must obey Brown and endure his insults. He has fantasies about killing Brown but just reports to his job every day and follows Brown's orders. But when the nasty Brown attacks Twain's brother, Twain finally lets it all out and gives Brown a sound beating. Although the ship's captain scolds Twain for attacking Brown, he lets him know that Brown really deserved it. When Brown goes to the captain and tells him that he won't work on the same boat as Twain, the captain tells the pilot he will have to leave the boat.

Visual Summary

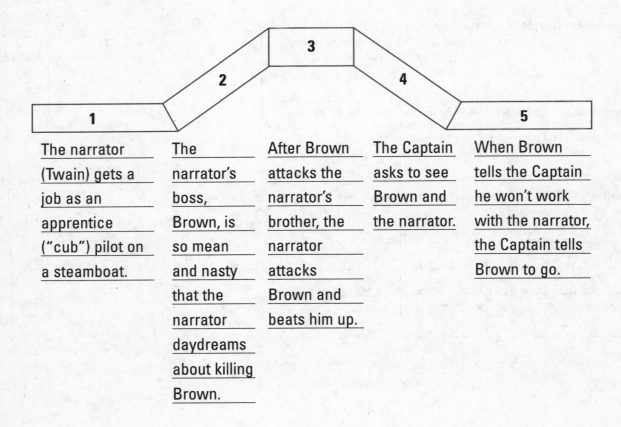

1 The narrator (Twain) gets a job as an apprentice ("cub") pilot on a steamboat.

2 The narrator's boss, Brown, is so mean and nasty that the narrator daydreams about killing Brown.

3 After Brown attacks the narrator's brother, the narrator attacks Brown and beats him up.

4 The Captain asks to see Brown and the narrator.

5 When Brown tells the Captain he won't work with the narrator, the Captain tells Brown to go.

Cub Pilot on the Mississippi
Mark Twain

When you are an apprentice learning a new job, sometimes you have to put up with a difficult boss and lots of criticism that you don't deserve.

During the two or two and a half years of my apprentice-ship[1] I served under many pilots, and had experience of many kinds of steamboatmen and many varieties of steam-boats. I am to this day profiting somewhat by that experi-ence; for in that brief, sharp schooling, I got personally and familiarly acquainted with about all the different types of human nature that are to be found in fiction, biography, or history.

The fact is daily borne in upon me that the average shore-employment requires as much as forty years to equip a man with this sort of an education. When I say I am still profiting by this thing, I do not mean that it has constituted me a judge of men—no, it has not done that, for judges of men are born, not made. My profit is various in kind and degree, but the feature of it which I value most is the zest which that early experience has given to my later reading. When I find a well-drawn character in fiction or biography I generally take a warm personal interest in him, for the reason that I have known him before—met him on the river.

The figure that comes before me oftenest, out of the shad-ows of that vanished time, is that of Brown, of the steamer *Pennsylvania*. He was a middle-aged, long, slim, bony, smooth-shaven, horse-faced, ignorant, stingy, malicious, snarling, fault-hunting, mote[2]-magnifying tyrant. I early got the habit of coming on watch with dread at my heart. No matter how good a time I might have been having with the off-watch below, and no matter how high my spirits might be when I started aloft, my soul became lead in my body the moment I approached the pilothouse.

I still remember the first time I ever entered the presence of that man. The boat had backed out from St. Louis and was "straightening down." I ascended to the pilothouse in high feather, and very proud to be semiofficially a member of the executive family of so fast and famous a boat. Brown was at the wheel. I paused in the middle of the room, all fixed to make my bow, but Brown did not look around. I thought he took a furtive glance at me out of the corner of

---

Vocabulary Development: furtive (fur´ tiv) *adj.* sly or done in secret

---

1. **apprenticeship** (ə pren´ tis ship) *n.* time a person spends working for a master craftsperson in a craft or trade in return for instruction.
2. **mote** (mōt) *n.* speck of dust.

◆ **Activate Prior Knowledge**

Have you or a friend ever worked for a difficult boss? List at least two problems that working for a difficult boss can lead to.

1. _____

_____

_____

2. _____

_____

_____

◆ **Literary Analysis**

Circle words in the bracketed para-graph that name character traits of Brown that might lead to **conflict between the characters**, Brown and Twain.

Mark the Text

◆ **Reading Strategy**

The **idiom** *in high feather* has an understood meaning that has noth-ing to do with feathers. Based on clues in the underlined sentence, do you think *in high feather* means "in a positive mood" or "in a quiet way"? Explain.

_____

_____

_____

_____

_____

_____

his eye, but as not even this notice was repeated, I judged I had been mistaken. By this time he was picking his way among some dangerous "breaks" abreast the woodyards; therefore it would not be proper to interrupt him; so I stepped softly to the high bench and took a seat.

There was silence for ten minutes; then my new boss turned and inspected me deliberately and painstakingly from head to heel for about—as it seemed to me—a quarter of an hour. After which he removed his countenance[3] and I saw it no more for some seconds; then it came around once more, and this question greeted me: "Are you Horace Bigsby's cub?"[4]

"Yes, sir."

After this there was a pause and another inspection. Then: "What's your name?"

I told him. He repeated it after me. It was probably the only thing he ever forgot; for although I was with him many months he never addressed himself to me in any other way than "Here!" and then his command followed.

"Where was you born?"

"In Florida, Missouri."

A pause. Then: "Dern sight better stayed there!"

By means of a dozen or so of pretty direct questions, he pumped my family history out of me.

The leads[5] were going now in the first crossing. This interrupted the inquest.[6] When the leads had been laid in he resumed:

"How long you been on the river?"

I told him. After a pause:

"Where'd you get them shoes?"

I gave him the information.

"Hold up your foot!"

I did so. He stepped back, examined the shoe minutely and contemptuously, scratching his head thoughtfully, tilting his high sugar-loaf hat well forward to facilitate the operation, then ejaculated, "Well, I'll be dod derned!" and returned to his wheel.

What occasion there was to be dod derned about it is a thing which is still as much of a mystery to me now as it was then. It must have been all of fifteen minutes—fifteen minutes of dull, homesick silence—before that long horse-face swung round upon me again—and then what a change! It was as red as fire, and every muscle in it was working. Now came this shriek: "Here! You going to set there all day?"

I lit in the middle of the floor, shot there by the electric suddenness of the surprise. As soon as I could get my voice I said apologetically: "I have had no orders, sir."

---

3. **countenance** (koun´ tə nəns) n. face.
4. **cub** (kub) n. beginner.
5. **leads** (ledz) n. weights that were lowered to test the depth of the river.
6. **inquest** (in´ kwest) n. investigation.

◆ Reading Strategy

The underlined sentence contains an **idiom.** Briefly explain how asking someone questions can be like using a pump.

_____

_____

_____

_____

_____

_____

◆ Reading Check

Based on the pilot's questions and comments, how does he seem to feel about the cub pilot?

_____

_____

_____

_____

_____

_____

"You've had no *orders*! My, what a fine bird we are! We must have *orders*! Our father was a *gentleman* —and *we've* been to *school*. Yes, *we* are a gentleman, *too,* and got to have *orders*! ORDERS, is it? ORDERS is what you want! Dod dern my skin, *I'll* learn you to swell yourself up and blow around *here* about your dod-derned *orders*! G'way from the wheel!" (I had approached it without knowing it.)

I moved back a step or two and stood as in a dream, all my senses stupefied by this frantic assault.

"What you standing there for? Take that ice-pitcher down to the texas-tender![7] Come, move along, and don't you be all day about it!"

The moment I got back to the pilothouse Brown said:

"Here! What was you doing down there all this time?"

"I couldn't find the texas-tender; I had to go all the way to the pantry."

"Derned likely story! Fill up the stove."

I proceeded to do so. He watched me like a cat. Presently he shouted: "Put down that shovel! Derndest numskull I ever saw—ain't even got sense enough to load up a stove."

All through the watch this sort of thing went on. Yes, and the subsequent watches were much like it during a stretch of months. As I have said, I soon got the habit of coming on duty with dread. The moment I was in the presence, even in the darkest night, I could feel those yellow eyes upon me, and knew their owner was watching for a <u>pretext</u> to spit out some venom on me. Preliminarily he would say: "Here! Take the wheel."

Two minutes later: "*Where* in the nation you going to? Pull her down! pull her down!"

After another moment: "Say! You going to hold her all day? Let her go—meet her! meet her!"

Then he would jump from the bench, snatch the wheel from me, and meet her himself, pouring out wrath upon me all the time.

George Ritchie was the other pilot's cub. He was having good times now; for his boss, George Ealer, was as kind-hearted as Brown wasn't. Ritchie had steered for Brown the season before; consequently, he knew exactly how to entertain himself and plague me, all by the one operation. Whenever I took the wheel for a moment on Ealer's watch, Ritchie would sit back on the bench and play Brown, with continual ejaculations of "Snatch her! Snatch her! Derndest mudcat I ever saw!" "Here! Where are you going *now*? Going to run over that snag?" "Pull her *down*! Don't you hear me?

Vocabulary Development: pretext (prē´ tekst) *n.* false reason or motive used to hide a real intention

---

7. **texas-tender** the waiter in the officers' quarters.

◆ **Literary Analysis**

Read the bracketed paragraph aloud, putting stress on the words in italics to bring out the bad feelings Brown has toward Twain.

◆ **Reading Strategy**

Circle an **idiom** involving an animal in the bracketed paragraph. Then, write its meaning on the lines below.

_____

_____

_____

_____

◆ **Literary Analysis**

Clarify the **conflict** between Brown and Twain by filling in the chart below (one item has already been entered). Include differences between them that might lead them to struggle with each other.

DIFFERENCES	
Twain	**Brown**
Young; inexperienced	Older; experienced

How does the other apprentice pilot, George Ritchie, "entertain himself and plague" Twain?

_____

_____

_____

◆ Literary Analysis

Underline a sentence in the bracketed paragraph that shows that the **conflict** with Brown is starting to take over Twain's mind and get in the way of his work.

◆ Reading Check

Why does Twain think that Brown is planning to set a trap for him?

_____

_____

_____

◆ Reading Strategy

How would you define the underlined idiom *I lost my head* if you were writing an **idiom** dictionary for new English speakers?

_____

_____

_____

Pull her *down*!" "There she goes! *Just* as I expected! I *told* you not to cramp that reef. G'way from the wheel!"

So I always had a rough time of it, no matter whose watch it was; and sometimes it seemed to me that Ritchie's good-natured badgering was pretty nearly as aggravating as Brown's dead-earnest nagging.

I often wanted to kill Brown, but this would not answer. A cub had to take everything his boss gave, in the way of vigorous comment and criticism; and we all believed that there was a United States law making it a penitentiary offense to strike or threaten a pilot who was on duty.

However, I could *imagine* myself killing Brown; there was no law against that; and that was the thing I used always to do the moment I was abed. Instead of going over my river in my mind, as was my duty, I threw business aside for pleasure, and killed Brown. I killed Brown every night for months; not in old, stale, commonplace ways, but in new and picturesque ones—ways that were sometimes surprising for freshness of design and ghastliness of situation and environment.

Brown was *always* watching for a pretext to find fault; and if he could find no plausible pretext, he would invent one. He would scold you for shaving a shore, and for not shaving it; for hugging a bar, and for not hugging it; for "pulling down" when not invited, and for *not* pulling down when not invited; for firing up without orders, and *for* waiting for orders. In a word, it was his invariable rule to find fault with *everything* you did and another invariable rule of his was to throw all his remarks (to you) into the form of an insult.

One day we were approaching New Madrid, bound down and heavily laden. Brown was at one side of the wheel, steering; I was at the other, standing by to "pull down" or "shove up." He cast a furtive glance at me every now and then. I had long ago learned what that meant; viz., he was trying to invent a trap for me. I wondered what shape it was going to take. By and by he stepped back from the wheel and said in his usual snarly way:

"Here! See if you've got gumption enough to round her to."

This was simply *bound* to be a success; nothing could prevent it; for he had never allowed me to round the boat to before; consequently, no matter how I might do the thing, he could find free fault with it. He stood back there with his greedy eye on me, and the result was what might have been foreseen: I lost my head in a quarter of a minute, and didn't know what I was about; I started too early to bring the boat around, but detected a green gleam of joy in Brown's eye, and corrected my mistake. I started around once more while too high up, but corrected myself again in time. I made other false moves, and still managed to save myself; but at last I grew so confused and anxious that I tumbled into the very worst blunder of all—I got too far *down* before beginning to fetch the boat around. Brown's chance was come.

His face turned red with passion; he made one bound, hurled me across the house with a sweep of his arm, spun the wheel down, and began to pour out a stream of vituperation[8] upon me which lasted till he was out of breath. In the course of this speech he called me all the different kinds of hard names he could think of, and once or twice I thought he was even going to swear—but he had never done that, and he didn't this time. "Dod dern" was the nearest he ventured to the luxury of swearing.

Two trips later I got into serious trouble. Brown was steering; I was "pulling down." My younger brother Henry appeared on the hurricane deck, and shouted to Brown to stop at some landing or other, a mile or so below. Brown gave no intimation that he had heard anything. But that was his way: he never condescended to take notice of an underclerk. The wind was blowing; Brown was deaf (although he always pretended he wasn't), and I very much doubted if he had heard the order. If I had had two heads, I would have spoken; but as I had only one, it seemed judicious to take care of it; so I kept still.

Presently, sure enough, we went sailing by that plantation. Captain Klinefelter appeared on the deck, and said: "Let her come around, sir, let her come around. Didn't Henry tell you to land here?"

"*No*, sir!"

"I sent him up to do it."

"He *did* come up; and that's all the good it done, the dodderned fool. He never said anything."

"Didn't *you* hear him?" asked the captain of me.

Of course I didn't want to be mixed up in this business, but there was no way to avoid it; so I said: "Yes, sir."

I knew what Brown's next remark would be, before he uttered it. It was: "Shut your mouth! You never heard anything of the kind."

I closed my mouth, according to instructions. An hour later Henry entered the pilothouse, unaware of what had been going on. He was a thoroughly inoffensive boy, and I was sorry to see him come, for I knew Brown would have no pity on him. Brown began, straightway: "Here! Why didn't you tell me we'd got to land at that plantation?"

Vocabulary Development: intimation (in´ tə mā´ shən) *n.* hint or suggestion
judicious (jōō dish´ əs) *adj.* showing sound judgment; wise and careful

---

8. **vituperation** (vī tōō´ pə rā´ shən) *n.* abusive language.

Cub Pilot on the Mississippi **31**

◆ **Stop to Reflect**

How much worse do you think the **conflict between Brown and Twain** can get? Make a prediction about what might happen next. Then, read ahead to see if your prediction is right.

_____

_____

_____

_____

◆ **Reading Check**

Based on the bracketed paragraph, why doesn't Twain repeat Henry's order to make sure that Brown heard it?

_____

_____

_____

_____

_____

_____

_____

_____

_____

In the bracketed passage, find three actions Twain takes that show that the **conflict** has reached a new level. Underline and number them.

Whom is Twain trying to defend when he hits Brown?

_____

_____

_____

_____

_____

Can you think of any other **idioms** that have almost the same meaning as "done for"? A sample is listed for you.

1. in hot water

2. _____

_____

3. _____

_____

"I did tell you, Mr. Brown."

"It's a lie!"

I said: "You lie, yourself. He did tell you."

Brown glared at me in unaffected surprise; and for as much as a moment he was entirely speechless; then he shouted to me: "I'll attend to your case in a half a minute!" then to Henry, "And you leave the pilothouse; out with you!"

It was pilot law, and must be obeyed. The boy started out, and even had his foot on the upper step outside the door, when Brown, with a sudden access of fury, picked up a ten-pound lump of coal and sprang after him; but I was between, with a heavy stool, and I hit Brown a good honest blow which stretched him out.

I had committed the crime of crimes—I had lifted my hand against a pilot on duty! I supposed I was booked for the penitentiary sure, and couldn't be booked any surer if I went on and squared my long account with this person while I had the chance; consequently I stuck to him and pounded him with my fists a considerable time. I do not know how long, the pleasure of it probably made it seem longer than it really was; but in the end he struggled free and jumped up and sprang to the wheel: a very natural solicitude, for, all this time, here was this steamboat tearing down the river at the rate of fifteen miles an hour and nobody at the helm! However, Eagle Bend was two miles wide at this bank-full stage, and correspondingly long and deep: and the boat was steering herself straight down the middle and taking no chances. Still, that was only luck—a body *might* have found her charging into the woods.

Perceiving at a glance that the *Pennsylvania* was in no danger, Brown gathered up the big spyglass, war-club fashion, and ordered me out of the pilothouse with more than ordinary bluster. But I was not afraid of him now; so, instead of going, I tarried, and criticized his grammar. I reformed his ferocious speeches for him, and put them into good English, calling his attention to the advantage of pure English over the dialect of the collieries⁹ whence he was extracted. He could have done his part to admiration in a crossfire of mere vituperation, of course; but he was not equipped for this species of controversy; so he presently laid aside his glass and took the wheel, muttering and shaking his head; and I retired to the bench. The racket had brought everybody to the hurricane deck, and I trembled when I saw the old captain looking up from amid the crowd. I said to myself, "Now I *am* done for!" for although, as a rule, he was so fatherly and indulgent toward the boat's family, and so

Vocabulary Development: indulgent (in dul´ jənt) *adj.* very mild and tolerant; not strict or critical

9. **collieries** (kal´ yər ēz) *n.* coal mines.

patient of minor shortcomings, he could be stern enough when the fault was worth it.

I tried to imagine what he *would* do to a cub pilot who had been guilty of such a crime as mine, committed on a boat guard-deep[10] with costly freight and alive with passengers. Our watch was nearly ended. I thought I would go and hide somewhere till I got a chance to slide ashore. So I slipped out of the pilothouse, and down the steps, and around to the texas-door, and was in the act of gliding within, when the captain confronted me! I dropped my head, and he stood over me in silence a moment or two, then said impressively: "Follow me."

I dropped into his wake; he led the way to his parlor in the forward end of the texas. We were alone now. He closed the afterdoor, then moved slowly to the forward one and closed that. He sat down; I stood before him. He looked at me some little time, then said: "So you have been fighting Mr. Brown?"

I answered meekly: "Yes, sir."

"Do you know that that is a very serious matter?"

"Yes, sir."

"Are you aware that this boat was plowing down the river fully five minutes with no one at the wheel?"

"Yes, sir."

"Did you strike him first?"

"Yes, sir."

"What with?"

"A stool, sir."

"Hard?"

"Middling, sir."

"Did it knock him down?"

"He—he fell, sir."

"Did you follow it up? Did you do anything further?"

"Yes, sir."

"What did you do?"

"Pounded him, sir."

"Pounded him?"

"Yes, sir."

"Did you pound him much? that is, severely?"

"One might call it that, sir, maybe."

"I'm deuced glad of it! Hark ye, never mention that I said that. You have been guilty of a great crime; and don't you ever be guilty of it again, on this boat. *But*—lay for him ashore! Give him a good sound thrashing, do you hear? I'll pay the expenses. Now go—and mind you, not a word of this to anybody. Clear out with you! You've been guilty of a great crime, you whelp!"[11]

---

10. guard-deep filled to the level of a wooden frame protecting the paddle wheel.
11. whelp (hwelp) *n.* here, a disrespectful young man.

Define the underlined **idiom**, *a close shave*. How do you think it got its meaning?

_____

_____

_____

_____

_____

Why does Twain feel like "an emancipated slave" at the end of this account?

_____

_____

_____

_____

_____

I slid out, happy with the sense of a close shave and a mighty deliverance; and I heard him laughing to himself and slapping his fat thighs after I had closed his door.

When Brown came off watch he went straight to the captain, who was talking with some passengers on the boiler deck, and demanded that I be put ashore in New Orleans—and added: "I'll never turn a wheel on this boat again while that cub stays."

The captain said: "But he needn't come round when you are on watch, Mr. Brown."

"I won't even stay on the same boat with him. One of us has got to go ashore."

"Very well," said the captain, "let it be yourself," and resumed his talk with the passengers.

During the brief remainder of the trip I knew how an emancipated slave feels, for I was an emancipated slave myself. While we lay at landings I listened to George Ealer's flute, or to his readings from his two Bibles, that is to say, Goldsmith and Shakespeare, or I played chess with him—and would have beaten him sometimes, only he always took back his last move and ran the game out differently.

Vocabulary Development: emancipated (i man´ sə pā´ təd) *v.* freed from the control or power of another

---

Reader's Response: Do you think the captain was right in backing up Twain instead of Brown? Explain.

_____

_____

_____

Thinking About the Skill: How can you figure out what an **idiom** means when it is used in a story?

_____

_____

_____

Harriet Tubman: Guide to Freedom

Ann Petry

Summary

Harriet Tubman, a former slave, was a brave and determined woman who repeatedly led runaway slaves to freedom in Canada. This is the story of one such trip, a dangerous month-long escape from Maryland to Canada in 1851. Harriet and the runaway slaves traveled by night and slept by day so that they would not be seen. The journey, entirely on foot, was cold and strenuous. The runaway slaves were dreadfully hungry and tired, and Tubman tried to keep up their morale. She urged them on, telling them of the joys of freedom and of the good people along the way who were sympathetic toward slaves and would provide food and shelter. When Tubman's party finally reached St. Catharines in what is now Ontario, Canada, they could begin their new lives in freedom.

Visual Summary

It helps to understand "Harriet Tubman: Guide to Freedom" if you think about the story's purpose. All the events of the story point in one direction: to show who Harriet Tubman was and why she thought it was so important to help slaves escape. If you ask yourself questions about the story's purpose, the events begin to fall into place. Fill out the following chart as you read to help you think about the story's purpose:

Questions	Harriet Tubman
Who was she?	
What did she do?	
When did she live?	
Where did she work and live?	
Why is she important?	
How did she help slaves escape?	

List two things that you have heard or read about how runaway slaves were treated before the Civil War.

1. _____

_____

2. _____

_____

A **third-person narrative** usually includes many third-person pronouns, such as *he*, *his*, *she*, *her*, *it*, or *they*. Circle any third-person pronouns you see in the bracketed passage.

On what night during the week did slave escapes usually occur? Why?

_____

_____

_____

_____

_____

_____

_____

_____

_____

Harriet Tubman: Guide to Freedom
Ann Petry

In the Bible, Moses led his people out of slavery in Egypt to freedom. In the years before the Civil War, former slave Harriet Tubman was sometimes called Moses because she led slaves from the South to freedom.

Along the Eastern Shore of Maryland, in Dorchester County, in Caroline County, the masters kept hearing whispers about the man named Moses, who was running off slaves. At first they did not believe in his existence. The stories about him were fantastic, unbelievable. Yet they watched for him. They offered rewards for his capture.

They never saw him. Now and then they heard whispered rumors to the effect that he was in the neighborhood. The woods were searched. The roads were watched. There was never anything to indicate his whereabouts. But a few days afterward, a goodly number of slaves would be gone from the plantation. Neither the master nor the overseer had heard or seen anything unusual in the quarter. Sometimes one or the other would vaguely remember having heard a whippoorwill call somewhere in the woods, close by, late at night. Though it was the wrong season for whippoorwills.

Sometimes the masters thought they had heard the cry of a hoot owl, repeated, and would remember having thought that the intervals between the low moaning cry were wrong, that it had been repeated four times in succession instead of three. There was never anything more than that to suggest that all was not well in the quarter. Yet when morning came, they invariably discovered that a group of the finest slaves had taken to their heels.

Unfortunately, the discovery was almost always made on a Sunday. Thus a whole day was lost before the machinery of pursuit could be set in motion. The posters offering rewards for the <u>fugitives</u> could not be printed until Monday. The men who made a living hunting for runaway slaves were out of reach, off in the woods with their dogs and their guns, in pursuit of four-footed game, or they were in camp meetings[1] saying their prayers with their wives and families beside them.

Harriet Tubman could have told them that there was far more involved in this matter of running off slaves than signaling the would-be runaways by imitating the call of a whippoorwill, or a hoot owl, far more involved than a matter

---

Vocabulary Development: fugitives (fyo͞o′ ji tivs′) *n.* people fleeing

---

1. **camp meetings** religious meetings held outdoors or in a tent.

of waiting for a clear night when the North Star was visible.

In December 1851, when she started out with the band of fugitives that she planned to take to Canada, she had been in the vicinity of the plantation for days, planning the trip, carefully selecting the slaves that she would take with her.

She had announced her arrival in the quarter by singing the forbidden spiritual[2] —"Go down, Moses, 'way down to Egypt Land"—singing it softly outside the door of a slave cabin, late at night. The husky voice was beautiful even when it was barely more than a murmur borne on the wind.

Once she had made her presence known, word of her coming spread from cabin to cabin. The slaves whispered to each other, ear to mouth, mouth to ear, "Moses is here." "Moses has come." "Get ready. Moses is back again." The ones who had agreed to go North with her put ashcake and salt herring in an old bandanna, hastily tied it into a bundle, and then waited patiently for the signal that meant it was time to start.

There were eleven in this party, including one of her brothers and his wife. It was the largest group that she had ever conducted, but she was determined that more and more slaves should know what freedom was like.

She had to take them all the way to Canada. The Fugitive Slave Law[3] was no longer a great many incomprehensible words written down on the country's lawbooks. The new law had become a reality. It was Thomas Sims, a boy, picked up on the streets of Boston at night and shipped back to Georgia. It was Jerry and Shadrach, arrested and jailed with no warning.

She had never been in Canada. The route beyond Philadelphia was strange to her. But she could not let the runaways who accompanied her know this. As they walked along she told them stories of her own first flight, she kept painting vivid word pictures of what it would be like to be free.

But there were so many of them this time. She knew moments of doubt when she was half-afraid, and kept looking back over her shoulder, imagining that she heard the sound of pursuit. They would certainly be pursued. Eleven of them. Eleven thousand dollars' worth of flesh and bone and muscle that belonged to Maryland planters. If they were caught, the eleven runaways would be whipped and sold South, but she—she would probably be hanged.

---

2. **forbidden spiritual** In 1831, a slave named Nat Turner encouraged an unsuccessful slave uprising in Virginia by talking about the biblical story of the Israelites' escape from Egypt. Afterwards, the singing of certain spirituals was forbidden, for fear of encouraging more uprisings.

3. **Fugitive Slave Law** This part of the Compromise of 1850 held that escaped slaves, even if found in free states, could be returned to their masters. As a result, fugitives were not safe until they reached Canada.

◆ **Reading Strategy**

A good **purpose**, or reason, for reading this true story is to learn who Harriet Tubman was and what she did. To help achieve this purpose look for details in the bracketed passage to help you answer the following questions:

1. When did Harriet start out on the trip described in this narrative?

_____

2. How many slaves is she helping to escape?

_____

3. Where is she taking the runaway slaves?

_____

4. Is this her first time leading runaway slaves to freedom?

_____

◆ **Reading Check**

Why does Harriet have to take the slaves all the way to Canada?

_____

_____

◆ **Literary Analysis**

In a **third-person narrative,** the narrator often describes a character's actions and also lets readers in on the character's thoughts. List two of Harriet Tubman's actions and two thoughts mentioned on this page.

Actions

1. _____

2. _____

Thoughts

1. _____

2. _____

◆ Reading Check

How does Harriet keep up the spirits of the people she is leading?

_____

_____

_____

_____

_____

◆ Reading Strategy

Will the slammed door, mentioned in the underlined sentence, stop Harriet? **Set a purpose** for reading ahead by writing two questions that you hope the next part of the story will answer.

1._____

_____

_____

_____

2._____

_____

_____

_____

They tried to sleep during the day but they never could wholly relax into sleep. She could tell by the positions they assumed, by their restless movements. And they walked at night. Their progress was slow. It took them three nights of walking to reach the first stop. She had told them about the place where they would stay, promising warmth and good food, holding these things out to them as an incentive to keep going.

When she knocked on the door of a farmhouse, a place where she and her parties of runaways had always been welcome, always been given shelter and plenty to eat, there was no answer. She knocked again, softly. A voice from within said, "Who is it?" There was fear in the voice.

She knew instantly from the sound of the voice that there was something wrong. She said, "A friend with friends," the password on the Underground Railroad.

The door opened, slowly. The man who stood in the doorway looked at her coldly, looked with unconcealed astonishment and fear at the eleven disheveled runaways who were standing near her. Then he shouted, "Too many, too many. It's not safe. My place was searched last week. It's not safe!" and slammed the door in her face.

She turned away from the house, frowning. She had promised her passengers food and rest and warmth, and instead of that, there would be hunger and cold and more walking over the frozen ground. Somehow she would have to instill courage into these eleven people, most of them strangers, would have to feed them on hope and bright dreams of freedom instead of the fried pork and corn bread and milk she had promised them.

They stumbled along behind her, half-dead for sleep, and she urged them on, though she was as tired and as discouraged as they were. She had never been in Canada but she kept painting wondrous word pictures of what it would be like. She managed to dispel their fear of pursuit, so that they would not become hysterical, panic-stricken. Then she had to bring some of the fear back, so that they would stay awake and keep walking though they drooped with sleep.

Yet during the day, when they lay down deep in a thicket, they never really slept, because if a twig snapped or the wind sighed in the branches of a pine tree, they jumped to their feet, afraid of their own shadows, shivering and shaking. It was very cold, but they dared not make fires because someone would see the smoke and wonder about it.

Vocabulary Development: incentive (in sent´ iv) *n.* something that stimulates one to action; encouragement **disheveled** (di shev´ əld) *adj.* untidy; messy

She kept thinking, eleven of them. Eleven thousand dollars' worth of slaves. And she had to take them all the way to Canada. Sometimes she told them about Thomas Garrett, in Wilmington. She said he was their friend even though he did not know them. He was the friend of all fugitives. He called them God's poor. He was a Quaker and his speech was a little different from that of other people. His clothing was different, too. He wore the wide-brimmed hat that the Quakers wear.

She said that he had thick white hair, soft, almost like a baby's, and the kindest eyes she had ever seen. He was a big man and strong, but he had never used his strength to harm anyone, always to help people. He would give all of them a new pair of shoes. Everybody. He always did. Once they reached his house in Wilmington, they would be safe. He would see to it that they were.

She described the house where he lived, told them about the store where he sold shoes. She said he kept a pail of milk and a loaf of bread in the drawer of his desk so that he would have food ready at hand for any of God's poor who should suddenly appear before him, fainting with hunger. There was a hidden room in the store. A whole wall swung open, and behind it was a room where he could hide fugitives. On the wall there were shelves filled with small boxes—boxes of shoes—so that you would never guess that the wall actually opened.

While she talked, she kept watching them. They did not believe her. She could tell by their expressions. They were thinking. New shoes, Thomas Garrett, Quaker, Wilmington—what foolishness was this? Who knew if she told the truth? Where was she taking them anyway?

That night they reached the next stop—a farm that belonged to a German. She made the runaways take shelter behind trees at the edge of the fields before she knocked at the door. She hesitated before she approached the door, thinking, suppose that he, too, should refuse shelter, suppose—Then she thought, Lord, I'm going to hold steady on to You and You've got to see me through—and knocked softly.

She heard the familiar guttural voice say, "Who's there?" She answered quickly, "A friend with friends."

He opened the door and greeted her warmly. "How many this time?" he asked.

"Eleven," she said and waited, doubting, wondering.

He said, "Good. Bring them in."

He and his wife fed them in the lamplit kitchen, their faces glowing, as they offered food and more food, urging them to eat, saying there was plenty for everybody, have more milk, have more bread, have more meat.

They spent the night in the warm kitchen. They really slept, all that night and until dusk the next day. When they

The third-person pronouns *he* and *she* are used often in the bracketed passage. Identify the two people:

He: _____

_____

She: _____

_____

Read the rest of this page with the following **purpose:** To compare what happens at the second stop with what happened at the first stop (on page 38). List two ways that the events are alike and two ways they are different.

Ways Alike

1. _____

_____

2. _____

_____

Ways Different

1. _____

_____

2. _____

_____

_____

_____

_____

How do you know that the stories that Harriet Tubman tells the fugitives in the bracketed paragraph are **third-person narratives** and not first-person narratives?

_____

_____

_____

_____

_____

Circle a word in the underlined sentence that shows that Harriet's first attempt to escape was unsuccessful.

Mark the Text

left, it was with reluctance. They had all been warm and safe and well-fed. It was hard to exchange the security offered by that clean, warm kitchen for the darkness and the cold of a December night.

Harriet had found it hard to leave the warmth and friend-liness, too. But she urged them on. For a while, as they walked, they seemed to carry in them a measure of content-ment; some of the serenity and the cleanliness of that big warm kitchen lingered on inside them. But as they walked farther and farther away from the warmth and the light, the cold and the darkness entered into them. They fell silent, sullen, suspicious. She waited for the moment when some one of them would turn <u>mutinous</u>. It did not happen that night.

Two nights later she was aware that the feet behind her were moving slower and slower. She heard the irritability in their voices, knew that soon someone would refuse to go on.

She started talking about William Still and the Philadelphia Vigilance Committee.[4] No one commented. No one asked any questions. She told them the story of William and Ellen Craft and how they escaped from Georgia. Ellen was so fair that she looked as though she were white, and so she dressed up in a man's clothing and she looked like a wealthy young planter. Her husband, William, who was dark, played the role of her slave. Thus they traveled from Macon, Georgia, to Philadelphia, riding on the trains, staying at the finest hotels. Ellen pretended to be very ill— her right arm was in a sling, and her right hand was bandaged, because she was supposed to have rheumatism. Thus she avoided having to sign the register at the hotels for she could not read or write. They finally arrived safely in Philadelphia, and then went on to Boston.

No one said anything. Not one of them seemed to have heard her.

She told them about Frederick Douglass, the most famous of the escaped slaves, of his eloquence, of his magnificent appearance. <u>Then she told them of her own first vain effort at running away, evoking the memory of that miserable life she had led as a child, reliving it for a moment in the telling.</u>

But they had been tired too long, hungry too long, afraid too long, footsore too long. One of them suddenly cried out in despair, "Let me go back. It is better to be a slave than to suffer like this in order to be free."

Vocabulary Development: mutinous (myo͞ot′ ən əs) *adj.* rebellious

---

4. **Philadelphia Vigilance Committee** group of citizens who helped escaped slaves. Its secretary was a free black man named William Still.

She carried a gun with her on these trips. She had never used it—except as a threat. Now as she aimed it, she experienced a feeling of guilt, remembering that time, years ago, when she had prayed for the death of Edward Brodas, the Master, and then not too long afterward had heard that great wailing cry that came from the throats of the field hands, and knew from the sound that the Master was dead.

One of the runaways said, again, "Let me go back. Let me go back," and stood still, and then turned around and said, over his shoulder, "I am going back."

She lifted the gun, aimed it at the despairing slave. She said, "Go on with us or die." The husky low-pitched voice was grim.

He hesitated for a moment and then he joined the others. They started walking again. She tried to explain to them why none of them could go back to the plantation. If a runaway returned, he would turn traitor, the master and the overseer would force him to turn traitor. The returned slave would disclose the stopping places, the hiding places, the cornstacks they had used with the full knowledge of the owner of the farm, the name of the German farmer who had fed them and sheltered them. These people who had risked their own security to help runaways would be ruined, fined, imprisoned.

She said, "We got to go free or die. And freedom's not bought with dust."

This time she told them about the long agony of the Middle Passage on the old slave ships, about the black horror of the holds, about the chains and the whips. They too knew these stories. But she wanted to remind them of the long hard way they had come, about the long hard way they had yet to go. She told them about Thomas Sims, the boy picked up on the streets of Boston and sent back to Georgia. She said when they got him back to Savannah, got him in prison there, they whipped him until a doctor who was standing by watching said, "You will kill him if you strike him again!" His master said, "Let him die!"

Thus she forced them to go on. Sometimes she thought she had become nothing but a voice speaking in the darkness, cajoling, urging, threatening. Sometimes she told them things to make them laugh, sometimes she sang to them, and heard the eleven voices behind her blending softly with hers, and then she knew that for the moment all was well with them.

She gave the impression of being a short, muscular, indomitable woman who could never be defeated. Yet at any

---

Vocabulary Development: cajoling (kə jōl′ iŋ) *v.* coaxing or persuading gently
indomitable (in däm′ it ə bəl) *adj.* not easily discouraged

Harriet Tubman: Guide to Freedom **41**

◆ **Reading Strategy**

Set a purpose to find out why Harriet carries a gun. Then write the answer below.

_____

_____

_____

◆ **Literary Analysis**

Underline quotes that contain first-person pronouns in the bracketed passage and circle the pronouns. Then, on the lines below, explain why a **third-person narrative** may sometimes contain first-person pronouns.

◆ **Reading Check**

What happened to Thomas Sims?

_____

_____

_____

Why does Harriet tell the fugitives about him?

_____

_____

_____

_____

Set a purpose as you read this paragraph to find out why Harriet suddenly fell asleep. Write the answer below:

_____

_____

_____

_____

◆ Literary Analysis

This paragraph contains both third-person and first-person pronouns. Identify the person referred to as *he* and the person referred to as *I*.

He: _____

I: _____

◆ Reading Check

Why is cold weather such a problem for the fugitives?

_____

_____

_____

_____

_____

_____

_____

_____

moment she was liable to be seized by one of those curious fits of sleep, which might last for a few minutes or for hours.[5]

Even on this trip, she suddenly fell asleep in the woods. The runaways, ragged, dirty, hungry, cold, did not steal the gun as they might have, and set off by themselves, or turn back. They sat on the ground near her and waited patiently until she awakened. They had come to trust her implicitly, totally. They, too, had come to believe her repeated statement, "We got to go free or die." She was leading them into freedom, and so they waited until she was ready to go on.

Finally, they reached Thomas Garrett's house in Wilmington, Delaware. Just as Harriet had promised, Garrett gave them all new shoes, and provided carriages to take them on to the next stop.

By slow stages they reached Philadelphia, where William Still hastily recorded their names, and the plantations whence they had come, and something of the life they had led in slavery. Then he carefully hid what he had written, for fear it might be discovered. In 1872 he published this record in book form and called it *The Underground Railroad*. In the foreword to his book he said: "While I knew the danger of keeping strict records, and while I did not then dream that in my day slavery would be blotted out, or that the time would come when I could publish these records, it used to afford me great satisfaction to take them down, fresh from the lips of fugitives on the way to freedom, and to preserve them as they had given them."

William Still, who was familiar with all the station stops on the Underground Railroad, supplied Harriet with money and sent her and her eleven fugitives on to Burlington, New Jersey.

Harriet felt safer now, though there were danger spots ahead. But the biggest part of her job was over. As they went farther and farther north, it grew colder; she was aware of the wind on the Jersey ferry and aware of the cold damp in New York. From New York they went on to Syracuse, where the temperature was even lower.

In Syracuse she met the Reverend J.W. Loguen, known as "Jarm" Loguen. This was the beginning of a lifelong friendship. Both Harriet and Jarm Loguen were to become friends and supporters of Old John Brown.[6]

---

5. **sleep . . . hours** When she was about 13, Harriet accidentally received a severe blow on the head. Afterwards, she often lost consciousness and could not be awakened until the episode was over.
6. **John Brown** white abolitionist (1800–1859) who was hanged for leading a raid on the arsenal at Harpers Ferry, Virginia, as part of a slave uprising.

From Syracuse they went north again, into a colder, snowier city—Rochester. Here they almost certainly stayed with Frederick Douglass, for he wrote in his autobiography:

"On one occasion I had eleven fugitives at the same time under my roof, and it was necessary for them to remain with me until I could collect sufficient money to get them to Canada. It was the largest number I ever had at any one time, and I had some difficulty in providing so many with food and shelter, but, as may well be imagined, they were not very <u>fastidious</u> in either direction, and were well content with very plain food, and a strip of carpet on the floor for a bed, or a place on the straw in the barnloft."

Late in December 1851, Harriet arrived in St. Catharines, Canada West (now Ontario), with the eleven fugitives. It had taken almost a month to complete this journey; most of the time had been spent getting out of Maryland.

That first winter in St. Catharines was a terrible one. Canada was a strange frozen land, snow everywhere, ice everywhere, and a bone-biting cold the like of which none of them had ever experienced before. Harriet rented a small frame house in the town and set to work to make a home. The fugitives boarded with her. They worked in the forests, felling trees, and so did she. Sometimes she took other jobs, cooking or cleaning house for people in the town. She cheered on these newly arrived fugitives, working herself, finding work for them, finding food for them, praying for them, sometimes begging for them.

Often she found herself thinking of the beauty of Maryland, the mellowness of the soil, the richness of the plant life there. The climate itself made for an ease of living that could never be duplicated in this bleak, barren countryside.

In spite of the severe cold, the hard work, she came to love St. Catharines, and the other towns and cities in Canada where black men lived. She discovered that freedom meant more than the right to change jobs at will, more than the right to keep the money that one earned. It was the right to vote and to sit on juries. It was the right to be elected to office. In Canada there were black men who were county officials and members of school boards. St. Catharines had a large colony of ex-slaves, and they owned their own homes, kept them neat and clean and in good repair. They lived in whatever part of town they chose and sent their children to the schools.

Vocabulary Development: fastidious (fas tid′ ē əs) *adj.* refined in an oversensitive way, so as to be easily disgusted or displeased

---

◆ **Reading Strategy**

Set a purpose as you read the bracketed passage to find reasons why Harriet liked St. Catharines and reasons why she liked Maryland. Underline details that help you meet your purpose. Then list several reasons below.

St. Catharines

_____

_____

_____

Maryland

_____

_____

_____

◆ **Reading Strategy**

Through the **third-person narrative**, the writer shows what kind of person Harriet Tubman is. List several of the qualities the narrator reveals.

_____

_____

_____

_____

_____

_____

Do you think the author admires
Harriet Tubman? Explain.

_____

_____

_____

_____

_____

_____

When spring came she decided that she would make this
small Canadian city her home—as much as any place could
be said to be home to a woman who traveled from Canada to
the Eastern Shore of Maryland as often as she did.

In the spring of 1852, she went back to Cape May, New
Jersey. She spent the summer there, cooking in a hotel.
That fall she returned, as usual, to Dorchester County, and
brought out nine more slaves, conducting them all the way
to St. Catharines, in Canada West, to the bone-biting cold,
the snow-covered forests—and freedom.

She continued to live in this fashion, spending the winter
in Canada, and the spring and summer working in Cape
May, New Jersey, or in Philadelphia. She made two trips a
year into slave territory, one in the fall and another in the
spring. She now had a definite crystallized purpose, and in
carrying it out, her life fell into a pattern which remained
unchanged for the next six years.

Reader's Response: Would you have trusted Harriet Tubman to
take you on a long, dangerous journey? Why or why not?

_____

_____

_____

Thinking About the Skill: How can **setting a purpose** before you
begin reading help you understand what you read better?

_____

_____

_____

Up the Slide

Jack London

Summary

Seventeen-year-old Clay Dilham and his partner, Swanson, are headed to the city of Dawson in Canada's Yukon territory. Clay leaves their campsite by dog sled to get a load of firewood, confident he'll return in half an hour. Swanson doubts that good firewood is so near. As he travels on the frozen river, Clay spots a tree on a nearby mountain cliff. But climbing the icy cliff proves perilous. Clay slips several times along the way. After felling the tree, he struggles to get down the cliff, but he slips many more items. Freezing, Clay struggles for hours before winding up in a gully, where he discovers a hidden grove of pine trees. Clay finally returns to Swanson. A week later, he and Swanson sell fifty cords of the pine wood in Dawson.

Visual Summary

Problem		Solution		Result
Clay Dilham goes out to gather wood to sell. He has trouble moving around on an icy cliff.	→	With bravery and skill, Dilham finally manages to get to the tree and work his way down the mountain.	→	Dilham ends up finding even more wood than he expected.

◆ **Activate Prior Knowledge**

Imagine you are traveling to the Yukon, where temperatures have been known to plunge to -80°F. List five items of clothing or pieces of equipment that you would bring with you.

1. _____

2. _____

3. _____

4. _____

5. _____

◆ **Reading Strategy**

One way to follow the events of a story is to **predict,** or guess, what is going to happen. Based on Swanson's and Clay's thoughts in the bracketed passage, predict whether Clay will carry out his task in thirty minutes. Complete the sentence below with your prediction.

I predict Clay (will   will not) complete the task on time because

_____

_____

_____

_____

◆ **Reading Check**

Why does Clay think he is the only one able to discover the dead pine tree?

_____

_____

_____

_____

Up the Slide
Jack London

Clay Dilham is one of the many prospectors who traveled to the Yukon Territory in search of gold and adventure during the 1890s. The Yukon is a region in northwest Canada, next to Alaska.

When Clay Dilham left the tent to get a sled-load of firewood, he expected to be back in half an hour. So he told Swanson, who was cooking the dinner. Swanson and he belonged to different outfits, located about twenty miles apart on the Stewart River, but they had become traveling partners on a trip down the Yukon to Dawson[1] to get the mail.

Swanson had laughed when Clay said he would be back in half an hour. It stood to reason, Swanson said, that good, dry firewood could not be found so close to Dawson; that whatever firewood there was originally had long since been gathered in; that firewood would not be selling at forty dollars a cord[2] if any man could go out and get a sled-load and be back in the time Clay expected to make it.

Then it was Clay's turn to laugh, as he sprang on the sled and mushed the dogs on the river-trail. For, coming up from the Siwash village the previous day, he had noticed a small dead pine in an out-of-the-way place, which had defied discovery by eyes less sharp than his. And his eyes were both young and sharp, for his seventeenth birthday was just cleared.

A swift ten minutes over the ice brought him to the place, and figuring ten minutes to get the tree and ten minutes to return made him certain that Swanson's dinner would not wait.

Just below Dawson, and rising out of the Yukon itself, towered the great Moosehide Mountain, so named by Lieutenant Schwatka long ere[3] the Yukon became famous. On the river side the mountain was scarred and gullied and gored; and it was up one of these gores or gullies that Clay had seen the tree.

Halting his dogs beneath, on the river ice, he looked up, and after some searching, rediscovered it. Being dead, its weatherbeaten gray so blended with the gray wall of rock that a thousand men could pass by and never notice it. Taking root in a cranny, it had grown up, <u>exhausted</u> its bit of soil,

Vocabulary Development: exhausted (eg zôst′ əd) *v.* used up; expended completely

1. **Yukon** (yo͞o kän) . . . **Dawson** (dô sən) Dawson is a town and former gold-mining center on the Yukon River.
2. **cord** (kôrd) *n.* a measure of wood cut for fuel, equal to a pile eight feet long, four feet high, and four feet wide.
3. **ere** (er) *prep.* old word for *before.*

and perished. Beneath it the wall fell sheer for a hundred feet to the river. All one had to do was to sink an ax into the dry trunk a dozen times and it would fall to the ice, and most probably smash conveniently to pieces. This Clay had figured on when confidently limiting the trip to half an hour.

He studied the cliff thoroughly before attempting it. So far as he was concerned, the longest way round was the shortest way to the tree. Twenty feet of nearly perpendicular climbing would bring him to where a slide sloped more gently in. By making a long zigzag across the face of this slide and back again, he would arrive at the pine.

Fastening his ax across his shoulders so that it would not interfere with his movements, he clawed up the broken rock, hand and foot, like a cat, till the twenty feet were cleared and he could draw breath on the edge of the slide.

The slide was steep and its snow-covered surface slippery. Further, the heelless, walrus-hide shoes of his *muclucs* were polished by much ice travel, and by his second step he realized how little he could depend upon them for clinging purposes. A slip at that point meant a plunge over the edge and a twenty-foot fall to the ice. A hundred feet farther along, and a slip would mean a fifty-foot fall.

He thrust his mittened hand through the snow to the earth to steady himself, and went on. But he was forced to exercise such care that the first zigzag consumed five minutes. Then, returning across the face of the slide toward the pine, he met with a new difficulty. The slope steepened considerably, so that little snow collected, while bent flat beneath this thin covering were long, dry last-year's grasses.

The surface they presented was as glassy as that of his muclucs, and when both surfaces came together his feet shot out, and he fell on his face, sliding downward and convulsively clutching for something to stay himself.

This he succeeded in doing, although he lay quiet for a couple of minutes to get back his nerve. He would have taken off his muclucs and gone at it in his socks, only the cold was thirty below zero, and at such temperature his feet would quickly freeze. So he went on, and after ten minutes of risky work made the safe and solid rock where stood the pine.

A few strokes of the ax felled it into the chasm, and peeping over the edge, he indulged a laugh at the startled dogs. They were on the verge of bolting when he called aloud to them, soothingly, and they were reassured.

Then he turned about for the trip back. Going down, he knew, was even more dangerous than coming up, but how dangerous he did not realize till he had slipped half a dozen times, and each time saved himself by what appeared to him

Vocabulary Development: thoroughly (thur´ ō lē) *adv.* accurately and with regard to detail

Explain how it is possible for the "longest way round" to be "the shortest way to the tree."

_____

_____

_____

_____

_____

◆ Literary Analysis

The **conflict** in this story is a struggle between a person and nature. In the bracketed paragraphs, circle words and phrases that make the slide seem like a force opposing Clay.

Mark the Text

◆ Reading Check

During which season of the year does the story take place? How can you tell?

_____

_____

_____

_____

Do you think Clay is right "to get down by going up"? Explain the pros and cons of his decision.

Pros

_____

_____

_____

Cons

_____

_____

_____

List different elements of nature that Clay has to battle as part of the **conflict**.

_____

_____

_____

After reading the bracketed passage, **predict** whether Clay's struggle will decrease or increase from this point on. Write your prediction in the second column of the chart below. In the first column, write the story clues that help you make your prediction. After you have finished the story, turn back to this chart and fill in the third column.

Story Clue	My Prediction	Actual Outcome

a miracle. Time and again he ventured upon the slide, and time and again he was balked when he came to the grasses.

He sat down and looked at the treacherous snow-covered slope. It was <u>manifestly</u> impossible for him to make it with a whole body, and he did not wish to arrive at the bottom shattered like the pine tree.

But while he sat inactive the frost was stealing in on him, and the quick chilling of his body warned him that he could not delay. He must be doing something to keep his blood circulating. If he could not get down by going down, there only remained to him to get down by going up. It was a herculean[4] task, but it was the only way out of the predicament.

From where he was he could not see the top of the cliff, but he reasoned that the gully in which lay the slide must give inward more and more as it approached the top. From what little he could see, the gully displayed this tendency; and he noticed, also, that the slide extended for many hundreds of feet upward, and that where it ended the rock was well broken up and favorable for climbing. . . .

So instead of taking the zigzag which led downward, he made a new one leading upward and crossing the slide at an angle of thirty degrees. The grasses gave him much trouble, and made him long for soft-tanned moosehide moccasins, which could make his feet cling like a second pair of hands.

He soon found that thrusting his mittened hands through the snow and clutching the grass roots was uncertain and unsafe. His mittens were too thick for him to be sure of his grip, so he took them off. But this brought with it new trouble. When he held on to a bunch of roots the snow, coming in contact with his bare warm hand, was melted, so that his hands and the wristbands of his woolen shirt were dripping with water. This the frost was quick to attack, and his fingers were numbed and made worthless.

Then he was forced to seek good footing, where he could stand erect unsupported, to put on his mittens, and to thrash his hands against his sides until the heat came back into them.

This constant numbing of his fingers made his progress very slow; but the zigzag came to an end finally, where the side of the slide was buttressed by a perpendicular rock, and he turned back and upward again. As he climbed higher and higher, he found that the slide was wedge-shaped, its rocky buttresses pinching it away as it reared its upper end. Each step increased the depth which seemed to yawn for him.

While beating his hands against his sides he turned and looked down the long slippery slope, and figured, in case he slipped, that he would be flying with the speed of an express

Vocabulary Development: manifestly (man´ ə fest´ lē) *adv.* clearly

4. **herculean** (hər kyoo´ lē ən) *adj.* very difficult; requiring tremendous effort.

train ere he took the final plunge into the icy bed of the Yukon.

He passed the first outcropping rock, and the second, and at the end of an hour found himself above the third, and fully five hundred feet above the river. And here, with the end nearly two hundred feet above him, the pitch of the slide was increasing.

Each step became more difficult and perilous, and he was faint from <u>exertion</u> and from lack of Swanson's dinner. Three or four times he slipped slightly and recovered himself; but, growing careless from exhaustion and the long tension on his nerves, he tried to continue with too great haste, and was rewarded by a double slip of each foot, which tore him loose and started him down the slope.

On account of the steepness there was little snow; but what little there was was displaced by his body, so that he became the nucleus of a young avalanche. He clawed desperately with his hands, but there was little to cling to, and he sped downward faster and faster.

The first and second outcroppings were below him, but he knew that the first was almost out of line, and pinned his hope on the second. Yet the first was just enough in line to catch one of his feet and to whirl him over and head downward on his back.

The shock of this was severe in itself, and the fine snow enveloped him in a blinding, maddening cloud; but he was thinking quickly and clearly of what would happen if he brought up head first against the outcropping. He twisted himself over on his stomach, thrust both hands out to one side, and pressed them heavily against the flying surface.

This had the effect of a brake, drawing his head and shoulders to the side. In this position he rolled over and over a couple of times, and then, with a quick jerk at the right moment, he got his body the rest of the way round.

And none too soon, for the next moment his feet drove into the outcropping, his legs doubled up, and the wind was driven from his stomach with the abruptness of the stop.

There was much snow down his neck and up his sleeves. At once and with unconcern he shook this out, only to discover, when he looked up to where he must climb again, that he had lost his nerve. He was shaking as if with a palsy, and sick and faint from a frightful nausea.

Fully ten minutes passed ere he could master these sensations and summon sufficient strength for the weary climb. His legs hurt him and he was limping, and he was conscious of a sore place in his back, where he had fallen on the ax.

In an hour he had regained the point of his tumble, and was contemplating the slide, which so suddenly steepened. It was plain to him that he could not go up with his hands and

Vocabulary Development: exertion (eg zur′ shən) *n.* energetic effort

---

◆ Reading Check

What internal problems are now affecting Clay?

_____

_____

_____

_____

_____

_____

_____

_____

◆ Literary Analysis

Based on the bracketed passage, who seems to be winning this struggle—Clay, or the slide? Explain your answer.

_____

_____

_____

_____

_____

_____

◆ Reading Check

Where is Clay now, and why has it taken him an hour to get here?

_____

_____

_____

_____

feet alone, and he was beginning to lose his nerve again when he remembered the ax.

Reaching upward the distance of a step, he brushed away the snow, and in the frozen gravel and crumbled rock of the slide chopped a shallow resting place for his foot. Then he came up a step, reached forward, and repeated the <u>maneuver</u>. And so, step by step, foot-hole by foot-hole, a tiny speck of toiling life poised like a fly on the face of Moosehide Mountain, he fought his upward way.

Twilight was beginning to fall when he gained the head of the slide and drew himself into the rocky bottom of the gully. At this point the shoulder of the mountain began to bend back toward the crest, and in addition to its being less steep, the rocks afforded better handhold and foothold. The worst was over, and the best yet to come!

The gully opened out into a miniature basin, in which a floor of soil had been deposited, out of which, in turn, a tiny grove of pines had sprung. The trees were all dead, dry and seasoned, having long since exhausted the thin skin of earth.

Clay ran his experienced eye over the timber, and estimated that it would chop up into fifty cords at least. Beyond, the gully closed in and became barren rock again. On every hand was barren rock, so the wonder was small that the trees had escaped the eyes of men. They were only to be discovered as he had discovered them—by climbing after them.

He continued the <u>ascent</u>, and the white moon greeted him when he came out upon the crest of Moosehide Mountain. At his feet, a thousand feet below, sparkled the lights of Dawson.

But the <u>descent</u> was precipitate and dangerous in the uncertain moonlight, and he elected to go down the mountain by its gentler northern flank. In a couple of hours he reached the Yukon at the Siwash village, and took the river-trail back to where he had left the dogs. There he found Swanson, with a fire going, waiting for him to come down.

And although Swanson had a hearty laugh at his expense, nevertheless, a week or so later, in Dawson, there were fifty cords of wood sold at forty dollars a cord, and it was he and Swanson who sold them.

Vocabulary Development: maneuver (mə n$\overline{oo}$′ vər) *n.* series of planned steps
ascent (ə sent′) *n.* act of climbing or rising
descent (dē sent′) *n.* act of climbing down

Reader's Response: Do you think the risks that Clay took were reasonable or foolish? Why?

_____

_____

Thank You, M'am
Langston Hughes

Summary

About eleven o'clock one night on the street, a boy tries to snatch the purse of a large woman. When he trips, the woman grabs him and scolds him. Annoyed by his dirty face, she drags him to her home to clean him up. The boy says he wanted money for a pair of blue suede shoes. When he says there's no one at his home, the woman makes dinner for the two of them. The boy has a chance to run away, but he doesn't. After eating, the woman gives him ten dollars for shoes and warns him never to steal again. The boy, nearly speechless, says, "Thank you, m'am," and leaves.

Visual Summary

A boy tries to steal a woman's purse.	→	The woman doesn't report the boy to the police but instead takes him to her home.	→	At home, the woman feeds the boy and shows him kindness instead of anger.

List two emotions you might feel if
you caught someone trying to steal
from you.

1. _____

2. _____

List two emotions you might feel if
you were caught trying to steal
from someone else.

1. _____

2. _____

◆ Reading Strategy

A good way to get involved in a
story is to **respond to characters'
actions** in a personal way. How do
you feel about Mrs. Jones's actions
during the purse snatching? Circle
one of the following responses, and
then explain your answer.

1. I feel sorry for her.

2. I admire her.

3. I am angry at her.

_____

_____

_____

_____

◆ Reading Check

What does Mrs. Jones threaten to
do to the boy?

_____

_____

_____

_____

Thank You M'am
Langston Hughes

*How would you respond if someone tried to steal your purse or
wallet? Mrs. Jones's response may surprise you.*

She was a large woman with a large purse that had everything in it but hammer and nails. It had a long strap and
she carried it slung across her shoulder. It was about eleven
o'clock at night, and she was walking alone, when a boy ran
up behind her and tried to snatch her purse. The strap
broke with the single tug the boy gave it from behind. But
the boy's weight, and the weight of the purse combined
caused him to lose his balance. Instead of taking off full
blast as he had hoped, the boy fell on his back on the sidewalk, and his legs flew up. The large woman simply turned
around and kicked him right square in his blue-jeaned sit-
ter. Then she reached down, picked the boy up by his shirt
front, and shook him until his teeth rattled.

After that the woman said, "Pick up my pocketbook, boy,
and give it here."

She still held him. But she bent down enough to permit
him to stoop and pick up her purse. Then she said, "Now
ain't you ashamed of yourself?"

Firmly gripped by his shirt front, the boy said, "Yes'm."

The woman said, "What did you want to do it for?"

The boy said, "I didn't aim to."

She said, "You a lie!"

By that time two or three people passed, stopped, turned
to look, and some stood watching.

"If I turn you loose, will you run?" asked the woman.

"Yes'm," said the boy.

"Then I won't turn you loose," said the woman. She did
not release him.

"Lady, I'm sorry," whispered the boy.

"Um-hum! Your face is dirty. I got a great mind to wash
your face for you. Ain't you got nobody home to tell you to
wash your face?"

"No'm," said the boy.

"Then it will get washed this evening," said the large
woman starting up the street, dragging the frightened boy
behind her.

He looked as if he were fourteen or fifteen, frail and wil-
low-wild, in tennis shoes and blue jeans.

The woman said, "You ought to be my son. I would teach
you right from wrong. Least I can do right now is to wash
your face. Are you hungry?"

"No'm," said the being-dragged boy. "I just want you to
turn me loose."

"Was I bothering *you* when I turned that corner?" asked the woman.

"No'm."

"But you put yourself in contact with *me*," said the woman. "If you think that that contact is not going to last awhile, you got another thought coming. When I get through with you, sir, you are going to remember Mrs. Luella Bates Washington Jones."

Sweat popped out on the boy's face and he began to struggle. Mrs. Jones stopped, jerked him around in front of her, put a half nelson[1] about his neck, and continued to drag him up the street. When she got to her door, she dragged the boy inside, down a hall, and into a large kitchenette-furnished room at the rear of the house. She switched on the light and left the door open. The boy could hear other roomers laughing and talking in the large house. Some of their doors were open, too, so he knew he and the woman were not alone. The woman still had him by the neck in the middle of her room.

She said, "What is your name?"

"Roger," answered the boy.

"Then, Roger, you go to that sink and wash your face," said the woman, whereupon she turned him loose—at last. Roger looked at the door—looked at the woman—looked at the door—*and went to the sink.*

"Let the water run until it gets warm," she said. "Here's a clean towel."

"You gonna take me to jail?" asked the boy, bending over the sink.

"Not with that face, I would not take you nowhere," said the woman. "Here I am trying to get home to cook me a bite to eat and you snatch my pocketbook! Maybe you ain't been to your supper either, late as it be. Have you?"

"There's nobody home at my house," said the boy.

"Then we'll eat," said the woman. "I believe you're hungry—or been hungry—to try to snatch my pocketbook."

"I wanted a pair of blue suede shoes," said the boy.

"Well, you didn't have to snatch *my* pocketbook to get some suede shoes," said Mrs. Luella Bates Washington Jones. "You could of asked me."

"M'am?"

The water dripping from his face, the boy looked at her. There was a long pause. A very long pause. After he had dried his face and not knowing what else to do dried it again, the boy turned around, wondering what next. The door was open. He could make a dash for it down the hall. He could run, run, run, *run!*

The woman was sitting on the day bed. After a while she

---

1. **half nelson** wrestling hold using one arm.

◆ **Reading Strategy**

Would you act the same way that Mrs. Jones does in the bracketed paragraph? Why or why not?

_____

_____

_____

_____

_____

_____

_____

◆ **Literary Analysis**

One way to discover an **implied theme,** or hidden message, of a story is to see how characters speak to each other. Complete the sentence below. Then underline statements in the bracketed dialogue that back up your opinion.

Mrs. Jones speaks to Roger in a(n)

_____ way.

◆ **Reading Check**

What do you expect Mrs. Jones to say next when you turn the page?

_____

_____

_____

What does the bracketed speech **imply** about Mrs. Jones's reasons for helping Roger?

_____

_____

_____

How do you feel about Roger now that his behavior seems to have changed, based on the bracketed passage? Explain.

_____

_____

_____

Based on the underlined sentence, what kind of person do you think Mrs. Jones is?

_____

_____

_____

Underline two final pieces of advice Mrs. Jones gives Roger. What message is she trying to get across to him?

Mark THE Text!

_____

_____

_____

_____

said, "I were young once and I wanted things I could not get."

There was another long pause. The boy's mouth opened. Then he frowned, but not knowing he frowned.

The woman said, "Um-hum! You thought I was going to say *but*, didn't you? You thought I was going to say, *but I didn't snatch people's pocketbooks*. Well, I wasn't going to say that." Pause. Silence. "I have done things, too, which I would not tell you, son—neither tell God, if He didn't already know. So you set down while I fix us something to eat. You might run that comb through your hair so you will look <u>presentable</u>."

In another corner of the room behind a screen was a gas plate and an icebox. Mrs. Jones got up and went behind the screen. The woman did not watch the boy to see if he was going to run now, nor did she watch her purse which she left behind her on the day bed. But the boy took care to sit on the far side of the room where he thought she could easily see him out of the corner of her eye, if she wanted to. He did not trust the woman not to trust him. And he did not want to be <u>mistrusted</u> now.

"Do you need somebody to go to the store," asked the boy, "maybe to get some milk or something?"

"Don't believe I do," said the woman, "unless you just want sweet milk yourself. I was going to make cocoa out of this canned milk I got here."

"That will be fine," said the boy.

She heated some lima beans and ham she had in the icebox, made the cocoa, and set the table. <u>The woman did not ask the boy anything about where he lived, or his folks, or anything else that would embarrass him.</u> Instead, as they ate, she told him about her job in a hotel beauty shop that stayed open late, what the work was like, and how all kinds of women came in and out, blondes, redheads, and brunettes. Then she cut him a half of her ten-cent cake.

"Eat some more, son," she said.

When they were finished eating she got up and said, "Now, here, take this ten dollars and buy yourself some blue suede shoes. And next time, do not make the mistake of <u>latching</u> onto *my* pocketbook *nor nobody else's*—because shoes come by devilish like that will burn your feet. I got to get my rest now. But from here on in, son, I hope you will behave yourself."

Vocabulary Development: presentable (prē zent´ ə bəl) *adj.* in proper order for being seen by others
mistrusted (mis´ trust´ əd) *v.* doubted
latching (lach´ iŋ) *v.* grasping or attaching oneself to

She led him down the hall to the front door and opened it. "Goodnight! Behave yourself, boy!" she said, looking out into the street.

The boy wanted to say something other than, "Thank you, m'am," to Mrs. Luella Bates Washington Jones, but although his lips moved, he couldn't even say that as he turned at the foot of the <u>barren</u> stoop and looked up at the large woman in the door. Then she shut the door.

---

barren (bar´ ən) *adj.* sterile; empty

Reader's Response: Do you think Mrs. Jones was right to trust Roger? Why or why not?

_____

_____

_____

Thinking About the Skill: In what way does **responding to how characters act** keep you involved in a story?

_____

_____

_____

Would you have been speechless at the end of the story like Roger? If not, what do you think you would have said to Mrs. Jones?

_____

_____

_____

_____

_____

Brown *vs.* Board of Education
Walter Dean Myers

Summary

In the 1950s, a number of states required or allowed African American and white students to attend separate public schools. Those who supported this practice claimed that education would be "separate but equal." Those who objected said that education could not be truly equal if the races were separated. In the case of *Brown* vs. *Board of Education of Topeka,* the Supreme Court of the United States ruled racial separation, or segregation, in public schools to be unconstitutional. The case began, in 1951, when Oliver Brown, an African American railroad worker, joined thirteen other families in suing the school board of Topeka, Kansas, for not allowing their children to attend an all-white school near their homes. Thurgood Marshall, who later became the first African American justice of the Supreme Court, presented the legal argument for Brown. The court ruled unanimously that segregated schools deprive minorities of equal educational opportunities. This ruling helped pave the way for other important gains by African Americans.

Visual Summary

Purpose of this Essay	Information to Achieve This Purpose
To show the historic importance of the Supreme Court decision *Brown* vs. *Board of Education*	1. History of school segregation 2. The life of the main lawyer on the case, Thurgood Marshall 3. The research the lawyer used 4. The Supreme Court's decision to end school segregation

Brown *vs.* Board of Education
Walter Dean Myers

The 1896 Supreme Court case of Plessy *vs.* Ferguson *upheld a law requiring "separate but equal" accommodations for African Americans and whites in railroad cars. For more than fifty years, that ruling was applied to segregate, or separate, the races in transportation, hotels, restaurants, and even in the public schools.*

It was not until 1954, in the Supreme Court decision of Brown *vs.* Board of Education of Topeka, *that segregation in public schools was declared unconstitutional. Walter Dean Myers explains how that decision, which led to the end of "separate but equal" accommodations, was largely the achievement of one man, Thurgood Marshall.*

There was a time when the meaning of freedom was easily understood. For an African crouched in the darkness of a tossing ship, wrists chained, men with guns standing on the decks above him, freedom was a physical thing, the ability to move away from his captors, to follow the dictates of his own heart, to listen to the voices within him that defined his values and showed him the truth of his own path. The plantation owners wanted to make the Africans feel helpless, inferior. They denied them images of themselves as Africans and told them that they were without beauty. They segregated them and told them they were without value.

Slowly, surely, the meaning of freedom changed to an <u>elusive</u> thing that even the strongest people could not hold in their hands. There were no chains on black wrists, but there were the shadows of chains, stretching for hundreds of years back through time, across black minds.

* * *

From the end of the Civil War in 1865 to the early 1950's, many public schools in both the North and South were seg-regated. Segregation was different in the different sections of the country. In the North most of the schools were segregat-ed *de facto*[1]; that is, the law allowed blacks and whites to go to school together, but they did not actually always attend the same schools. Since a school is generally attended by children living in its neighborhood, wherever there were <u>predominantly</u> African-American neighborhoods there were, "in fact," segregated schools. In many parts of the country,

---

> **Vocabulary Development: elusive** (i loo´ siv) *adj.* hard to grasp or retain mentally
> **predominantly** (pri däm´ ə nənt lē) *adj.* mainly; most noticeably

---

1. *de facto* (dē fak´ tō) Latin for "existing in actual fact."

◆ Activate Prior Knowledge

Write two things you know about segregation in the United States.

1. _____
_____
_____
_____
_____

2. _____
_____
_____
_____
_____

◆ Reading Strategy

Because American legal practices are modeled on legal practices of ancient Rome, many of our legal terms have **origins** in Latin. In the bracketed passage, how can you tell that *de facto* is a legal term?

_____
_____
_____
_____

◆ Reading Check

From 1865 to the early 1950s, in what way were most public schools segregated in the North?

_____
_____
_____
_____
_____

Why do you think the writer uses Latin terms that he then translates for the reader?

_____

_____

_____

_____

What was the main claim made by parents in the law suit against the Topeka school board?

_____

_____

_____

_____

What did the *Brown* vs. *Board of Education of Topeka* case mean for young Linda Brown, for the African American parents of the children involved, and for the N.A.A.C.P. legal team?

_____

_____

_____

_____

_____

_____

_____

_____

however, and especially in the South, the segregation was *de jure,*[2] meaning that there were laws which forbade blacks to attend the same schools as whites.

The states with segregated schools relied upon the ruling of the Supreme Court in the 1896 *Plessy* vs. *Ferguson* case for legal justification: Facilities that were "separate but equal" were legal.

In the early 1950's the National Association for the Advancement of Colored People (N.A.A.C.P.) sponsored five cases that eventually reached the Supreme Court. One of the cases involved the school board of Topeka, Kansas.

Thirteen families sued the Topeka school board, claiming that to segregate the children was harmful to the children and, therefore, a violation of the equal protection clause of the Fourteenth Amendment. The names on the Topeka case were listed in alphabetical order, with the father of seven-year-old Linda Brown listed first.

"I didn't understand why I couldn't go to school with my playmates. I lived in an integrated neighborhood and played with children of all nationalities, but when school started they went to a school only four blocks from my home and I was sent to school across town," she says.

For young Linda the case was one of convenience and of being made to feel different, but for African-American parents it had been a long, hard struggle to get a good education for their children. It was also a struggle waged by lawyers who had worked for years to overcome segregation. The head of the legal team who presented the school cases was Thurgood Marshall.

*   *   *

The city was Baltimore, Maryland, and the year was 1921. Thirteen-year-old Thurgood Marshall struggled to balance the packages he was carrying with one hand while he tried to get his bus fare out of his pocket with the other. It was almost Easter, and the part-time job he had would provide money for flowers for his mother. Suddenly he felt a violent tug at his right arm that spun him around, sending his packages sprawling over the floor of the bus.

"Don't you never push in front of no white lady again!" an angry voice spat in his ear.

Thurgood turned and threw a punch . . . . The man charged into Thurgood, throwing punches that mostly missed, and tried to wrestle the slim boy to the ground. A policeman broke up the fight, grabbing Thurgood with one

---

2. *de jure* (dē jur´ ə) Latin for "by right or legal establishment."

huge black hand and pushing him against the side of the bus. Within minutes they were in the local courthouse.

Thurgood was not the first of his family to get into a good fight. His father's father had joined the Union Army during the Civil War, taking the names Thorough Good to add to the one name he had in bondage. His grandfather on his mother's side was a man brought from Africa and, according to Marshall's biography, "so ornery that his owner wouldn't sell him out of pity for the people who might buy him, but gave him his freedom instead and told him to clear out of the county."

Thurgood's frequent scrapes earned him a reputation as a young boy who couldn't be trusted to get along with white folks.

His father, Will Marshall, was a steward at the Gibson Island Yacht Club near Baltimore, and his mother, Norma, taught in a segregated school. The elder Marshall felt he could have done more with his life if his education had been better, but there had been few opportunities available for African Americans when he had been a young man. When it was time for the Marshall boys to go to college, he was more than willing to make the sacrifices necessary to send them.

Young people of color from all over the world came to the United States to study at Lincoln University, a predominantly black institution in southeastern Pennsylvania. Here Marshall majored in predentistry, which he found boring, and joined the Debating Club, which he found interesting. By the time he was graduated at the age of twenty-one, he had decided to give up dentistry for the law. Three years later he was graduated, first in his class, from Howard University Law School.

At Howard there was a law professor, Charles Hamilton Houston, who would affect the lives of many African-American lawyers and who would influence the legal aspects of the civil rights movement. Houston was a great teacher, one who demanded that his students be not just good lawyers but great lawyers. If they were going to help their people—and for Houston the only reason for African Americans to become lawyers was to do just that—they would have to have absolute understanding of the law, and be diligent in the preparation of their cases. At the time, Houston was an attorney for the N.A.A.C.P. and fought against discrimination in housing and in jobs.

After graduation, Thurgood Marshall began to do some work for the N.A.A.C.P., trying the difficult civil rights cases. He not only knew about the effects of discrimination by reading about

---

Vocabulary Development: diligent (dil′ ə jənt) *adj.* done with careful, steady effort; hardworking

---

◆ **Literary Analysis**

What facts about Thurgood Marshall's family do you learn in the bracketed passage?

_____

_____

_____

_____

◆ **Stop to Reflect**

In the underlined passage, circle the clues to why Marshall gave up dentistry. How did his experience in the Debating Club influence his decision?

Mark the Text

_____

_____

_____

_____

_____

◆ **Reading Check**

What profession, or type of work, did Marshall choose?

_____

_____

_____

_____

_____

_____

_____

An **informative essay** sometimes includes word choices that express the writer's point of view, or opinion. What do the underlined words in the bracketed passage tell you about Myers's attitude toward Marshall and his fellow lawyers? For example, does he think of them primarily as teachers or as fighters? Explain.

_____

_____

_____

_____

_____

_____

◆ Reading Check

In the bracketed paragraph, circle a passage that describes a result of segregation— something that resulted from the separation of whites and African Americans. Describe the result in your own words.

_____

_____

_____

_____

_____

_____

_____

_____

it, he was still living it when he was graduated from law school in 1933. In 1936 Marshall began working full-time for the N.A.A.C.P., and in 1940 became its chief counsel.

It was Thurgood Marshall and a battery of N.A.A.C.P. attorneys who began to challenge segregation throughout the country. These men and women were <u>warriors</u> in the <u>cause</u> of freedom for African Americans, taking their <u>battles</u> into courtrooms across the country. They understood the process of American justice and the power of the Constitution.

In *Brown* vs. *Board of Education of Topeka,* Marshall argued that segregation was a violation of the Fourteenth Amendment—that even if the facilities and all other "tangibles" were equal, which was the heart of the case in *Plessy* vs. *Ferguson,* a violation still existed. There were <u>intangible</u> factors, he argued, that made the education unequal.

Everyone involved understood the significance of the case: that it was much more than whether black children could go to school with white children. If segregation in the schools was declared <u>unconstitutional</u>, then *all* segregation in public places could be declared unconstitutional.

Southerners who argued against ending school segregation were caught up, as then-Congressman Brooks Hays of Arkansas put it, in "a lifetime of adventures in that gap between law and custom." The law was one thing, but most Southern whites felt just as strongly about their customs as they did the law.

Dr. Kenneth B. Clark, an African-American psychologist, testified for the N.A.A.C.P. He presented clear evidence that the effect of segregation was harmful to African-American children. Describing studies conducted by black and white psychologists over a twenty-year period, he showed that black children felt inferior to white children. In a particularly dramatic study that he had supervised, four dolls, two white and two black, were presented to African-American children. From the responses of the children to the dolls, identical in every way except color, it was clear that the children were rejecting the black dolls. African-American children did not just feel separated from white children, they felt that the separation was based on their inferiority.

Dr. Clark understood fully the principles and ideas of those people who had held Africans in bondage and had

---

Vocabulary Development: intangible (in tan´ jə bəl) *adj.* not able to be grasped
unconstitutional (un´ kän stə too´ shə nəl) *adj.* not in accordance with the U.S. Constitution

tried to make slaves of captives. By isolating people of African descent, by barring them from certain actions or places, they could make them feel inferior. The social scientists who testified at *Brown* vs. *Board of Education* showed that children who felt inferior also performed poorly.

The Justice Department argued that racial segregation was objectionable to the Eisenhower Administration and hurt our relationships with other nations.

On May 17, 1954, after <u>deliberating</u> for nearly a year and a half, the Supreme Court made its ruling. The Court stated that it could not use the intentions of 1868, when the Fourteenth Amendment was passed, as a guide to its ruling, or even those of 1896, when the decision in *Plessy* vs. *Ferguson* was handed down. Chief Justice Earl Warren wrote:

> We must consider public education in the light of its full development and its present place in American life throughout the nation. We must look instead to the effect of segregation itself on public education.

The Court went on to say that "modern authority" supported the idea that segregation deprived African Americans of equal opportunity. "Modern authority" referred to Dr. Kenneth B. Clark and the weight of evidence that he and the other social scientists had presented.

The high court's decision in *Brown* vs. *Board of Education* signaled an important change in the struggle for civil rights. It signaled clearly that the legal prohibitions that <u>oppressed</u> African Americans would have to fall. Equally important was the idea that the nature of the fight for equality would change. Ibrahima, Cinqué, Nat Turner, and George Latimer had struggled for freedom by fighting against their captors or fleeing from them. The 54th had fought for African freedom on the battlefields of the Civil War. Ida B. Wells had fought for equality with her pen. Lewis H. Latimer and Meta Vaux Warrick had tried to earn equality with their work. In *Brown* vs. *Board of Education* Thurgood Marshall, Kenneth B. Clark, and the lawyers and social scientists, both black and white, who helped them had won for African Americans a victory that would bring them closer to full equality than they had ever been in North America. There would still be legal battles to be won, but the major struggle would be in the hearts and minds of people and "in that gap between law and custom."

Vocabulary Development: deliberating (di lib′ ə rā tiŋ) *v.* thinking carefully
oppressed (ə prest′) *v.* kept down by injustice

◆ **Literary Analysis**

Look at the proposed outline for this **informative essay.** Then, below the miniature outline "page," record an important fact or detail for each of the three main categories in the outline.

I. History of School Segregation
  A.
  B.
  C.
II. Thurgood Marshall's Life
  A.
  B.
  C.
III. The *Brown* vs. *Board of Education* Decision
  A.
  B.
  C.

I.A. _____

_____

_____

_____

II.A. _____

_____

_____

_____

III.A. _____

_____

_____

_____

What important change in the struggle for civil rights resulted from the Supreme Court's decision in *Brown* vs. *Board of Education*?

_____

_____

_____

_____

_____

_____

_____

_____

_____

_____

In 1967 Thurgood Marshall was appointed by President Lyndon B. Johnson as an associate justice of the U.S. Supreme Court. He retired in 1991.

"I didn't think of my father or the other parents as being heroic at the time," Linda Brown says. "I was only seven. But as I grew older and realized how far-reaching the case was and how it changed the complexion of the history of this country, I was just thrilled that my father and the others here in Topeka were involved."

Reader's Response: How do you think the Supreme Court's decision in *Brown* vs. *Board of Education* has affected your life?

_____

_____

_____

_____

_____

Thinking About the Skill: How did analyzing word origins help you to understand an important distinction in this essay?

_____

_____

_____

_____

_____

A Retrieved Reformation

O. Henry

Summary

Jimmy Valentine, a safecracker, walks out of prison with a smile. He intends to go right back to cracking safes. He is soon back at it. He uses special tools to open vaults that others can't open. One day, Jimmy travels to a small town, falls in love at first sight with the local banker's daughter, and decides to reform. He assumes a new identity, opens a successful shoe store, and is about to marry the banker's daughter. He is planning to give away his special thief's tools and start life over. But the detective who has been pursuing Jimmy shows up and plans to arrest him. Then, Jimmy's fiancée's niece gets locked in the bank's vault. With his special tools Jimmy opens the vault and saves the little girl. Once the detective sees Jimmy's act of kindness, he changes his mind and doesn't arrest Jimmy.

Visual Summary

Events in the Story
• Jimmy Valentine is released from prison. • He goes back to "cracking" safes. • In a town he visits, he falls in love with the banker's daughter. • He gives up his criminal ways and changes his life. • A detective has been following him to arrest him. • Jimmy's fiancée's niece gets locked in the bank vault. • Jimmy uses his safe-cracking skills to open the vault to save her. • The detective sees him do this.

What We Expect to Happen	What Really Happens
After the detective travels so far to find the safecracker, he will arrest him.	When the detective sees that the safecracker is doing good deeds, he lets him go.

A Retrieved Reformation
O. Henry

*This is the story of Jimmy Valentine, a convicted safecracker who
gets out of prison. Then, something happens that puts him in danger of
returning to prison.*

A guard came to the prison shoe-shop, where Jimmy
Valentine was <u>assiduously</u> stitching uppers, and escorted
him to the front office. There the warden handed Jimmy his
pardon, which had been signed that morning by the governor. Jimmy took it in a tired kind of way. He had served
nearly ten months of a four-year sentence. He had expected
to stay only about three months, at the longest. When a man
with as many friends on the outside as Jimmy Valentine had
is received in the "stir" it is hardly worthwhile to cut his
hair.

"Now, Valentine," said the warden, "you'll go out in the
morning. Brace up, and make a man of yourself. You're not
a bad fellow at heart. Stop cracking safes, and live straight."

"Me?" said Jimmy, in surprise. "Why, I never cracked a
safe in my life."

"Oh, no," laughed the warden. "Of course not. Let's see,
now. How was it you happened to get sent up on that
Springfield job? Was it because you wouldn't prove an alibi
for fear of compromising somebody in extremely high-toned
society? Or was it simply a case of a mean old jury that had
it in for you? It's always one or the other with you innocent
victims."

"Me?" said Jimmy, still blankly <u>virtuous</u>. "Why, warden, I
never was in Springfield in my life!"

"Take him back, Cronin," smiled the warden, "and fix him
up with outgoing clothes. Unlock him at seven in the morning, and let him come to the bullpen.[1] Better think over my
advice, Valentine."

At a quarter past seven on the next morning Jimmy stood
in the warden's outer office. He had on a suit of the villain-
ously fitting, ready-made clothes and a pair of the stiff,
squeaky shoes that the state furnishes to its discharged
compulsory guests.

The clerk handed him a railroad ticket and the five-dollar
bill with which the law expected him to rehabilitate himself
into good citizenship and prosperity. The warden gave him a

Vocabulary Development: assiduously (ə sij′ ōō wəs lē) *adv.* carefully and busily
virtuous (vʉr′ chōō wəs) *adj.* moral;
upright

---

1. **bullpen** *n.* barred room in a jail, where prisoners are kept temporarily.

cigar, and shook hands. Valentine, 9762, was chronicled on the books "Pardoned by Governor," and Mr. James Valentine walked out into the sunshine.

Disregarding the song of the birds, the waving green trees, and the smell of the flowers, Jimmy headed straight for a restaurant. There he tasted the first sweet joys of liberty in the shape of a chicken dinner. From there he proceeded leisurely to the depot and boarded his train. Three hours set him down in a little town near the state line. He went to the café of one Mike Dolan and shook hands with Mike, who was alone behind the bar.

"Sorry we couldn't make it sooner, Jimmy, me boy," said Mike. "But we had that protest from Springfield to buck against, and the governor nearly balked. Feeling all right?"

"Fine," said Jimmy. "Got my key?"

He got his key and went upstairs, unlocking the door of a room at the rear. Everything was just as he had left it. There on the floor was still Ben Price's collar-button that had been torn from that eminent detective's shirt-band when they had overpowered Jimmy to arrest him.

Pulling out from the wall a folding-bed, Jimmy slid back a panel in the wall and dragged out a dust-covered suitcase. He opened this and gazed fondly at the finest set of burglar's tools in the East. It was a complete set, made of specially tempered steel, the latest designs in drills, punches, braces and bits, jimmies, clamps, and augers,[2] with two or three novelties invented by Jimmy himself, in which he took pride. Over nine hundred dollars they had cost him to have made at —, a place where they make such things for the profession.

In half an hour Jimmy went downstairs and through the café. He was now dressed in tasteful and well-fitting clothes, and carried his dusted and cleaned suitcase in his hand.

"Got anything on?" asked Mike Dolan, genially.

"Me?" said Jimmy, in a puzzled tone. "I don't understand. I'm representing the New York Amalgamated Short Snap Biscuit Cracker and Frazzled Wheat Company."

This statement delighted Mike to such an extent that Jimmy had to take a seltzer-and-milk on the spot. He never touched "hard" drinks.

A week after the release of Valentine, 9762, there was a neat job of safe-burglary done in Richmond, Indiana, with no clue to the author. A scant eight hundred dollars was all that was secured. Two weeks after that a patented, improved, burglar-proof safe in Logansport was opened like a cheese to the tune of fifteen hundred dollars, currency; securities and silver untouched. That began to interest the rogue-catchers.[3] Then an old-fashioned bank-safe in

2. **drills . . . augers** (ô´ gərz) *n.* tools used in metalwork.
3. **rogue-catchers** *n.* police.

© Pearson Education, Inc.

◆ Stop to Reflect

What do you think Mike is referring to in the bracketed passage? Write your ideas on the lines below, and circle the words and phrases in the passage that give you clues.

_____

_____

_____

_____

_____

_____

_____

◆ Reading Strategy

Asking questions about a story's characters and events can help you understand what you read. What question could you ask yourself about Valentine's actions in the bracketed paragraph?

_____

_____

_____

_____

_____

◆ Reading Check

What are the first things Jimmy does after being released from prison?

_____

_____

_____

_____

Question	Answer

Who is Ben Price?

_____

_____

_____

_____

_____

_____

_____

_____

_____

_____

_____

_____

_____

Jefferson City became active and threw out of its crater an eruption of bank-notes amounting to five thousand dollars. The losses were now high enough to bring the matter up into Ben Price's class of work. By comparing notes, a remarkable similarity in the methods of the burglaries was noticed. Ben Price investigated the scenes of the robberies, and was heard to remark:

"That's Dandy Jim Valentine's autograph. He's resumed business. Look at that combination knob—jerked out as easy as pulling up a radish in wet weather. He's got the only clamps that can do it. And look how clean those tumblers were punched out! Jimmy never has to drill but one hole. Yes, I guess I want Mr. Valentine. He'll do his bit next time without any short-time or clemency foolishness."

Ben Price knew Jimmy's habits. He had learned them while working up the Springfield case. Long jumps, quick getaways, no confederates,[4] and a taste for good society— these ways had helped Mr. Valentine to become noted as a successful dodger of <u>retribution</u>. It was given out that Ben Price had taken up the trail of the elusive cracksman, and other people with burglar-proof safes felt more at ease.

One afternoon, Jimmy Valentine and his suitcase climbed out of the mail hack[5] in Elmore, a little town five miles off the railroad down in the blackjack country of Arkansas. Jimmy, looking like an athletic young senior just home from college, went down the board sidewalk toward the hotel.

A young lady crossed the street, passed him at the corner and entered a door over which was the sign "The Elmore Bank." Jimmy Valentine looked into her eyes, forgot what he was, and became another man. She lowered her eyes and colored slightly. Young men of Jimmy's style and looks were scarce in Elmore.

Jimmy collared a boy that was loafing on the steps of the bank as if he were one of the stockholders, and began to ask him questions about the town, feeding him dimes at intervals. By and by the young lady came out, looking royally unconscious of the young man with the suitcase, and went her way.

"Isn't that young lady Miss Polly Simpson?" asked Jimmy, with specious guile.[6]

"Naw," said the boy. "She's Annabel Adams. Her pa owns this bank. What'd you come to Elmore for? Is that a gold watch chain? I'm going to get a bulldog. Got any more dimes?"

Vocabulary Development: retribution (re′ trə byoo′ shən) *n.* punishment for wrongdoing

---

4. **confederates** (kən fed′ ər its) *n.* accomplices.
5. **mail hack** *n.* horse and carriage used to deliver mail.
6. **specious guile** (spē′ shəs gīl′) *n.* crafty, indirect way of obtaining information.

Jimmy went to the Planters' Hotel, registered as Ralph D. Spencer, and engaged a room. He leaned on the desk and declared his platform[7] to the clerk. He said he had come to Elmore to look for a location to go into business. How was the shoe business, now, in the town? He had thought of the shoe business. Was there an opening?

The clerk was impressed by the clothes and manner of Jimmy. He, himself, was something of a pattern of fashion to the thinly gilded[8] youth of Elmore, but he now perceived his shortcomings. While trying to figure out Jimmy's manner of tying his four-in-hand,[9] he cordially gave information.

Yes, there ought to be a good opening in the shoe line. There wasn't an exclusive shoe store in the place. The dry-goods and general stores handled them. Business in all lines was fairly good. Hoped Mr. Spencer would decide to locate in Elmore. He would find it a pleasant town to live in, and the people very sociable.

Mr. Spencer thought he would stop over in the town a few days and look over the situation. No, the clerk needn't call the boy. He would carry up his suitcase, himself: it was rather heavy.

Mr. Ralph Spencer, the phoenix[10] that arose from Jimmy Valentine's ashes—ashes left by the flame of a sudden and alterative attack of love—remained in Elmore, and prospered. He opened a shoe store and secured a good run of trade.

Socially he was also a success, and made many friends. And he accomplished the wish of his heart. He met Miss Annabel Adams, and became more and more captivated by her charms.

At the end of a year the situation of Mr. Ralph Spencer was this: he had won the respect of the community, his shoe store was flourishing, and he and Annabel were engaged to be married in two weeks. Mr. Adams, the typical, plodding, country banker, approved of Spencer. Annabel's pride in him almost equaled her affection. He was as much at home in the family of Mr. Adams and that of Annabel's married sister as if he were already a member.

One day Jimmy sat down in his room and wrote this letter, which he mailed to the safe address of one of his old friends in St. Louis:

Dear Old Pal:

I want you to be at Sullivan's place, in Little Rock, next Wednesday night, at nine o'clock. I want you to wind up some little matters for me. And, also, I want to make you a present of my kit of tools. I know you'll be glad to get them—you

---

7. **platform** *n.* here, a statement of intention.
8. **thinly gilded** *adj.* coated with a thin layer of gold; here, appearing well dressed.
9. **four-in-hand** *n.* necktie.
10. **phoenix** (fē´ niks) *n.* in Egyptian mythology, a beautiful bird that lived for about 600 years and then burst into flames. A new bird arose from its ashes.

◆ Reading Check

When and why does Jimmy Valentine decide to change his name and type of work?

_____

_____

_____

_____

◆ Stop to Reflect

Why do you think O. Henry compares Jimmy Valentine to a phoenix in the underlined passage? Use the information in the footnote as a clue.

_____

_____

_____

_____

◆ Literary Analysis

Mark the Text O. Henry is known for startling his readers with a **surprise ending**. What does the bracketed paragraph encourage you to guess about how Jimmy's new life will develop?

_____

_____

_____

_____

_____

_____

_____

◆ Reading Strategy

What **question** do you have about Ben Price's plans? Circle any words or phrases in the underlined passage that give you a clue to those plans.

Mark THE Text!

_____

_____

_____

_____

_____

◆ Stop to Reflect

Underline the parts of Annabel's comment that are ironic—amusing because of something she does not know, which the reader does know. What does the reader know that Annabel does not?

Mark THE Text!

_____

_____

_____

_____

_____

_____

couldn't duplicate the lot for a thousand dollars. Say, Billy, I've quit the old business—a year ago. I've got a nice store. I'm making an honest living, and I'm going to marry the finest girl on earth two weeks from now. It's the only life, Billy—the straight one. I wouldn't touch a dollar of another man's money now for a million. After I get married I'm going to sell out and go West, where there won't be so much danger of having old scores brought up against me. I tell you, Billy, she's an angel. She believes in me; and I wouldn't do another crooked thing for the whole world. Be sure to be at Sully's, for I must see you. I'll bring along the tools with me.

> Your old friend,
> Jimmy.

On the Monday night after Jimmy wrote this letter, Ben Price jogged <u>unobtrusively</u> into Elmore in a livery buggy.[11] He lounged about town in his quiet way until he found out what he wanted to know. From the drugstore across the street from Spencer's shoe store he got a good look at Ralph D. Spencer.

<u>"Going to marry the banker's daughter are you, Jimmy?" said Ben to himself, softly. "Well, I don't know!"</u>

The next morning Jimmy took breakfast at the Adamses. He was going to Little Rock that day to order his wedding suit and buy something nice for Annabel. That would be the first time he had left town since he came to Elmore. It had been more than a year now since those last professional "jobs," and he thought he could safely venture out.

After breakfast quite a family party went downtown together—Mr. Adams, Annabel, Jimmy, and Annabel's married sister with her two little girls, aged five and nine. They came by the hotel where Jimmy still boarded, and he ran up to his room and brought along his suitcase. Then they went on to the bank. There stood Jimmy's horse and buggy and Dolph Gibson, who was going to drive him over to the railroad station.

All went inside the high, carved oak railings into the banking-room—Jimmy included, for Mr. Adams's future son-in-law was welcome anywhere. The clerks were pleased to be greeted by the good-looking, agreeable young man who was going to marry Miss Annabel. Jimmy set his suitcase down. Annabel, whose heart was bubbling with happiness and lively youth, put on Jimmy's hat, and picked up the suitcase. "Wouldn't I make a nice drummer?"[12] said Annabel. "My! Ralph, how heavy it is! Feels like it was full of gold bricks."

Vocabulary Development: unobtrusively (un´ əb trōō´ siv lē) *adv.* without calling attention to oneself

---

11. **livery buggy** *n.* horse and carriage for hire.
12. **drummer** *n.* traveling salesman.

"Lot of nickel-plated shoehorns in there," said Jimmy, coolly, "that I'm going to return. Thought I'd save express charges by taking them up. I'm getting awfully economical."

The Elmore Bank had just put in a new safe and vault. Mr. Adams was very proud of it, and insisted on an inspection by everyone. The vault was a small one, but it had a new, patented door. It fastened with three solid steel bolts thrown simultaneously with a single handle, and had a time lock. Mr. Adams beamingly explained its workings to Mr. Spencer, who showed a courteous but not too intelligent interest. The two children, May and Agatha, were delighted by the shining metal and funny clock and knobs.

While they were thus engaged Ben Price sauntered in and leaned on his elbow, looking casually inside between the railings. He told the teller that he didn't want anything; he was just waiting for a man he knew.

Suddenly there was a scream or two from the women, and a commotion. Unperceived by the elders, May, the nine-year-old girl, in a spirit of play, had shut Agatha in the vault. She had then shot the bolts and turned the knob of the combination as she had seen Mr. Adams do.

The old banker sprang to the handle and tugged at it for a moment. "The door can't be opened," he groaned. "The clock hasn't been wound nor the combination set."

Agatha's mother screamed again, hysterically.

"Hush!" said Mr. Adams, raising his trembling hand. "All be quiet for a moment. Agatha!" he called as loudly as he could. "Listen to me." During the following silence they could just hear the faint sound of the child wildly shrieking in the dark vault in a panic of terror.

"My precious darling!" wailed the mother. "She will die of fright! Open the door! Oh, break it open! Can't you men do something?"

"There isn't a man nearer than Little Rock who can open that door," said Mr. Adams, in a shaky voice. "My God! Spencer, what shall we do? That child—she can't stand it long in there. There isn't enough air, and, besides, she'll go into convulsions from fright."

Agatha's mother, frantic now, beat the door of the vault with her hands. Somebody wildly suggested dynamite. Annabel turned to Jimmy, her large eyes full of anguish, but not yet despairing. To a woman nothing seems quite impossible to the powers of the man she worships.

"Can't you do something, Ralph—try, won't you?"

◆ **Reading Check**

What is the reason for Jimmy's suitcase being so heavy?

_____

_____

_____

_____

◆ **Reading Strategy**

What **question** do you have about Ben Price's behavior based on the bracketed passage?

_____

_____

_____

_____

_____

_____

_____

_____

_____

◆ **Reading Check**

Summarize the problem that is described in the bracketed passage.

_____

_____

_____

_____

_____

_____

Vocabulary Development: simultaneously (sī´ məl tā´ nē əs lē) *adv.* occurring at the same time
anguish (aŋ´ gwish) *n.* great suffering from worry

What **question** could you ask yourself based on the bracketed passage?

_____

_____

_____

What happens to Agatha?

_____

_____

_____

Are you **surprised** that Jimmy opens the door of the vault? Why or why not?

_____

_____

_____

_____

_____

Explain what is **surprising** about this **ending** to the story based on the bracketed passage.

_____

_____

_____

_____

_____

_____

He looked at her with a queer, soft smile on his lips and in his keen eyes.

"Annabel," he said, "give me that rose you are wearing, will you?"

Hardly believing that she heard him aright, she unpinned the bud from the bosom of her dress, and placed it in his hand. Jimmy stuffed it into his vest pocket, threw off his coat and pulled up his shirt sleeves. With that act Ralph D. Spencer passed away and Jimmy Valentine took his place. "Get away from the door, all of you," he commanded, shortly. He set his suitcase on the table, and opened it out flat. From that time on he seemed to be unconscious of the presence of anyone else. He laid out the shining, queer implements swiftly and orderly, whistling softly to himself as he always did when at work. In a deep silence and immovable, the others watched him as if under a spell.

In a minute Jimmy's pet drill was biting smoothly into the steel door. In ten minutes—breaking his own burglarious record—he threw back the bolts and opened the door. Agatha, almost collapsed, but safe, was gathered into her mother's arms.

Jimmy Valentine put on his coat, and walked outside the railings toward the front door. As he went he thought he heard a far-away voice that he once knew call "Ralph!" But he never hesitated.

At the door a big man stood somewhat in his way. "Hello, Ben!" said Jimmy, still with his strange smile. "Got around at last, have you? Well, let's go. I don't know that it makes much difference, now."

And then Ben Price acted rather strangely.

"Guess you're mistaken, Mr. Spencer," he said. "Don't believe I recognize you. Your buggy's waiting for you, ain't it?"

And Ben Price turned and strolled down the street.

Reader's Response: Would you have done what Ben Price did? Explain your answer.

_____

_____

_____

Thinking About the Skill: How did asking questions help you to understand the characters and events in this story? Give an example.

_____

_____

_____

Gentleman of Río en Medio

Juan A. A. Sedillo

Summary

"Gentleman of Río en Medio" focuses on Don Anselmo. He is an old Spanish American gentleman who is very honest and proud. Don Anselmo refuses to accept extra money for the sale of his land when it turns out that he has twice as much land as he thought. The new American owners are not happy, however, when the neighborhood children keep playing in the orchard that is part of the land they bought. They bring back Don Anselmo, who tells the Americans that he planted the trees for each of the children in town and that they belong to the children, not to him. Because Don Anselmo was so honest in refusing to accept extra money for his land, the Americans decide to solve the problem by buying each of the trees from the other families.

Visual Summary

Key Traits of Don Anselmo

Honesty

He won't take more for the land than he first agreed to.

Generosity

He donates trees on his land to the children.

Don Anselmo

Loyalty

He stands up for the rights of the children to play among the trees he has given them.

When you buy something, you assume that you and the seller agree to certain things. List the terms, or main points, of an agreement between a buyer and a seller.

1._____

_____

2._____

_____

3._____

_____

4._____

_____

◆ **Reading Strategy**

When story writers do not state things directly, they may give you clues about characters or situations. From these details you can **draw inferences,** or make educated guesses. For example, in the bracketed passage, the old man bows to everyone. From this action you can draw the inference that he is respectful. Underline more details in this passage that help you to draw inferences about the old man. Write the inferences below.

1._____

_____

2._____

_____

3._____

_____

◆ **Reading Check**

Why has the old man come down from his village?

_____

_____

Gentleman of Río en Medio
Juan A. A. Sedillo

Don Anselmo, the main character in this story, lives in a tiny Spanish American village in the Sangre de Cristo mountains of northern New Mexico. His ancestors were among the early Spanish settlers who came to the Southwest in the 1600s.

It took months of negotiation to come to an understanding with the old man. He was in no hurry. What he had the most of was time. He lived up in Río en Medio,[1] where his people had been for hundreds of years. He tilled the same land they had tilled. His house was small and wretched, but quaint. The little creek ran through his land. His orchard was gnarled and beautiful.

The day of the sale he came into the office. His coat was old, green and faded. I thought of Senator Catron,[2] who had been such a power with these people up there in the mountains. Perhaps it was one of his old Prince Alberts.[3] He also wore gloves. They were old and torn and his fingertips showed through them. He carried a cane, but it was only the skeleton of a worn-out umbrella. Behind him walked one of his innumerable kin—a dark young man with eyes like a gazelle.

The old man bowed to all of us in the room. Then he removed his hat and gloves, slowly and carefully. Chaplin[4] once did that in a picture, in a bank—he was the janitor. Then he handed his things to the boy, who stood obediently behind the old man's chair.

There was a great deal of conversation, about rain and about his family. He was very proud of his large family. Finally we got down to business. Yes, he would sell, as he had agreed, for twelve hundred dollars, in cash. We would buy, and the money was ready. "Don[5] Anselmo," I said to him in Spanish, "we have made a discovery. You remember that we sent that surveyor, that engineer, up there to survey your land so as to make the deed. Well, he finds that you

Vocabulary Development: negotiation (ni gō′ shē ā′ shən) *n.* discussion to reach an agreement
gnarled (närld) *adj.* knotty and twisted
innumerable (i nōō′ mər ə bəl) *adj.* too many to be counted

1. **Río en Medio** (rē′ ō en mā′ dē ō)
2. **Senator Catron** Thomas Benton Catron, senator from New Mexico, 1912–1917.
3. **Prince Alberts** long, double-breasted coats.
4. **Chaplin** Charlie Chaplin (1889–1977), actor and producer of silent films in the United States.
5. **don** Spanish title of respect, similar to *sir* in English.

own more than eight acres. He tells us that your land extends across the river and that you own almost twice as much as you thought." He didn't know that. "And now, Don Anselmo," I added, "these Americans are *buena gente*,[6] they are good people, and they are willing to pay you for the additional land as well, at the same rate per acre, so that instead of twelve hundred dollars you will get almost twice as much, and the money is here for you."

The old man hung his head for a moment in thought. Then he stood up and stared at me. "Friend," he said, "I do not like to have you speak to me in that manner." I kept still and let him have his say. "I know these Americans are good people, and that is why I have agreed to sell to them. But I do not care to be insulted. I have agreed to sell my house and land for twelve hundred dollars and that is the price."

I argued with him but it was useless. Finally he signed the deed and took the money but refused to take more than the amount agreed upon. Then he shook hands all around, put on his ragged gloves, took his stick and walked out with the boy behind him.

A month later my friends had moved into Río en Medio. They had replastered the old adobe house, pruned the trees, patched the fence, and moved in for the summer. One day they came back to the office to complain. The children of the village were overrunning their property. They came every day and played under the trees, built little play fences around them, and took blossoms. When they were spoken to they only laughed and talked back good-naturedly in Spanish.

I sent a messenger up to the mountains for Don Anselmo. It took a week to arrange another meeting. When he arrived he repeated his previous preliminary performance. He wore the same faded cutaway,[7] carried the same stick and was accompanied by the boy again. He shook hands all around, sat down with the boy behind his chair, and talked about the weather. Finally I <u>broached</u> the subject. "Don Anselmo, about the ranch you sold to these people. They are good people and want to be your friends and neighbors always. When you sold to them you signed a document, a deed, and in that deed you agreed to several things. One thing was that they were to have the complete possession of the property. Now, Don Anselmo, it seems that every day the children of the village overrun the orchard and spend most of their time there. We would like to know if you, as the most respected man in

---

Vocabulary Development: broached (brōcht) *v.* started a discussion about a topic

---

6. ***buena gente*** (bwā´ nä hen´ tā) Spanish for "good people."
7. **cutaway** (kut´ ə wā´) *n.* coat worn by men for formal daytime occasions.

◆ **Literary Analysis**

A **conflict** is a struggle between two opposing forces. A conflict in a story usually leads to a resolution, or solution. The old man and the narrator disagree about what to do after they find out the land is bigger and more valuable than they thought. How is this conflict resolved?

_____

_____

_____

_____

_____

◆ **Reading Strategy**

What **inference** can you draw about Don Anselmo, based on his refusal to accept more money?

_____

_____

_____

_____

_____

◆ **Reading Check**

What unexpected problems have come up after the sale of Don Anselmo's land?

1. _____

_____

2. _____

_____

What **inferences** can you draw about Don Anselmo's ideas about owning land, compared with the ideas of the narrator and his friends?

_____

_____

_____

_____

_____

_____

_____

_____

◆ Literary Analysis

How do the narrator and his friends finally resolve the **conflict** about the trees?

_____

_____

_____

_____

Why do they choose this complicated way of resolving the conflict?

_____

_____

_____

_____

_____

_____

_____

the village, could not stop them from doing so in order that these people may enjoy their new home more in peace."

Don Anselmo stood up. "We have all learned to love these Americans," he said, "because they are good people and good neighbors. I sold them my property because I knew they were good people, but I did not sell them the trees in the orchard."

This was bad. "Don Anselmo," I pleaded, "when one signs a deed and sells real property one sells also everything that grows on the land, and those trees, every one of them, are on the land and inside the boundaries of what you sold."

"Yes, I admit that," he said. "You know," he added, "I am the oldest man in the village. Almost everyone there is my relative and all the children of Río en Medio are my *sobrinos* and *nietos*,[8] my descendants. Every time a child has been born in Río en Medio since I took possession of that house from my mother I have planted a tree for that child. The trees in that orchard are not mine, Señor, they belong to the children of the village. Every person in Río en Medio born since the railroad came to Santa Fe owns a tree in that orchard. I did not sell the trees because I could not. They are not mine."

There was nothing we could do. Legally we owned the trees but the old man had been so generous, refusing what amounted to a fortune for him. It took most of the following winter to buy the trees, individually, from the descendants of Don Anselmo in the valley of Río en Medio.

---

8. ***sobrinos*** (sō brē´ nōs) **and** ***nietos*** (nyā´ tōs) Spanish for "nieces and nephews" and "grandchildren."

Reader's Response: If you had bought Don Anselmo's property, how would you feel after hearing his explanation of why he had not sold you the orchard trees? Give reasons for your answer.

_____

_____

_____

Thinking About the Skill: How does drawing inferences help you to understand the characters' actions in this story? Give an example to support your answer.

_____

_____

_____

from The People, Yes
Carl Sandburg

Summary

This selection is excerpted from a two-hundred page poem. In the poem, Sandburg declares his faith in the common American people. This part of the poem talks about the wild stories and adventures of well-known characters in American tall tales, such as Pecos Bill (sometimes called Pete), Paul Bunyan, and John Henry.

Visual Summary

MAIN IDEA

**America's folklore
shows a land of great variety**

People	Places	Events
Pecos Pete	Missouri	Cyclones
Paul Bunyan	Texas	Mutiny
John Henry	Rocky Mountains	Watch swallowed by cow
	California	Thick fog
	Nebraska	Cattle lost in a redwood tree
	Dakotas	

Write the name of a hero you know from American folktales or tall tales. Then, briefly tell about one of his or her exploits.

_____

_____

_____

◆ **Reading Strategy**

Carl Sandburg includes many **cultural references**—details of his American heritage or traditions—in this poem. Circle names of American places or heroes named in the bracketed passage.

Mark the Text

◆ **Literary Analysis**

In these bracketed lines, the poet follows **oral tradition** using exaggeration to create humor. Which story seems the most exaggerated or funny to you? Explain.

Mark the Text

_____

_____

_____

_____

_____

_____

_____

_____

_____

from The People, Yes
Carl Sandburg

Tall tales may not always be true, but they are fun to listen to and retell to others.

They have yarns
Of a skyscraper so tall they had to put hinges
On the two top stories so to let the moon go by,
Of one corn crop in Missouri when the roots
5   Went so deep and drew off so much water
The Mississippi riverbed that year was dry,
Of pancakes so thin they had only one side,
Of "a fog so thick we shingled the barn and six feet
    out on the fog,"
Of Pecos Pete straddling a cyclone in Texas and
    riding it to the west coast where "it rained out
    under him,"
10 Of the man who drove a swarm of bees across
    the Rocky Mountains and the Desert "and didn't
    lose a bee,"
Of a mountain railroad curve where the engineer
    in his cab can touch the caboose and spit in the
    conductor's eye,
Of the boy who climbed a cornstalk growing so fast
    he would have starved to death if they hadn't
    shot biscuits up to him,
Of the old man's whiskers: "When the wind was with
    him his whiskers arrived a day before he did,"
Of the hen laying a square egg and cackling, "Ouch!"
    and of hens laying eggs with the dates printed on
    them,
15 Of the ship captain's shadow: it froze to the deck
    one cold winter night,
Of <u>mutineers</u> on that same ship put to chipping
    rust with rubber hammers,
Of the sheep counter who was fast and accurate: "I
    just count their feet and divide by four,"
Of the man so tall he must climb a ladder to shave
    himself,
Of the <u>runt</u> so teeny-weeny it takes two men and a boy
    to see him,
20 Of <u>mosquitoes</u>: one can kill a dog, two of them
    a man,

Vocabulary Development: **mutineers** (myo͞ot′ ən irz′) *n.* crew members on a ship who revolt against their officers
runt (runt) *n.* the smallest animal in a litter
mosquitoes (mə skēt′ ōz) *n.* insects having two wings, the females of which extract blood from animals and people

Of a cyclone that sucked cookstoves out of the kitchen,
    up the chimney <u>flue</u>, and on to the next town,
Of the same cyclone picking up wagontracks in
    Nebraska and dropping them over in the Dakotas,
Of the hook-and-eye snake[1] unlocking itself into
    forty pieces, each piece two inches long, then in
    nine seconds flat snapping itself together again,
Of the watch swallowed by the cow—when they
    butchered her a year later the watch was running
    and had the correct time,
25 Of horned snakes, hoop snakes that roll themselves where
    they want to go, and rattlesnakes carrying bells
    instead of rattles on their tails,
Of the herd of cattle in California getting lost in a giant
    redwood tree that had hollowed out,
Of the man who killed a snake by putting its tail in its
    mouth so it swallowed itself,
Of railroad trains whizzing along so fast they reach the
    station before the whistle,
Of pigs so thin the farmer had to tie knots in their
    tails to keep them from crawling through the cracks
    in their pens,
30 Of Paul Bunyan's big blue ox, Babe, measuring
    between the eyes forty-two ax-handles and a plug of
    Star tobacco exactly,
Of John Henry's hammer and the curve of its swing
    and his singing of it as "a rainbow round my
    shoulder."

Vocabulary Development: flue (flo͞o) *n.* the pipe in a chimney that
    leads the smoke outside

---

1. **hook-and-eye snake** here, a snake that is fastened together with metal hooks.

Reader's Response: Which story in the poem would you want to
pass along to a younger family member? Why?

_____

_____

_____

Thinking About the Skill: How does looking for references to
American culture help you understand the poem's message better?

_____

_____

Circle a detail in line 22 (bracketed)
that storytellers might have varied
as they passed the story on in the
oral tradition. Then, on the lines
below, write how you might exag-
gerate this detail even further.

_____

_____

_____

_____

_____

◆ Reading Strategy

Which two traditional American folk
heroes are named near the end of
the poem?

1. _____

2. _____

How did each (or people doing the
same jobs) help America grow?

_____

_____

_____

_____

_____

_____

_____

_____

_____

_____

_____

_____

from Travels with Charley

John Steinbeck

Summary

The writer, John Steinbeck, decides to leave his New York home and drive across the United States. As an American writer, he feels an obligation to observe the country and its people firsthand. He buys a special pick-up truck mounted with a small house. Steinbeck doesn't tell people he is a writer because he wants people to feel free to open up to him. His only companion is his French poodle, Charley. In North Dakota, Steinbeck is frightened by the wind in a desolate area. He dislikes the Bad Lands, where he meets a stranger who has little to say to him. In the late afternoon, however, the hills lose their dreadful look and take on a beautiful glow. On a gorgeous night, as he prepares to sleep, Steinbeck realizes that the Bad Lands are Good Lands.

Visual Summary

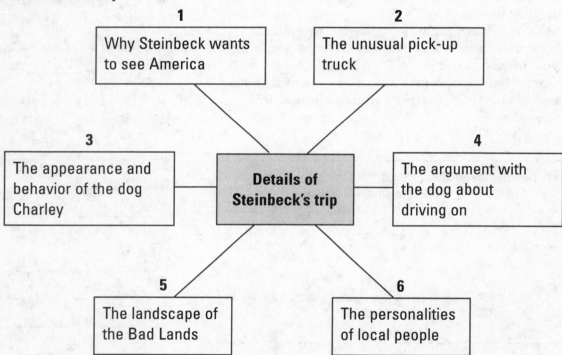

1. Why Steinbeck wants to see America

2. The unusual pick-up truck

3. The appearance and behavior of the dog Charley

Details of Steinbeck's trip

4. The argument with the dog about driving on

5. The landscape of the Bad Lands

6. The personalities of local people

from Travels with Charley
John Steinbeck

Where would you go to get to know America? John Steinbeck describes a place he visited that made a strong impression on him.

My plan was clear, concise, and reasonable, I think. For many years I have traveled in many parts of the world. In America I live in New York, or dip into Chicago or San Francisco. But New York is no more America than Paris is France or London is England. Thus I discovered that I did not know my own country. I, an American writer, writing about America, was working from memory, and the memory is at best a faulty, warpy reservoir. I had not heard the speech of America, smelled the grass and trees and sewage, seen its hills and water, its color and quality of light. I knew the changes only from books and newspapers. But more than this, I had not felt the country for twenty-five years. In short, I was writing of something I did not know about, and it seems to me that in a so-called writer this is criminal. My memories were distorted by twenty-five intervening years.

Once I traveled about in an old bakery wagon, double-doored rattler with a mattress on its floor. I stopped where people stopped or gathered, I listened and looked and felt, and in the process had a picture of my country the accuracy of which was impaired only by my own shortcomings.

So it was that I determined to look again, to try to rediscover this monster land. Otherwise, in writing, I could not tell the small <u>diagnostic</u> truths which are the foundations of the larger truth. One sharp difficulty presented itself. In the intervening twenty-five years my name had become reasonably well known. And it has been my experience that when people have heard of you, favorably or not, they change; they become, through shyness or the other qualities that publicity inspires, something they are not under ordinary circumstances. This being so, my trip demanded that I leave my name and my identity at home. I had to be <u>peripatetic</u> eyes and ears, a kind of moving gelatin plate.[1] I could not sign hotel registers, meet people I knew, interview others, or even ask searching questions. Furthermore, two or more people disturb the ecologic complex of an area. I had to go alone

---

Vocabulary Development: diagnostic (dī´ əg näs´ tik) *adj.* providing a distinguishing sign or characteristic as evidence
peripatetic (per´ i pə tet´ ik) *adj.* moving from place to place; walking about

---

1. **gelatin plate** sensitive glass plate used to reproduce pictures.

◆ **Activate Prior Knowledge**

List a place in the United States you have never seen but would like to visit. Explain why.

_____

_____

_____

_____

_____

_____

_____

_____

◆ **Reading Check**

How and when did Steinbeck travel around America previously?

_____

_____

_____

_____

_____

◆ **Reading Strategy**

One way to **clarify details** you don't understand is to look for notes or explanations on the page. How can you determine what a "gelatin plate" is?

_____

_____

_____

_____

◆ **Reading Strategy**

Reread to determine Steinbeck's purpose for using the truck. Read ahead to discover his needs. Then, fill in the chart below.

Purpose:
Needs:

◆ **Reading Strategy**

As you read ahead on pages 80 and 81, find five "controversies" that worry Steinbeck's friends. Mark them with large numbers in the margins next to the text. The first one has been marked for you.

_____

_____

_____

_____

_____

_____

_____

_____

_____

_____

_____

and I had to be self-contained, a kind of casual turtle carrying his house on his back.

With all this in mind I wrote to the head office of a great corporation which manufactures trucks. I specified my purpose and my needs.

I wanted a three-quarter-ton pick-up truck, capable of going anywhere under possibly rigorous conditions, and on this truck I wanted a little house built like the cabin of a small boat. A trailer is difficult to maneuver on mountain roads, is impossible and often illegal to park, and is subject to many restrictions. In due time, specifications came through, for a tough, fast, comfortable vehicle, mounting a camper top—a little house with double bed, a four-burner stove, a heater, refrigerator and lights operating on butane, a chemical toilet, closet space, storage space, windows screened against insects—exactly what I wanted. It was delivered in the summer to my little fishing place at Sag Harbor near the end of Long Island. Although I didn't want to start before Labor Day, when the nation settles back to normal living, I did want to get used to my turtle shell, to equip it and learn it. It arrived in August, a beautiful thing, powerful and yet lithe. It was almost as easy to handle as a passenger car. And because my planned trip had aroused some satiric remarks among my friends, I named it Rocinante, which you will remember was the name of Don Quixote's[2] horse.

Since I made no secret of my project, a number of controversies arose among my friends and advisers. (A projected journey spawns advisers in schools.) I was told that since my photograph was as widely distributed as my publisher could make it, I would find it impossible to move about without being recognized. Let me say in advance that in over ten thousand miles, in thirty-four states, I was not recognized even once. I believe that people identify things only in context. Even those people who might have known me against a background I am supposed to have, in no case identified me in Rocinante.

I was advised that the name Rocinante painted on the side of my truck in sixteenth-century Spanish script would cause curiosity and inquiry in some places. I do not know how

1

Vocabulary Development: **rigorous** (rig′ ər əs) *adj.* very strict or harsh
maneuver (mə n$\overline{oo}$′ vər) *v.* to manage; lead; control
inquiry (in′ kwə rē) *n.* an investigation or examination; questioning

---

2. **Don Quixote** (dän′ kē hōt′ ē) hero of an early 17th-century satirical romance by Cervantes, who tries in a chivalrous but unrealistic way to rescue the oppressed and fight evil.

many people recognized the name, but surely no one ever asked about it.

Next, I was told that a stranger's purpose in moving about the country might cause inquiry or even suspicion. For this reason I racked a shotgun, two rifles, and a couple of fishing rods in my truck, for it is my experience that if a man is going hunting or fishing his purpose is understood and even applauded. Actually, my hunting days are over. I no longer kill or catch anything I cannot get into a frying pan; I am too old for sport killing. This stage setting turned out to be unnecessary.

It was said that my New York license plates would arouse interest and perhaps questions, since they were the only outward identifying marks I had. And so they did—perhaps twenty or thirty times in the whole trip. But such contacts followed an invariable pattern, somewhat as follows:

Local man: "New York, huh?"

Me: "Yep."

Local man: "I was there in nineteen thirty-eight—or was it thirty-nine? Alice, was it thirty-eight or thirty-nine we went to New York?"

Alice: "It was thirty-six. I remember because it was the year Alfred died."

Local man: "Anyway, I hated it. Wouldn't live there if you paid me."

There was some genuine worry about my traveling alone, open to attack, robbery, assault. It is well known that our roads are dangerous. And here I admit I had senseless qualms. It is some years since I have been alone, nameless, friendless, without any of the safety one gets from family, friends, and accomplices. There is no reality in the danger. It's just a very lonely, helpless feeling at first—a kind of desolate feeling. For this reason I took one companion on my journey—an old French gentleman poodle known as Charley.

Actually his name is Charles le Chien.[3] He was born in Bercy on the outskirts of Paris and trained in France, and while he knows a little poodle-English, he responds quickly only to commands in French. Otherwise he has to translate, and that slows him down. He is a very big poodle, of a color called bleu, and he is blue when he is clean. Charley is a born diplomat. He prefers negotiation to fighting, and properly so, since he is very bad at fighting. Only once in his ten years has he been in trouble—when he met a dog who refused to negotiate. Charley lost a piece of his right ear that time. But he is a good watch dog—has a roar like a lion, designed to conceal from night-wandering strangers the fact that he couldn't bite his way out of a *cornet de papier*.[4] He is a good friend and traveling companion, and would rather

---

3. **Charles le Chien** (shärl′ lə shē un′) French for "Charles the dog."
4. *cornet de papier* (kôr nā′ də pà pyā′) French for "paper bag."

travel about than anything he can imagine. If he occurs at length in this account, it is because he contributed much to the trip. A dog, particularly an exotic like Charley, is a bond between strangers. Many conversations en route began with "What degree of a dog is that?"

The techniques of opening conversation are universal. I knew long ago and rediscovered that the best way to attract attention, help, and conversation is to be lost.

* * *

The night was loaded with omens. The grieving sky turned the little water to a dangerous metal and then the wind got up—not the gusty, rabbity wind of the seacoasts I know but a great bursting sweep of wind with nothing to inhibit it for a thousand miles in any direction. Because it was a wind strange to me, and therefore mysterious, it set up mysterious responses in me. In terms of reason, it was strange only because I found it so. But a goodly part of our experience which we find <u>inexplicable</u> must be like that. To my certain knowledge, many people conceal experiences for fear of ridicule. How many people have seen or heard or felt something which so outraged their sense of what should be that the whole thing was brushed quickly away like dirt under a rug?

For myself, I try to keep the line open even for things I can't understand or explain, but it is difficult in this frightened time. At this moment in North Dakota I had a reluctance to drive on that amounted to fear. At the same time, Charley wanted to go—in fact, made such a commotion about going that I tried to reason with him.

"Listen to me, dog. I have a strong impulse to stay amounting to <u>celestial</u> command. If I should overcome it and go and a great snow should close in on us, I would recognize it as a warning disregarded. If we stay and a big snow should come I would be certain I had a pipeline to prophecy."

Charley sneezed and paced restlessly. "All right, *mon cur*,[5] let's take your side of it. You want to go on. Suppose we do, and in the night a tree should crash down right where we are presently standing. It would be you who have the attention of the gods. And there is always that chance. I could tell you many stories about faithful animals who saved their

---

Vocabulary Development: inexplicable (in eks´ pli kə bəl) *adj.* that cannot be explained or understood
celestial (sə les´ chəl) *adj.* of heaven; divine

---

5. *mon cur* (mōn kʉr´) French slang for "my dear mutt."

masters, but I think you are just bored and I'm not going to flatter you." Charley leveled at me his most cynical eye. I think he is neither a romantic nor a mystic. "I know what you mean. If we go, and no tree crashes down, or stay and no snow falls—what then? I'll tell you what then. We forget the whole episode and the field of prophecy is in no way injured. I vote to stay. You vote to go. But being nearer the pinnacle of creation than you, and also president, I cast the deciding vote."

We stayed and it didn't snow and no tree fell, so naturally we forgot the whole thing and are wide open for more mystic feelings when they come. And in the early morning swept clean of clouds and telescopically clear, we crunched around on the thick white ground cover of frost and got under way. The caravan of the arts was dark but the dog barked as we ground up to the highway.

Someone must have told me about the Missouri River at Bismarck, North Dakota, or I must have read about it. In either case, I hadn't paid attention. I came on it in amazement. Here is where the map should fold. Here is the boundary between east and west. On the Bismarck side it is eastern landscape, eastern grass, with the look and smell of eastern America. Across the Missouri on the Mandan side, it is pure west, with brown grass and water scorings and small outcrops. The two sides of the river might well be a thousand miles apart. As I was not prepared for the Missouri boundary, so I was not prepared for the Bad Lands. They deserve this name. They are like the work of an evil child. Such a place the Fallen Angels might have built as a spite to Heaven, dry and sharp, desolate and dangerous, and for me filled with foreboding. A sense comes from it that it does not like or welcome humans. But humans being what they are, and I being human, I turned off the highway on a shaley road and headed in among the buttes, but with a shyness as though I crashed a party. The road surface tore viciously at my tires and made Rocinante's overloaded springs cry with anguish. What a place for a colony of troglodytes, or better, of trolls. And here's an odd thing. Just as I felt unwanted in this land, so do I feel a reluctance in writing about it.

Presently I saw a man leaning on a two-strand barbed-wire fence, the wires fixed not to posts but to crooked tree limbs stuck in the ground. The man wore a dark hat, and jeans and long jacket washed palest blue with lighter places at knees and elbows. His pale eyes were frosted with sun glare and his lips scaly as snakeskin. A .22 rifle leaned against the fence beside him and on the ground lay a little heap of fur and feathers—rabbits and small birds. I pulled up to speak to him, saw his eyes wash over Rocinante, sweep up the details, and then retire into their sockets. And I found I had nothing to say to him. The "Looks like an

◆ **Literary Analysis**

List two factual details about the Bad Lands that Steinbeck includes in the bracketed passage.

1. _____

_____

2. _____

_____

List two impressions he includes.

1. _____

_____

2. _____

_____

◆ **Reading Strategy**

What details in the last paragraph show that the local man is used to being outdoors?

_____

_____

_____

_____

_____

early winter," or "Any good fishing hereabouts?" didn't seem to apply. And so we simply brooded at each other.

"Afternoon!"

"Yes, sir," he said.

"Any place nearby where I can buy some eggs?"

"Not real close by 'less you want to go as far as Galva or up to Beach."[6]

"I was set for some scratch-hen eggs."

"Powdered," he said. "My Mrs. gets powdered."

"Lived here long?"

"Yep."

I waited for him to ask something or to say something so we could go on, but he didn't. And as the silence continued, it became more and more impossible to think of something to say. I made one more try. "Does it get very cold here winters?"

"Fairly."

"You talk too much."

He grinned. "That's what my Mrs. says."

"So long," I said, and put the car in gear and moved along. And in my rear-view mirror I couldn't see that he looked after me. He may not be a typical Badlander, but he's one of the few I caught.

A little farther along I stopped at a small house, a section of war-surplus barracks, it looked, but painted white with yellow trim, and with the dying vestiges of a garden, frosted-down geraniums and a few clusters of chrysanthemums, little button things yellow and red-brown. I walked up the path with the certainty that I was being regarded from behind the white window curtains. An old woman answered my knock and gave me the drink of water I asked for and nearly talked my arm off. She was hungry to talk, frantic to talk, about her relatives, her friends, and how she wasn't used to this. For she was not a native and she didn't rightly belong here. Her native clime was a land of milk and honey and had its share of apes and ivory and peacocks. Her voice rattled on as though she was terrified of the silence that would settle when I was gone. As she talked it came to me that she was afraid of this place and, further, that so was I. I felt I wouldn't like to have the night catch me here.

I went into a state of flight, running to get away from the unearthly landscape. And then the late afternoon changed everything. As the sun angled, the buttes and coulees, the cliffs and sculptured hills and ravines lost their burned and dreadful look and glowed with yellow and rich browns and a hundred variations of red and silver gray, all picked out by streaks of coal black. It was so beautiful that I stopped near a thicket of dwarfed and wind-warped cedars and junipers,

---

6. **Galva . . . Beach** cities in western North Dakota near the border of Montana.

◆ **Reading Strategy**

Where are Galva and Beach located?

_____

_____

How do you know?

_____

_____

_____

◆ **Reading Strategy**

Circle details in the bracketed passage that support the idea in the underlined sentence.

◆ **Literary Analysis**

Which details or impressions in this part of the travel essay might convince you to visit the Bad Lands?

_____

_____

_____

_____

_____

and once stopped I was caught, trapped in color and dazzled by the clarity of the light. Against the descending sun the battlements were dark and clean-lined, while to the east, where the uninhibited light poured slantwise, the strange landscape shouted with color. And the night, far from being frightful, was lovely beyond thought, for the stars were close, and although there was no moon the starlight made a silver glow in the sky. The air cut the nostrils with dry frost. And for pure pleasure I collected a pile of dry dead cedar branches and built a small fire just to smell the perfume of the burning wood and to hear the excited crackle of the branches. My fire made a dome of yellow light over me, and nearby I heard a screech owl hunting and a barking of coyotes, not howling but the short chuckling bark of the dark of the moon. This is one of the few places I have ever seen where the night was friendlier than the day. And I can easily see how people are driven back to the Bad Lands.

Before I slept I spread a map on my bed, a Charley-tromped map. Beach was not far away, and that would be the end of North Dakota. And coming up would be Montana, where I had never been. That night was so cold that I put on my insulated underwear for pajamas, and when Charley had done his duties and had his biscuits and consumed his usual gallon of water and finally curled up in his place under the bed, I dug out an extra blanket and covered him—all except the tip of his nose—and he sighed and wriggled and gave a great groan of pure ecstatic comfort. And I thought how every safe generality I gathered in my travels was canceled by another. In the night the Bad Lands had become Good Lands. I can't explain it. That's how it was.

Reader's Response: Would you enjoy traveling with Steinbeck and Charley in Rocinante? Why or why not?

_____

_____

_____

Thinking About the Skill: What are some ways that a travel essay is different from a short story?

_____

_____

_____

© Pearson Education, Inc.

◆ **Stop to Reflect**

How and why have Steinbeck's feelings about the Bad Lands changed?

_____

_____

_____

_____

_____

_____

◆ **Reading Strategy**

What details indicate that Steinbeck intends to move on now?

_____

_____

_____

_____

_____

_____

_____

_____

_____

_____

_____

_____

_____

_____

The White Umbrella

Gish Jen

Summary

In "The White Umbrella," two young Chinese American sisters are concerned because their mother has taken a job. The job makes their mother late for family duties. The narrator seems embarrassed and insecure about the fact that her mother must work, while her sister, Mona, doesn't seem to mind as much. When the sisters have a piano lesson, the mother is late picking them up because of her job. Mona agrees to wait inside, out of the rain, while the narrator insists on waiting outside because she wants to believe that her mother will show up any minute. The narrator happily accepts the piano teacher's beautiful umbrella as a gift. She tries to hide it when the mother picks the girls up, but after it contributes to a car accident, she throws her umbrella away. She wants to ease her own guilty feelings about accepting it.

Visual Summary

"The White Umbrella" focuses on the personalities of its four key characters.

Character	Key Traits
The narrator	insecure, talented, emotional
Mona	secure, confident, practical
The mother	proud, hardworking, nervous
Miss Crosman	kindhearted, lonely

The White Umbrella
Gish Jen

The young Chinese American girl who tells this story wants her mother to stop working and pay better attention to her and her sister. She also wants a special white umbrella. Trying to get what she wants makes her take a closer look at herself.

When I was twelve, my mother went to work without telling me or my little sister.

"Not that we need the second income." The lilt of her accent drifted from the kitchen up to the top of the stairs, where Mona and I were listening.

"No," said my father, in a barely audible voice. "Not like the Lee family."

The Lees were the only other Chinese family in town. I remembered how sorry my parents had felt for Mrs. Lee when she started waitressing downtown the year before; and so when my mother began coming home late, I didn't say anything, and tried to keep Mona from saying anything either.

"But why shouldn't I?" she argued. "Lots of people's mothers work."

"Those are American people," I said.

"So what do you think we are? I can do the pledge of allegiance with my eyes closed."

Nevertheless, she tried to be <u>discreet</u>; and if my mother wasn't home by 5:30, we would start cooking by ourselves, to make sure dinner would be on time. Mona would wash the vegetables and put on the rice; I would chop.

For weeks we wondered what kind of work she was doing. I imagined that she was selling perfume, testing dessert recipes for the local newspaper. Or maybe she was working for the florist. Now that she had learned to drive, she might be delivering boxes of roses to people.

"<u>I don't think so</u>," said Mona as we walked to our piano lesson after school. "<u>She would've hit something by now.</u>"

A gust of wind littered the street with leaves.

"Maybe we better hurry up," she went on, looking at the sky. "It's going to pour."

"But we're too early." Her lesson didn't begin until 4:00, mine until 4:30, so we usually tried to walk as slowly as we could. "And anyway, those aren't the kind of clouds that rain. Those are cumulus clouds."[1]

Vocabulary Development: discreet (di skrēt´) *adj.* careful about what one says or does; prudent

---

1. **cumulus** (kyōō´ myōō ləs) **clouds** *n.* fluffy, white clouds that usually indicate fair weather.

◆ Activate Prior Knowledge

The white umbrella is something that the narrator of the story wants very badly. Briefly describe a time when you really wanted to have an item of clothing, a CD, a book, a videotape, a toy, or a piece of athletic equipment.

_____

_____

_____

_____

_____

_____

◆ Literary Analysis

Based on the opening of the story, list two **character traits,** or personality qualities, of the narrator and two of her mother.

Narrator:

1._____

2._____

Her mother:

1._____

2._____

◆ Reading Check

What does Mona's underlined comment mean?

_____

_____

_____

_____

_____

_____

_____

_____

_____

_____

_____

_____

_____

_____

_____

◆ Reading Strategy

Making predictions can help you focus on your reading. Predict what is going to happen with the umbrella mentioned in the underlined sentence. Write your prediction in the chart below.

My Prediction	Based On

We arrived out of breath and wet.

"Oh, you poor, poor dears," said old Miss Crosman. "Why don't you call me the next time it's like this out? If your mother won't drive you, I can come pick you up."

"No, that's okay," I answered. Mona wrung her hair out on Miss Crosman's rug. "We just couldn't get the roof of our car to close, is all. We took it to the beach last summer and got sand in the mechanism." I pronounced this last word carefully, as if the credibility of my lie depended on its middle syllable. "It's never been the same." I thought for a second. "It's a convertible."

"Well then make yourselves at home." She exchanged looks with Eugenie Roberts, whose lesson we were interrupting. Eugenie smiled good-naturedly. "The towels are in the closet across from the bathroom."

Huddling at the end of Miss Crosman's nine-foot leatherette couch, Mona and I watched Eugenie play. She was a grade ahead of me and, according to school rumor, had a boyfriend in high school. I believed it. . . . She had auburn hair, blue eyes, and, I noted with a particular pang, a pure white folding umbrella.

"I can't see," whispered Mona.

"So clean your glasses."

"My glasses _are_ clean. You're in the way."

I looked at her. "They look dirty to me."

"That's because _your_ glasses are dirty."

Eugenie came bouncing to the end of her piece.

"Oh! Just stupendous!" Miss Crosman hugged her, then looked up as Eugenie's mother walked in. "Stupendous!" she said again. "Oh! Mrs. Roberts! Your daughter has a gift, a real gift. It's an honor to teach her."

Mrs. Roberts, radiant with pride, swept her daughter out of the room as if she were royalty, born to the piano bench. Watching the way Eugenie carried herself, I sat up, and concentrated so hard on sucking in my stomach that I did not realize until the Robertses were gone that Eugenie had left her umbrella. As Mona began to play, I jumped up and ran to the window, meaning to call to them—only to see their brake lights flash then fade at the stop sign at the corner. As if to allow them passage, the rain had let up; a quivering sun lit their way.

The umbrella glowed like a scepter on the blue carpet while Mona, slumping over the keyboard, managed to eke out[2] a fair rendition of a catfight. At the end of the piece, Miss Crosman asked her to stand up.

Vocabulary Development: credibility (kred´ ə bil´ ə tē) _n._ believability

---

2. **eke** (ēk) **out** barely manage to play.

"Stay right there," she said, then came back a minute later with a towel to cover the bench. "You must be cold," she continued. "Shall I call your mother and have her bring over some dry clothes?"

"No," answered Mona. "She won't come because she . . ."

"She's too busy," I broke in from the back of the room.

"I see." Miss Crosman sighed and shook her head a little. "Your glasses are filthy, honey," she said to Mona. "Shall I clean them for you?"

Sisterly embarrassment seized me. Why hadn't Mona wiped her lenses when I told her to? As she resumed abuse of the piano, I stared at the umbrella. I wanted to open it, twirl it around by its slender silver handle; I wanted to dangle it from my wrist on the way to school the way the other girls did. I wondered what Miss Crosman would say if I offered to bring it to Eugenie at school tomorrow. She would be impressed with my consideration for others; Eugenie would be pleased to have it back; and I would have possession of the umbrella for an entire night. I looked at it again, toying with the idea of asking for one for Christmas. I knew, however, how my mother would react.

"Things," she would say. "What's the matter with a raincoat? All you want is things, just like an American."

Sitting down for my lesson, I was careful to keep the towel under me and sit up straight.

"I'll bet you can't see a thing either," said Miss Crosman, reaching for my glasses. "And you can relax, you poor dear." She touched my chest, in an area where she never would have touched Eugenie Roberts. "This isn't a boot camp."[3]

When Miss Crosman finally allowed me to start playing I played extra well, as well as I possibly could. See, I told her with my fingers. You don't have to feel sorry for me.

"That was wonderful," said Miss Crosman. "Oh! Just wonderful."

An entire constellation rose in my heart.

"And guess what," I announced proudly. "I have a surprise for you."

Then I played a second piece for her, a much more difficult one that she had not assigned.

"Oh! That was stupendous," she said without hugging me. "Stupendous! You are a genius, young lady. If your mother

---

Vocabulary Development: constellation (kän′ stə lā′ shən) *n.* group of stars named after, and thought to resemble, an object, an animal, or a mythological character in outline

---

3. **boot camp** place where soldiers receive basic training and are disciplined severely.

© Pearson Education, Inc.

◆ **Literary Analysis**

Two **character traits** of Miss Crosman are being kind and considerate. Circle actions described on this page that illustrate these two traits.

Mark the Text

◆ **Reading Strategy**

Based on the bracketed passage, do you want to change your **prediction** about the umbrella or keep it the same? Explain.

_____

_____

_____

_____

_____

◆ **Stop to Reflect**

Do you think Miss Crosman is a good teacher? Why or why not?

_____

_____

_____

_____

_____

_____

_____

Is the narrator's mother really a
concert pianist? If you are unsure,
review the opening of the story to
determine if the statement is true.

_____

_____

_____

_____

◆ Reading Strategy

Predict if the girls will tell Miss
Crosman why their mother is late.
Write your prediction in the chart
below.

My Prediction	Based On

had started you younger, you'd be playing like Eugenie
Roberts by now!"

I looked at the keyboard, wishing that I had still a third,
even more difficult piece to play for her. I wanted to tell her
that I was the school spelling bee champion, that I wasn't
ticklish, that I could do karate.

"My mother is a concert pianist," I said.

She looked at me for a long moment, then finally, without
saying anything, hugged me. I didn't say anything about
bringing the umbrella to Eugenie at school.

The steps were dry when Mona and I sat down to wait for
my mother.

"Do you want to wait inside?" Miss Crosman looked
anxiously at the sky.

"No," I said. "Our mother will be here any minute."

"In a while," said Mona.

"Any minute," I said again, even though my mother had
been at least twenty minutes late every week since she started working.

According to the church clock across the street we had
been waiting twenty-five minutes when Miss Crosman came
out again.

"Shall I give you ladies a ride home?"

"No," I said. "Our mother is coming any minute."

"Shall I at least give her a call and remind her you're
here? Maybe she forgot about you."

"I don't think she _forgot_," said Mona.

"Shall I give her a call anyway? Just to be safe?"

"I bet she already left," I said. "How could she forget
about us?"

Miss Crosman went in to call.

"There's no answer," she said, coming back out.

"See, she's on her way," I said.

"Are you sure you wouldn't like to come in?"

"No," said Mona.

"Yes," I said. I pointed at my sister. "She meant yes too.
She meant no, she wouldn't like to go in."

Miss Crosman looked at her watch. "It's 5:30 now, ladies.
My pot roast will be coming out in fifteen minutes. Maybe
you'd like to come in and have some then?"

"My mother's almost here," I said. "She's on her way."

We watched and watched the street. I tried to imagine
what my mother was doing; I tried to imagine her writing
messages in the sky, even though I knew she was afraid of
planes. I watched as the branches of Miss Crosman's big

Vocabulary Development: anxiously (aŋk´ shəs lē) _adv._ in a worried
way

willow tree started to sway; they had all been trimmed to exactly the same height off the ground, so that they looked beautiful, like hair in the wind.

It started to rain.

"Miss Crosman is coming out again," said Mona.

"Don't let her talk you into going inside," I whispered.

"Why not?"

"Because that would mean Mom isn't really coming any minute."

"But she isn't," said Mona. "She's *working*."

"Shhh! Miss Crosman is going to hear you."

"She's working! She's working! She's working!"

I put my hand over her mouth, but she licked it, and so I was wiping my hand on my wet dress when the front door opened.

"We're getting even *wetter*," said Mona right away. "Wetter and wetter."

"Shall we all go in?" Miss Crosman pulled Mona to her feet. "Before you young ladies catch pneumonia? You've been out here an hour already."

"We're *freezing*." Mona looked up at Miss Crosman. "Do you have any hot chocolate? We're going to catch *pneumonia*."

"I'm not going in," I said. "My mother's coming any minute."

"Come on," said Mona. "Use your *noggin*."[4]

"Any minute."

"Come on, Mona," Miss Crosman opened the door. "Shall we get you inside first?"

"See you in the hospital," said Mona as she went in. "See you in the hospital with pneumonia."

I stared out into the empty street. The rain was pricking me all over; I was cold; I wanted to go inside. I wanted to be able to let myself go inside. If Miss Crosman came out again, I decided, I would go in.

She came out with a blanket and the white umbrella.

I could not believe that I was actually holding the umbrella, opening it. It sprang up by itself as if it were alive, as if that were what it wanted to do—as if it belonged in my hands, above my head. I stared up at the network of silver spokes, then spun the umbrella around and around and around. It was so clean and white that it seemed to glow, to illuminate everything around it.

"It's beautiful," I said.

Miss Crosman sat down next to me, on one end of the blanket. I moved the umbrella over so that it covered that too. I could feel the rain on my left shoulder and shivered. She put her arm around me.

"You poor, poor dear."

---

4. **Use your *noggin*** (näg´ in) informal expression for "use your head" or "think."

◆ Reading Strategy

Predict what Miss Crosman will do when it starts raining.

_____

_____

_____

Predict what the girls will do.

_____

_____

_____

◆ Literary Analysis

List two **character traits** of each sister that are revealed in the bracketed dialogue.

Narrator:

1. _____

2. _____

Her sister:

1. _____

2. _____

◆ Reading Strategy

On the lines below, **predict** what the narrator will do with the umbrella. Circle any details in the bracketed passage that helped you make your prediction.

_____

_____

_____

_____

© Pearson Education, Inc.

The White Umbrella **91**

What **character traits** do
the narrator's actions in
the underlined sen-
tence demonstrate?

_____

_____

_____

_____

_____

_____

◆ Reading Check

What mistaken idea about the
white umbrella did the narrator
have?

_____

_____

_____

_____

◆ Literary Analysis

What do you learn about the narrator's **character traits,** or qualities of
personality, from the bracketed
passage? For example, what do you
learn from the fact that she makes
the remark, and what do you learn
from the fact that she feels bad
about making it?

_____

_____

_____

_____

_____

_____

I knew that I was in store for another bolt of sympathy,
and braced myself by staring up into the umbrella.

"You know, I very much wanted to have children when I
was younger," she continued.

"You did?"

She stared at me a minute. Her face looked dry and
crusty, like day-old frosting.

"I did. But then I never got married."

I twirled the umbrella around again.

"This is the most beautiful umbrella I have ever seen," I
said. "Ever, in my whole life."

"Do you have an umbrella?"

"No. But my mother's going to get me one just like this for
Christmas."

"Is she? I tell you what. You don't have to wait until
Christmas. You can have this one."

"But this one belongs to Eugenie Roberts," I protested. "I
have to give it back to her tomorrow in school."

"Who told you it belongs to Eugenie? It's not Eugenie's.
It's mine. And now I'm giving it to you, so it's yours."

"It is?"

She hugged me tighter. "That's right. It's all yours."

"It's mine?" I didn't know what to say. "Mine?" Suddenly I
was jumping up and down in the rain. "It's beautiful! Oh! It's
beautiful!" I laughed.

Miss Crosman laughed too, even though she was getting
all wet.

"Thank you, Miss Crosman. Thank you very much.
Thanks a zillion. It's beautiful. It's _stupendous_!"

"You're quite welcome," she said.

"Thank you," I said again, but that didn't seem like
enough. Suddenly I knew just what she wanted to hear. "I
wish you were my mother."

Right away I felt bad.

"You shouldn't say that," she said, but her face was opening into a huge smile as the lights of my mother's car cautiously turned the corner. I quickly collapsed the umbrella
and put it up my skirt, holding onto it from the outside,
through the material.

"Mona!" I shouted into the house. "Mona! Hurry up!
Mom's here! I told you she was coming!"

Then I ran away from Miss Crosman, down to the curb.
Mona came tearing up to my side as my mother neared the
house. We both backed up a few feet, so that in case she
went onto the curb, she wouldn't run us over.

"But why didn't you go inside with Mona?" my mother
asked on the way home. She had taken off her own coat to
put over me, and had the heat on high.

"She wasn't using her noggin," said Mona, next to me in
the back seat.

"I should call next time," said my mother. "I just don't like to say where I am."

That was when she finally told us that she was working as a check-out clerk in the A&P. She was supposed to be on the day shift, but the other employees were unreliable, and her boss had promised her a promotion if she would stay until the evening shift filled in.

For a moment no one said anything. Even Mona seemed to find the <u>revelation</u> disappointing.

"A promotion already!" she said, finally.

I listened to the windshield wipers.

"You're so quiet." My mother looked at me in the rear view mirror. "What's the matter?"

"I wish you would quit," I said after a moment.

She sighed. "The Chinese have a saying: one beam cannot hold the roof up."

"But Eugenie Roberts's father supports their family."

She sighed once more. "Eugenie Roberts's father is Eugenie Roberts's father," she said.

As we entered the downtown area, Mona started leaning hard against me every time the car turned right, trying to push me over. Remembering what I had said to Miss Crosman, I tried to maneuver the umbrella under my leg so she wouldn't feel it.

"What's under your skirt?" Mona wanted to know as we came to a traffic light. My mother, watching us in the rear view mirror again, rolled slowly to a stop.

"What's the matter?" she asked.

"There's something under her skirt!" said Mona, pulling at me.

"Under her skirt?"

Meanwhile, a man crossing the street started to yell at us.

"Who do you think you are, lady?" he said. "You're blocking the whole crosswalk."

We all froze. Other people walking by stopped to watch.

"Didn't you hear me?" he went on, starting to thump on the hood with his fist. "Don't you speak English?"

My mother began to back up, but the car behind us honked. Luckily, the light turned green right after that. She sighed in relief.

"What were you saying, Mona?" she asked.

We wouldn't have hit the car behind us that hard if he hadn't been moving too, but as it was our car bucked violently, throwing us all first back and then forward.

Vocabulary Development: revelation (rev´ ə lā´ shən) *n.* something revealed; a disclosure of something not previously known or realized

---

◆ **Reading Check**

What kind of job does the narrator's mother have?

_____

_____

_____

How do the girls feel about the job?

_____

_____

_____

◆ **Literary Analysis**

What **character trait(s)** does the narrator show when she tries to hide the umbrella?

_____

_____

_____

◆ **Reading Check**

Mark the Text

Find the following events in the bracketed passage and number them in the order they occur. Write the numbers both in the text and in the list below.

____ The family gets in an auto accident.

____ A man pounds on the car hood.

____ The narrator tries to hide the umbrella.

____ The mother stops the car.

Why does the narrator scream?

_____

_____

_____

_____

_____

Explain how you feel about the narrator's action in the final sentence. Was it a good or bad thing to do? In her place would you have done the same thing? Why or why not?

_____

_____

_____

_____

_____

_____

_____

_____

"Uh oh," said Mona when we stopped. "*Another* accident."

I was relieved to have attention diverted from the umbrella. Then I noticed my mother's head, tilted back onto the seat. Her eyes were closed.

"Mom!" I screamed. "Mom! Wake up!"

She opened her eyes. "Please don't yell," she said. "Enough people are going to yell already."

"I thought you were dead," I said, starting to cry. "I thought you were dead."

She turned around, looked at me intently, then put her hand to my forehead.

"Sick," she confirmed. "Some kind of sick is giving you crazy ideas."

As the man from the car behind us started tapping on the window, I moved the umbrella away from my leg. Then Mona and my mother were getting out of the car. I got out after them; and while everyone else was inspecting the damage we'd done, I threw the umbrella down a sewer.

Reader's Response: What is your opinion of the narrator of the story? Did you like her? Why or why not?

_____

_____

_____

Thinking About the Skill: How did making predictions as you read help you focus on what was happening in the story?

_____

_____

_____

from An American Childhood
Annie Dillard

Summary

Annie Dillard grew up in America in the 1950s. She remembers a vivid childhood experience she had when she was five years old. Each night, something scary casts a pale glow as it travels across Annie's dark bedroom. Just before it reaches Annie, it roars and shrinks away. Only Annie sees it. Her younger sister sleeps innocently through the entire event. Annie finally figures out what this scary thing is after many fearful nights. It is the light reflection from a passing car. The roaring noise she hears is the car's engine changing gears as it pulls away from a stop sign. This experience teaches Annie about imagination and reason. Annie uses her thought process to solve the mystery. She also learns about what her imagination does with the world of things that exist outside her room.

Visual Summary

Event
The author is frightened by mysterious, moving lights she sees in her bedroom at night.

Cause
Lights from a passing car are reflected onto her bedroom wall.

Main Idea
She realizes that the world outside and the world inside her home are connected.

Briefly describe a time in childhood when you made an important discovery on your own about how the world works. For example, you might have discovered that you can float more easily in salt water than you can in fresh water.

_____

_____

_____

_____

_____

_____

_____

_____

_____

_____

_____

_____

What did Dillard see in her room each night when she was five?

_____

_____

_____

How did Dillard feel about what she saw in her room?

_____

_____

_____

_____

from An American Childhood
Annie Dillard

The author tells of a childhood experience that frightened her and how her fear eventually led to understanding.

When I was five, growing up in Pittsburgh in 1950, I would not go to bed willingly because something came into my room. This was a private matter between me and it. If I spoke of it, it would kill me.

Who could breathe as this thing searched for me over the very corners of the room? Who could ever breathe freely again? I lay in the dark.

My sister Amy, two years old, was asleep in the other bed. What did she know? She was innocent of evil. Even at two she composed herself attractively for sleep. She folded the top sheet tidily under her prettily outstretched arm; she laid her perfect head lightly on an unwrinkled pillow, where her thick curls spread evenly in rays like petals. All night long she slept smoothly in a series of pleasant and serene, if artificial-looking, positions, a faint smile on her closed lips, as if she were posing for an ad for sheets. There was no messiness in her, no roughness for things to cling to, only a charming and charmed innocence that seemed then to protect her, an innocence I needed but couldn't muster. Since Amy was asleep, furthermore, and since when I needed someone most I was afraid to stir enough to wake her, she was useless.

I lay alone and was almost asleep when the . . . thing entered the room by flattening itself against the open door and sliding in. It was a transparent, luminous oblong. I could see the door whiten at its touch; I could see the blue wall turn pale where it raced over it, and see the maple headboard of Amy's bed glow. It was a swift spirit; it was an awareness. It made noise. It had two joined parts, a head and a tail, like a Chinese dragon. It found the door, wall, and headboard; and it swiped them, charging them with its luminous glance. After its fleet, searching passage, things looked the same, but weren't.

I dared not blink or breathe; I tried to hush my whooping blood. If it found another awareness, it would destroy it.

Every night before it got to me it gave up. It hit my wall's corner and couldn't get past. It shrank completely into itself and vanished like a cobra down a hole. I heard the rising roar it made when it died or left. I still couldn't breathe. I knew—it was the worst fact I knew, a very hard fact—that it

---

Vocabulary Development: luminous (lo͞o′ mə nəs) *adj.* giving off light; shining; bright

could return again alive that same night.

Sometimes it came back, sometimes it didn't. Most often, restless, it came back. The light stripe slipped in the door, ran searching over Amy's wall, stopped, stretched lunatic at the first corner, raced wailing toward my wall, and vanished into the second corner with a cry. So I wouldn't go to bed.

It was a passing car whose windshield reflected the corner streetlight outside. I figured it out one night.

Figuring it out was as memorable as the oblong itself. Figuring it out was a long and forced <u>ascent</u> to the very rim of being, to the <u>membrane</u> of skin that both separates and connects the inner life and the outer world. I climbed deliberately from the depths like a diver who releases the monster in his arms and hauls himself hand over hand up an anchor chain till he meets the ocean's sparkling membrane and bursts through it; he sights the sunlit, becalmed hull of his boat, which had bulked so ominously from below.

I recognized the noise it made when it left. That is, the noise it made called to mind, at last, my daytime sensations when a car passed—the sight and noise together. A car came roaring down hushed Edgerton Avenue in front of our house, stopped at the corner stop sign, and passed on shrieking as its engine shifted up the gears. What, precisely, came into the bedroom? A reflection from the car's oblong windshield. Why did it travel in two parts? The window sash split the light and cast a shadow.

Night after night I labored up the same long chain of reasoning, as night after night the thing burst into the room where I lay awake and Amy slept prettily and my loud heart thrashed and I froze.

There was a world outside my window and <u>contiguous</u> to it. If I was so all-fired bright, as my parents, who had patently no basis for comparison, seemed to think, why did I have to keep learning this same thing over and over? For I had learned it a summer ago, when men with jackhammers broke up Edgerton Avenue. I had watched them from the yard; the street came up in jagged slabs like floes. When I lay to nap, I listened. One restless afternoon I connected the new noise in my bedroom with the jackhammer men I had been seeing outside. I understood abruptly that these worlds met, the outside and the inside. I traveled the route in my mind: You walked downstairs from here, and outside from

Vocabulary Development: **ascent** (ə sent´) *n.* the act of rising or climbing
membrane (mem´ brān) *n.* a thin, soft sheet or layer serving as a covering
contiguous (kən tig´ yo͞o əs) *adj.* in physical contact; near or next to

from An American Childhood **97**

◆ **Reading Strategy**

When you **evaluate the text**, you pause to judge how well the writer has written it. Evaluate the **originality** of the bracketed passage. What characteristics make this description unusual?

_____

_____

◆ **Reading Check**

To what process does Dillard compare the process of figuring out what she saw and heard?

_____

_____

_____

◆ **Reading Strategy**

After reading the bracketed passage, **evaluate its coherence**. How logically do the writer's ideas build on one another? Explain.

_____

_____

_____

_____

◆ **Reading Check**

What does Dillard force herself to do, and why?

_____

_____

_____

_____

What does Dillard begin to understand about the world "outside"?

_____

_____

_____

◆ **Reading Check**

What important thing does Dillard discover she can do? Circle the paragraph in which she describes this discovery.

_____

_____

_____

_____

_____

◆ **Literary Analysis**

A **vignette** is a brief narrative of a memorable experience. How does the final paragraph of this vignette show why the writer's experience was so memorable? For example, how can you tell from this paragraph that Dillard's experience gave her a new sense of power?

_____

_____

_____

_____

_____

_____

_____

downstairs. "Outside," then, was <u>conceivably</u> just beyond my windows. It was the same world I reached by going out the front or the back door. I forced my imagination yet again over this route.

The world did not have me in mind; it had no mind. It was a <u>coincidental</u> collection of things and people, of items, and I myself was one such item—a child walking up the sidewalk, whom anyone could see or ignore. The things in the world did not necessarily cause my overwhelming feelings; the feelings were inside me, beneath my skin, behind my ribs, within my skull. They were even, to some extent, under my control.

I could be connected to the outer world by reason, if I chose, or I could yield to what amounted to a narrative fiction, to a tale of terror whispered to me by the blood in my ears, a show in light projected on the room's blue walls. As time passed, I learned to amuse myself in bed in the darkened room by entering the fiction deliberately and replacing it by reason deliberately.

When the low roar drew nigh and the oblong slid in the door, I threw my own switches for pleasure. It's coming after me; it's a car outside. It's after me. It's a car. It raced over the wall, lighting it blue wherever it ran; it bumped over Amy's maple headboard in a rush, paused, slithered <u>elongate</u> over the corner, shrank, flew my way, and vanished into itself with a wail. It was a car.

Vocabulary Development: conceivably (kən sē′ və blē) *adv.* possibly
coincidental (kō in′ sə dent′ əl) *adj.* occurring without plan, by accident
elongate (i lôŋ′ gāt) *adj.* long and narrow

Reader's Response: Do you find Dillard's childhood fears understandable? Explain.

_____

_____

_____

Thinking About the Skill: What does evaluating Dillard's text help you to appreciate about her writing?

_____

_____

_____

The Adventure of the Speckled Band
Sir Arthur Conan Doyle

Summary

Sherlock Holmes is a popular fictional English detective. His friend and associate, Dr. Watson, tells how Holmes solves a mystery. Miss Helen Stoner seeks help from Holmes because she is upset over her twin sister's mysterious death and fears for her own life. She tells Holmes the facts of Julia's death and her sister's final words about a speckled band. Holmes looks at the dead sister's room, now used by Helen Stoner, and her stepfather's room, too. Holmes then suspects a murder plot. To prove it, he and Watson must stay in Helen Stoner's room overnight. Holmes uses his skills of observation and his research on Helen Stoner's family history to determine that the "speckled band" refers to a poisonous snake. In proving this, he prevents Helen Stoner's murder, but causes the death of the murderer.

Visual Summary

Characters	Conflict	Clues
Sherlock Holmes Dr. Watson Helen Stoner Julia Stoner Dr. Roylott	Helen Stoner fears for her life. Holmes attempts to catch the suspected criminal, Dr. Roylott, before he carries out a deadly plot against her.	whistle Indian animals bed bolted to floor dummy bell-rope ventilator a saucer of milk a safe Julia's last words

◆ **Activate Prior Knowledge**

List three famous fictional detectives you have read about or seen in films or on television. Then, tell what makes each one special.

1._____

_____

_____

2._____

_____

_____

3._____

_____

_____

◆ **Literary Analysis**

A **mystery story** is a fictional tale that tells how a detective solves a crime. How the crime is solved depends on the personality of the detective. Review the first three paragraphs and circle details that reveal the personality and methods of Sherlock Holmes.

The Adventure of the Speckled Band
Sir Arthur Conan Doyle

Dr. Watson, the companion of the great English detective Sherlock Holmes, tells how Holmes takes a case regarding a mysterious death that occurred two years earlier. The setting is an ancient manor house, occupied by a young woman, her ill-tempered stepfather, and his "pets," a baboon and a cheetah. Holmes solves the case through a combination of brilliant thinking and prompt action.

On glancing over my notes of the seventy odd cases in which I have during the last eight years studied the methods of my friend Sherlock Holmes, I find many tragic, some comic, a large number merely strange, but none commonplace; for, working as he did rather for the love of his art than for the acquirement of wealth, he refused to associate himself with any investigation which did not tend towards the unusual, and even the fantastic. Of all these varied cases, however, I cannot recall any which presented more singular features than that which was associated with the well-known Surrey family of the Roylotts of Stoke Moran. The events in question occurred in the early days of my association with Holmes when we were sharing rooms as bachelors in Baker Street. It is possible that I might have placed them upon record before but a promise of secrecy was made at the time, from which I have only been freed during the last month by the untimely death of the lady to whom the pledge was given. It is perhaps as well that the facts should now come to light, for I have reasons to know that there are widespread rumors as to the death of Dr. Grimesby Roylott which tend to make the matter even more terrible than the truth.

It was early in April in the year 1883 that I woke one morning to find Sherlock Holmes standing, fully dressed, by the side of my bed. He was a late riser, as a rule, and as the clock on the mantelpiece showed me that it was only a quarter past seven, I blinked up at him in some surprise, and perhaps just a little resentment, for I was myself regular in my habits.

"Very sorry to wake you up, Watson," said he, "but it's the common lot this morning. Mrs. Hudson has been awakened, she retorted upon me, and I on you."

"What is it, then—a fire?"

"No; a client. It seems that a young lady has arrived in a considerable state of excitement who insists upon seeing me. She is waiting now in the sitting room. Now, when young ladies wander about the metropolis at this hour of the morning, and get sleepy people up out of their beds, I presume that it is something very pressing which they have to communicate. Should it prove to be an interesting case, you would, I am sure, wish to follow it from the outset. I thought, at any rate, that I should call you and give you the chance."

"My dear fellow, I would not miss it for anything."

I had no keener pleasure than in following Holmes in his professional investigations, and in admiring the rapid deductions, as swift as intuitions, and yet always founded on a logical basis, with which he unraveled the problems which were submitted to him. I rapidly threw on my clothes and was ready in a few minutes to accompany my friend down to the sitting room. A lady dressed in black and heavily veiled, who had been sitting in the window, rose as we entered.

"Good morning, madam," said Holmes cheerily. "My name is Sherlock Holmes. This is my intimate friend and associate, Dr. Watson, before whom you can speak as freely as before myself. Ha! I am glad to see that Mrs. Hudson has had the good sense to light the fire. Pray draw up to it, and I shall order you a cup of hot coffee, for I observe that you are shivering."

"It is not cold which makes me shiver," said the woman in a low voice, changing her seat as requested.

"What, then?"

"It is fear, Mr. Holmes. It is terror." She raised her veil as she spoke, and we could see that she was indeed in a pitiable state of agitation, her face all drawn and gray, with restless, frightened eyes, like those of some hunted animal. Her features and figure were those of a woman of thirty, but her hair was shot with premature gray, and her expression was weary and haggard. Sherlock Holmes ran her over with one of his quick, all-comprehensive glances.

"You must not fear," said he soothingly, bending forward and patting her forearm. "We shall soon set matters right, I have no doubt. You have come in by train this morning, I see."

"You know me, then?"

"No, but I observe the second half of a return ticket in the palm of your left glove. You must have started early, and yet you had a good drive in a dogcart[1] along heavy roads, before you reached the station."

The lady gave a violent start and stared in bewilderment at my companion.

"There is no mystery, my dear madam," said he, smiling. "The left arm of your jacket is spattered with mud in no less than seven places. The marks are perfectly fresh. There is no vehicle save a dogcart which throws up mud in that way, and then only when you sit on the left-hand side of the driver."

"Whatever your reasons may be, you are perfectly correct," said she. "I started from home before six, reached

---

1. **dogcart** small horse-drawn carriage with seats arranged back-to-back.

◆ Reading Check

Why are Holmes and Watson awake at an early hour?

_____

_____

_____

_____

_____

◆ Reading Check

What is the relationship between Watson and Holmes?

_____

_____

What does Watson admire about Holmes's detective skills?

_____

_____

_____

_____

_____

◆ Reading Strategy

Identify the **evidence,** or proof, that Holmes uses to draw the underlined conclusion. Read the paragraphs that follow, and circle the observations and thoughts that led him to his conclusion.

Mark the Text

_____

_____

_____

_____

_____

In the bracketed passage, what does Holmes's comment about payment for his services reveal about him?

_____

_____

_____

_____

_____

Why has the woman come to Sherlock Holmes for help, rather than to someone else?

_____

_____

_____

_____

_____

Leatherhead at twenty past, and came in by the first train to Waterloo. Sir, I can stand this strain no longer; I shall go mad if it continues. I have no one to turn to—none, save only one, who cares for me, and he, poor fellow, can be of little aid. I have heard of you, Mr. Holmes. I have heard of you from Mrs. Farintosh, whom you helped in the hour of her sore need. It was from her that I had your address. Oh, sir, do you not think that you could help me, too, and at least throw a little light through the dense darkness which surrounds me? At present it is out of my power to reward you for your service, but in a month or six weeks I shall be married, with the control of my own income, and then at least you shall not find me ungrateful."

Holmes turned to his desk and, unlocking it, drew out a small case book, which he consulted.

"Farintosh," said he. "Ah yes, I recall the case; it was concerned with an opal tiara. I think it was before your time, Watson. I can only say, madam, that I shall be happy to devote the same care to your case as I did to that of your friend. As to reward, my profession is its own reward; but you are at liberty to defray whatever expenses I may be put to, at the time which suits you best. And now I beg that you will lay before us everything that may help us in forming an opinion upon the matter."

"Alas!" replied our visitor, "the very horror of my situation lies in the fact that my fears are so vague, and my suspicions depend so entirely upon small points, which might seem trivial to another, that even he to whom of all others I have a right to look for help and advice looks upon all that I tell him about it as fancy. He does not say so, but I can read it from his soothing answers and averted eyes. But I have heard, Mr. Holmes, that you can see deeply into the manifold wickedness of the human heart. You may advise me how to walk amid the dangers which encompass me."

"I am all attention, madam."

"My name is Helen Stoner, and I am living with my stepfather, who is the last survivor of one of the oldest Saxon families in England: the Roylotts of Stoke Moran, on the western border of Surrey."

Holmes nodded his head. "The name is familiar to me," said he.

"The family was at one time among the richest in England, and the estates extended over the borders into Berkshire in the north, and Hampshire in the west. In the

---

Vocabulary Development: defray (di frā´) _v._ to pay or furnish the money for
manifold (man´ ə fōld´) _adj._ many and varied

last century, however, four successive heirs were of a dissolute and wasteful disposition, and the family ruin was eventually completed by a gambler in the days of the Regency. <u>Nothing was left save a few acres of ground, and the two-hundred-year-old house, which is itself crushed under a heavy mortgage. The last squire dragged out his existence there, living the horrible life of an aristocratic pauper;</u> but his only son, my stepfather, seeing that he must adapt himself to the new conditions, obtained an advance from a relative, which enabled him to take a medical degree and went out to Calcutta, where, by his professional skill and his force of character, he established a large practice. In a fit of anger, however, caused by some robberies which had been perpetrated in the house, he beat his native butler to death and narrowly escaped a capital sentence. As it was, he suffered a long term of imprisonment and afterwards returned to England a <u>morose</u> and disappointed man.

"When Dr. Roylott was in India he married my mother, Mrs. Stoner, the young widow of Major-General Stoner, of the Bengal Artillery. My sister Julia and I were twins, and we were only two years old at the time of my mother's remarriage. She had a considerable sum of money—not less than £1000 a year[2]—and this she bequeathed to Dr. Roylott entirely while we resided with him, with a provision that a certain annual sum should be allowed to each of us in the event of our marriage. Shortly after our return to England my mother died—she was killed eight years ago in a railway accident near Crewe. Dr. Roylott then abandoned his attempts to establish himself in practice in London and took us to live with him in the old ancestral house at Stoke Moran. The money which my mother had left was enough for all our wants, and there seemed to be no obstacle to our happiness.

"But a terrible change came over our stepfather about this time. Instead of making friends and exchanging visits with our neighbors, who had at first been overjoyed to see a Roylott of Stoke Moran back in the old family seat, he shut himself up in his house and seldom came out save to indulge in ferocious quarrels with whoever might cross his path. Violence of temper approaching to mania has been hereditary in the men of the family, and in my stepfather's case it had, I believe, been intensified by his long residence in the tropics. A series of disgraceful brawls took place, two of which ended in the police court, until at last he became the terror of the village,

---

Vocabulary Development: morose (mə rōs´) *adj.* gloomy; ill-tempered; sullen

---

2. £1000 one thousand pounds; £ is the symbol for pound(s), the British unit of money.

◆ Literary Analysis

Mystery stories often include settings that are unfamiliar, isolated, in ruins, or dangerous. Why might the setting described in the underlined passage be a suitable scene for a crime?

_____

_____

_____

◆ Reading Strategy

Identify evidence, or proof, for conclusions about who committed the crime by using a chart like the one below. In the bracketed passage, circle a detail about Dr. Roylott that might be evidence. Enter it under the evidence column of the chart. Next to it, write a prediction suggested by the evidence.

Evidence	Prediction

Do you think that the presence of the cheetah and the baboon is **evidence** related to the crime? Why or why not?

_____

_____

_____

_____

_____

_____

◆ Reading Check

Whose death does Helen Stoner want Holmes to investigate?

_____

_____

◆ Reading Strategy

Gather **evidence** to solve the crime by using the information in the bracketed paragraph to draw a sketch of the bedrooms and their layout.

and the folks would fly at his approach, for he is a man of immense strength, and absolutely uncontrollable in his anger.

"Last week he hurled the local blacksmith over a parapet into a stream, and it was only by paying over all the money which I could gather together that I was able to avert another public exposure. He had no friends at all save the wandering gypsies, and he would give these vagabonds leave to encamp upon the few acres of bramble-covered land which represent the family estate, and would accept in return the hospitality of their tents, wandering away with them sometimes for weeks on end. He has a passion also for Indian animals, which are sent over to him by a correspondent, and he has at this moment a cheetah and a baboon, which wander freely over his grounds and are feared by the villagers almost as much as is their master.

"You can imagine from what I say that my poor sister Julia and I had no great pleasure in our lives. No servant would stay with us, and for a long time we did all the work of the house. She was but thirty at the time of her death, and yet her hair had already begun to whiten, even as mine has."

"Your sister is dead, then?"

"She died just two years ago, and it is of her death that I wish to speak to you. You can understand that, living the life which I have described, we were little likely to see anyone of our own age and position. We had, however, an aunt, my mother's maiden sister, Miss Honoria Westphail, who lives near Harrow, and we were occasionally allowed to pay short visits at this lady's house. Julia went there at Christmas two years ago, and met there a major in the Marines, to whom she became engaged. My stepfather learned of the engagement when my sister returned and offered no objection to the marriage; but within a fortnight of the day which had been fixed for the wedding, the terrible event occurred which has deprived me of my only companion."

Sherlock Holmes had been leaning back in his chair with his eyes closed and his head sunk in a cushion, but he half opened his lids now and glanced across at his visitor.

"Pray be precise as to details," said he.

"It is easy for me to be so, for every event of that dreadful time is seared into my memory. The manor house is, as I have already said, very old, and only one wing is now inhabited. The bedrooms in this wing are on the ground floor, the sitting rooms being in the central block of the buildings. Of these bedrooms the first is Dr. Roylott's, the second my sister's, and the third my own. There is no communication between them, but they all open out into the same corridor. Do I make myself plain?"

"Perfectly so."

"The windows of the three rooms open out upon the lawn.

That fatal night Dr. Roylott had gone to his room early, though we knew that he had not retired to rest, for my sister was troubled by the smell of the strong Indian cigars which it was his custom to smoke. She left her room, therefore, and came into mine, where she sat for some time, chatting about her approaching wedding. At eleven o'clock she rose to leave me, but she paused at the door and looked back.

"'Tell me, Helen,' said she, 'have you ever heard anyone whistle in the dead of the night?'

"'Never,' said I.

"'I suppose that you could not possibly whistle, yourself, in your sleep?'

"'Certainly not. But why?'

"'Because during the last few nights I have always, about three in the morning, heard a low, clear whistle. I am a light sleeper, and it has awakened me. I cannot tell where it came from—perhaps from the next room, perhaps from the lawn. I thought that I would just ask you whether you had heard it.'

"'No, I have not. It must be the gypsies in the plantation.'

"'Very likely. And yet if it were on the lawn, I wonder that you did not hear it also.'

"'Ah, but I sleep more heavily than you.'

"'Well, it is of no great consequence, at any rate.' She smiled back at me, closed my door, and a few moments later I heard her key turn in the lock."

"Indeed," said Holmes. "Was it your custom always to lock yourselves in at night?"

"Always."

"And why?"

"I think that I mentioned to you that the doctor kept a cheetah and a baboon. We had no feeling of security unless our doors were locked."

"Quite so. Pray proceed with your statement."

"I could not sleep that night. A vague feeling of impending misfortune impressed me. My sister and I, you will recollect, were twins, and you know how subtle are the links which bind two souls which are so closely allied. It was a wild night. The wind was howling outside, and the rain was beating and splashing against the windows. Suddenly, amid all the hubbub of the gale, there burst forth the wild scream of a terrified woman. I knew that it was my sister's voice. I sprang from my bed, wrapped a shawl round me, and rushed into the corridor. As I opened my door I seemed to hear a low whistle, such as my sister described, and a few moments later a clanging sound, as if a mass of metal had fallen. As I ran down the passage, my sister's door was unlocked, and revolved slowly upon its hinges. I stared at it horror-stricken, not knowing what was about to issue from it. By the light of the corridor lamp I saw my sister appear at the opening, her face blanched with terror, her hands grop-

◆ **Reading Strategy**

In the bracketed passage, circle one clue that could turn out to be an important piece of **evidence**. What question does this clue raise?

_____

_____

_____

_____

_____

_____

_____

_____

◆ **Literary Analysis**

The details in the underlined passage are included in the setting of many **mystery stories.** What do they add here?

_____

_____

_____

_____

_____

© **PEARSON Education, Inc.**   The Adventure of the Speckled Band **105**

_____

_____

_____

◆ Reading Strategy

In the bracketed passage, circle three pieces of **evidence** on which Sherlock Holmes seems to focus. Then, on the lines below, make your own educated guesses about them.

Mark the Text

1._____

_____

_____

2._____

_____

_____

3._____

_____

_____

◆ Reading Check

What does the coroner say about Julia's death?

_____

_____

_____

_____

ing for help, her whole figure swaying to and fro like that of a drunkard. I ran to her and threw my arms round her, but at that moment her knees seemed to give way and she fell to the ground. She writhed as one who is in terrible pain, and her limbs were dreadfully <u>convulsed</u>. At first I thought that she had not recognized me, but as I bent over her she suddenly shrieked out in a voice which I shall never forget, 'Oh, Helen! It was the band! The speckled band!' There was something else which she would fain have said, and she stabbed with her finger into the air in the direction of the doctor's room, but a fresh convulsion seized her and choked her words. I rushed out, calling loudly for my stepfather, and I met him hastening from his room in his dressing gown. When he reached my sister's side she was unconscious, and though he poured brandy down her throat and sent for medical aid from the village, all efforts were in vain, for she slowly sank and died without having recovered her consciousness. Such was the dreadful end of my beloved sister."

"One moment," said Holmes; "are you sure about this whistle and metallic sound? Could you swear to it?"

"That was what the county coroner asked me at the inquiry. It is my strong impression that I heard it, and yet, among the crash of the gale and the creaking of an old house, I may possibly have been deceived."

"Was your sister dressed?"

"No, she was in her nightdress. In her right hand was found the charred stump of a match, and in her left a matchbox."

"Showing that she had struck a light and looked about her when the alarm took place. That is important. And what conclusions did the coroner come to?"

"He investigated the case with great care, for Dr. Roylott's conduct had long been notorious in the county, but he was unable to find any satisfactory cause of death. My evidence showed that the door had been fastened upon the inner side, and the windows were blocked by old-fashioned shutters with broad iron bars, which were secured every night. The walls were carefully sounded, and were shown to be quite solid all round, and the flooring was also thoroughly examined, with the same result. The chimney is wide, but is barred up by four large staples. It is certain, therefore, that my sister was quite alone when she met her end. Besides, there were no marks of any violence upon her."

"How about poison?"

"The doctors examined her for it, but without success."

"What do you think that this unfortunate lady died of, then?"

Vocabulary Development: convulsed (kən vulst´) *adj.* taken over by violent, involuntary spasms

"It is my belief that she died of pure fear and nervous shock, though what it was that frightened her I cannot imagine."

"Were there gypsies in the plantation at the time?"

"Yes, there are nearly always some there."

"Ah, and what did you gather from this allusion to a band—a speckled band?"

"Sometimes I have thought that it was merely the wild talk of delirium, sometimes that it may have referred to some band of people, perhaps to these very gypsies in the plantation. I do not know whether the spotted handkerchiefs which so many of them wear over their heads might have suggested the strange adjective which she used."

Holmes shook his head like a man who is far from being satisfied.

"These are very deep waters," said he; "pray go on with your narrative."

"Two years have passed since then, and my life has been until lately lonelier than ever. A month ago, however, a dear friend, whom I have known for many years, has done me the honor to ask my hand in marriage. His name is Armitage— Percy Armitage—the second son of Mr. Armitage, of Crane Water, near Reading. My stepfather has offered no opposition to the match, and we are to be married in the course of the spring. Two days ago some repairs were started in the west wing of the building, and my bedroom wall has been pierced, so that I have had to move into the chamber in which my sister died, and to sleep in the very bed in which she slept. Imagine, then, my thrill of terror when last night, as I lay awake, thinking over her terrible fate, I suddenly heard in the silence of the night the low whistle which had been the herald of her own death. I sprang up and lit the lamp, but nothing was to be seen in the room. I was too shaken to go to bed again, however, so I dressed, and as soon as it was daylight I slipped down, got a dogcart at the Crown Inn, which is opposite, and drove to Leatherhead, from whence I have come on this morning with the one object of seeing you and asking your advice."

"You have done wisely," said my friend. "But have you told me all?"

"Yes, all."

"Miss Roylott, you have not. You are screening your stepfather."

"Why, what do you mean?"

For answer Holmes pushed back the frill of black lace which fringed the hand that lay upon our visitor's knee. Five little livid spots, the marks of four fingers and a thumb, were printed upon the white wrist.

"You have been cruelly used," said Holmes.

The lady colored deeply and covered over her injured

The Adventure of the Speckled Band **107**

◆ **Reading Strategy**

The "speckled band" may be an important piece of **evidence**. On the lines below, indicate three possible things to which it may refer. Remember that *speckled* means "covered with small spots or marks" and *band* can mean "something that ties together; strip of cloth, wood, metal, rubber; group of people or musicians."

1. _____

_____

2. _____

_____

3. _____

_____

◆ **Reading Check**

Why does Helen Stoner feel she may be in danger?

_____

_____

_____

_____

_____

◆ **Reading Check**

Who or what has caused the marks on Helen's wrist?

_____

_____

_____

_____

What plan of action will Holmes and Watson follow?

_____

_____

_____

_____

_____

_____

Based on the **evidence**, in the bracketed passage who do you think is closer to guessing what happened—Holmes, or Watson? Explain your answer.

_____

_____

_____

_____

_____

_____

_____

wrist. "He is a hard man," she said, "and perhaps he hardly knows his own strength."

There was a long silence, during which Holmes leaned his chin upon his hands and stared into the crackling fire. "This is a very deep business," he said at last. "There are a thousand details which I should desire to know before I decide upon our course of action. Yet we have not a moment to lose. If we were to come to Stoke Moran today, would it be possible for us to look over these rooms without the knowledge of your stepfather?"

"As it happens, he spoke of coming into town today upon some most important business. It is probable that he will be away all day and that there would be nothing to disturb you. We have a housekeeper now, but I could easily get her out of the way."

"Excellent. You are not averse to this trip, Watson?"

"By no means."

"Then we shall both come. What are you going to do yourself?"

"I have one or two things which I would wish to do now that I am in town. But I shall return by the twelve o'clock train, so as to be there in time for your coming."

"And you may expect us early in the afternoon. I have myself some small business matters to attend to. Will you not wait and breakfast?"

"No, I must go. My heart is lightened already since I have confided my trouble to you. I shall look forward to seeing you again this afternoon." She dropped her thick black veil over her face and glided from the room.

"And what do you think of it all, Watson?" asked Sherlock Holmes, leaning back in his chair.

"It seems to me to be a most dark and sinister business."

"Dark enough and sinister enough."

"Yet if the lady is correct in saying that the flooring and walls are sound, and that the door, window, and chimney are impassable, then her sister must have been undoubtedly alone when she met her mysterious end."

"What becomes, then, of these nocturnal whistles, and what of the very peculiar words of the dying woman?"

"I cannot think."

"When you combine the ideas of whistles at night, the presence of a band of gypsies who are on intimate terms with this old doctor, the fact that we have every reason to believe that the doctor has an interest in preventing his stepdaughter's marriage, the dying allusion to a band, and, finally, the fact that Miss Helen Stoner heard a metallic clang, which might have been caused by one of those metal bars that secured the shutters, falling back into its place, I think that there is good ground to think that the mystery may be cleared along those lines."

"But what, then, did the gypsies do?"

"I cannot imagine."

"I see many objections to any such theory."

"And so do I. It is precisely for that reason that we are going to Stoke Moran this day. I want to see whether the objections are fatal, or if they may be explained away. But what in the name of the devil!"

The ejaculation had been drawn from my companion by the fact that our door had been suddenly dashed open, and that a huge man had framed himself in the aperture. His costume was a peculiar mixture of the professional and of the agricultural, having a black top hat, a long frock coat, and a pair of high gaiters,[3] with a hunting crop swinging in his hand. So tall was he that his hat actually brushed the crossbar of the doorway, and his breadth seemed to span it across from side to side. A large face, seared with a thousand wrinkles, burned yellow with the sun, and marked with every evil passion, was turned from one to the other of us, while his deep-set, bile-shot eyes, and his high, thin, fleshless nose, gave him somewhat the resemblance to a fierce old bird of prey.

"Which of you is Holmes?" asked this apparition.

"My name, sir; but you have the advantage of me," said my companion quietly.

"I am Dr. Grimesby Roylott, of Stoke Moran."

"Indeed, Doctor," said Holmes blandly. "Pray take a seat."

"I will do nothing of the kind. My stepdaughter has been here. I have traced her. What has she been saying to you?"

"It is a little cold for the time of the year," said Holmes.

"What has she been saying to you?" screamed the old man furiously.

"But I have heard that the crocuses promise well," continued my companion imperturbably.

"Ha! You put me off, do you?" said our new visitor, taking a step forward and shaking his hunting crop. "I know you, you scoundrel! I have heard of you before. You are Holmes, the meddler."

My friend smiled.

"Holmes, the busybody!"

His smile broadened.

"Holmes, the Scotland Yard Jack-in-office!"

Holmes chuckled heartily. "Your conversation is most entertaining," said he. "When you go out close the door, for there is a decided draft."

"I will go when I have said my say. Don't you dare to meddle with my affairs. I know that Miss Stoner has been here. I traced her! I am a dangerous man to fall foul of! See

---

Vocabulary Development: imperturbably (im′ pər tʉr′ bə blē) *adv.*
unexcitedly; impassively

---

3. **gaiters** (gāt′ ərz) *n.* cloth or leather coverings for the ankles and calves of legs.

◆ Literary Analysis

The plot, or sequence of events, in a **mystery story** develops around a **conflict** between a character who has committed a crime and the character who is trying to solve it. Based on the description of Dr. Roylott, do you think he will be a difficult opponent for Holmes? Why or why not?

_____

_____

_____

_____

_____

_____

_____

◆ Literary Analysis

The **conflict** between Roylott and Holmes is obvious from the start. In the face of Roylott's threats and insults, why do you think Holmes smiles and keeps calm?

_____

_____

_____

_____

◆ Reading Check

Why does Dr. Roylott pay a visit to Holmes?

_____

_____

_____

_____

Gather **evidence** by circling the numbers in the underlined passage. Then, on the lines below, do the mathematics to show how much money Dr. Roylott would lose each year if one or both stepdaughters married. What do your calculations suggest about the doctor's possible motive for murder?

_____

_____

_____

_____

_____

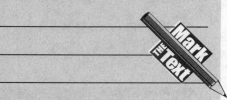

Is this motive by itself evidence of Dr. Roylott's guilt? Explain why or why not.

_____

_____

_____

_____

◆ **Stop to Reflect**

Ask yourself what Holmes means by the underlined remark. In what way might a gun be an "argument"?

_____

_____

_____

_____

_____

_____

_____

here." He stepped swiftly forward, seized the poker, and bent it into a curve with his huge brown hands.

"See that you keep yourself out of my grip," he snarled, and hurling the twisted poker into the fireplace he strode out of the room.

"He seems a very amiable person," said Holmes, laughing. "I am not quite so bulky, but if he had remained I might have shown him that my grip was not much more feeble than his own." As he spoke he picked up the steel poker and, with a sudden effort, straightened it out again.

"Fancy his having the insolence to confound me with[4] the official detective force! This incident gives zest to our investigation, however, and I only trust that our little friend will not suffer from her imprudence in allowing this brute to trace her. And now, Watson, we shall order breakfast, and afterwards I shall walk down to Doctors' Commons, where I hope to get some data which may help us in this matter."

It was nearly one o'clock when Sherlock Holmes returned from his excursion. He held in his hand a sheet of blue paper, scrawled over with notes and figures.

"I have seen the will of the deceased wife," said he. "To determine its exact meaning I have been obliged to work out the present prices of the investments with which it is concerned. <u>The total income, which at the time of the wife's death was little short of £1100, is now, through the fall in agricultural prices, not more than £750. Each daughter can claim an income of £250, in case of marriage.</u> It is evident, therefore, that if both girls had married, this beauty would have had a mere pittance,[5] while even one of them would cripple him to a very serious extent. My morning's work has not been wasted, since it has proved that he has the very strongest motives for standing in the way of anything of the sort. And now, Watson, this is too serious for dawdling, especially as the old man is aware that we are interesting ourselves in his affairs; so if you are ready, we shall call a cab and drive to Waterloo. I should be very much obliged if you would slip your revolver into your pocket. <u>An Eley's No. 2 is an excellent argument with gentlemen who can twist steel pokers into knots.</u> That and a toothbrush are, I think, all that we need."

At Waterloo we were fortunate in catching a train for Leatherhead, where we hired a trap at the station inn and drove for four or five miles through the lovely Surrey lanes. It was a perfect day, with a bright sun and a few fleecy clouds in the heavens. The trees and wayside hedges were just throwing out their first green shoots, and the air was full of the pleasant smell of the moist earth. To me at least

---

4. **confound . . . with** mistake me for.
5. **pittance** (pit´ əns) *n.* small or barely sufficient allowance of money.

there was a strange contrast between the sweet promise of the spring and this sinister quest upon which we were engaged. My companion sat in the front of the trap, his arms folded, his hat pulled down over his eyes, and his chin sunk upon his breast, buried in the deepest thought. Suddenly, however, he started, tapped me on the shoulder, and pointed over the meadows.

"Look there!" said he.

A heavily timbered park stretched up in a gentle slope, thickening into a grove at the highest point. From amid the branches there jutted out the gray gables and high rooftop of a very old mansion.

"Stoke Moran?" said he.

"Yes, sir, that be the house of Dr. Grimesby Roylott," remarked the driver.

"There is some building going on there," said Holmes; "that is where we are going."

"There's the village," said the driver, pointing to a cluster of roofs some distance to the left; "but if you want to get to the house, you'll find it shorter to get over this stile, and so by the footpath over the fields. There it is, where the lady is walking."

"And the lady, I fancy, is Miss Stoner," observed Holmes, shading his eyes. "Yes, I think we had better do as you suggest."

We got off, paid our fare, and the trap rattled back on its way to Leatherhead.

"I thought it as well," said Holmes as we climbed the stile, "that this fellow should think we had come here as architects, or on some definite business. It may stop his gossip. Good afternoon, Miss Stoner. You see that we have been as good as our word."

Our client of the morning had hurried forward to meet us with a face which spoke her joy. "I have been waiting so eagerly for you," she cried, shaking hands with us warmly. "All has turned out splendidly. Dr. Roylott has gone to town, and it is unlikely that he will be back before evening."

"We have had the pleasure of making the doctor's acquaintance," said Holmes, and in a few words he sketched out what had occurred. Miss Stoner turned white to the lips as she listened.

"Good heavens!" she cried, "he has followed me, then."

"So it appears."

"He is so cunning that I never know when I am safe from him. What will he say when he returns?"

"He must guard himself, for he may find that there is someone more cunning than himself upon his track. You must lock yourself up from him tonight. If he is violent, we

◆ Reading Check

Where are Holmes and Watson going, and for what purpose?

_____

_____

_____

_____

_____

_____

◆ Reading Check

Holmes tells Watson he wants to prevent the driver's "gossip." How might gossip interfere with their plans?

_____

_____

_____

◆ Literary Analysis

Who is " 'someone more cunning' " than Dr. Roylott?

_____

How might the "more cunning" person affect the outcome of the **conflict** in this **mystery**?

_____

_____

_____

What **evidence** might Holmes be looking for when he examines "the outsides of the windows," as noted in the underlined passage?

_____

_____

_____

_____

Underline details in the bracketed passage that represent important pieces of **evidence**. Then, on the lines below, explain what you can guess, based on this evidence.

_____

_____

_____

_____

_____

_____

_____

_____

What **evidence** proves that Holmes guessed incorrectly that someone entered through the window?

_____

_____

_____

shall take you away to your aunt's at Harrow. Now, we must make the best use of our time, so kindly take us at once to the rooms which we are to examine."

The building was of gray, lichen-blotched[6] stone, with a high central portion and two curving wings, like the claws of a crab, thrown out on each side. In one of these wings the windows were broken and blocked with wooden boards, while the roof was partly caved in, a picture of ruin. The central portion was in little better repair, but the right-hand block was comparatively modern, and the blinds in the windows, with the blue smoke curling up from the chimneys, showed that this was where the family resided. Some scaffolding had been erected against the end wall, and the stonework had been broken into, but there were no signs of any workmen at the moment of our visit. Holmes walked slowly up and down the ill-trimmed lawn and examined with deep attention the outsides of the windows.

"This, I take it, belongs to the room in which you used to sleep, the center one to your sister's, and the one next to the main building to Dr. Roylott's chamber?"

"Exactly so. But I am now sleeping in the middle one."

"Pending the alterations, as I understand. By the way, there does not seem to be any very pressing need for repairs at that end wall."

"There were none. I believe that it was an excuse to move me from my room."

"Ah! that is suggestive. Now, on the other side of this narrow wing runs the corridor from which these three rooms open. There are windows in it, of course?"

"Yes, but very small ones. Too narrow for anyone to pass through."

"As you both locked your doors at night, your rooms were unapproachable from that side. Now, would you have the kindness to go into your room and bar your shutters?"

Miss Stoner did so, and Holmes, after a careful examination through the open window, endeavored in every way to force the shutter open, but without success. There was no slit through which a knife could be passed to raise the bar. Then with his lens he tested the hinges, but they were of solid iron, built firmly into the massive masonry. "Hum!" said he, scratching his chin in some perplexity. "My theory certainly presents some difficulties. No one could pass through these shutters if they were bolted. Well, we shall see if the inside throws any light upon the matter."

A small side door led into the whitewashed corridor from which the three bedrooms opened. Holmes refused to examine the third chamber, so we passed at once to the second, that in which Miss Stoner was now sleeping, and in which her sister had met with her fate. It was a homely little room,

---

6. **lichen-blotched** (lī′ kən blächt) *adj.* covered with patches of fungus.

with a low ceiling and a gaping fireplace, after the fashion of old country houses. A brown chest of drawers stood in one corner, a narrow white-counterpaned bed in another, and a dressing table on the left-hand side of the window. These articles, with two small wickerwork chairs, made up all the furniture in the room save for a square of Wilton carpet in the center. The boards round and the paneling of the walls were of brown, worm-eaten oak, so old and discolored that it may have dated from the original building of the house. Holmes drew one of the chairs into a corner and sat silent, while his eyes traveled round and round and up and down, taking in every detail of the apartment.

"Where does that bell communicate with?" he asked at last, pointing to a thick bell-rope which hung down beside the bed, the tassel actually lying upon the pillow.

"It goes to the housekeeper's room."

"It looks newer than the other things?"

"Yes, it was only put there a couple of years ago."

"Your sister asked for it, I suppose?"

"No, I never heard of her using it. We used always to get what we wanted for ourselves."

"Indeed, it seemed unnecessary to put so nice a bell-pull there. You will excuse me for a few minutes while I satisfy myself as to this floor." He threw himself down upon his face with his lens in his hand and crawled swiftly backward and forward, examining minutely the cracks between the boards. Then he did the same with the woodwork with which the chamber was paneled. Finally he walked over to the bed and spent some time in staring at it and in running his eye up and down the wall. Finally he took the bell-rope in his hand and gave it a brisk tug.

"Why, it's a dummy," said he.

"Won't it ring?"

"No, it is not even attached to a wire. This is very interesting. You can see now that it is fastened to a hook just above where the little opening for the ventilator is."

"How very absurd! I never noticed that before!"

"Very strange!" muttered Holmes, pulling at the rope. "There are one or two very singular points about this room. For example, what a fool a builder must be to open a ventilator into another room, when, with the same trouble, he might have communicated with the outside air!"

"That is also quite modern," said the lady.

"Done about the same time as the bell-rope?" remarked Holmes.

"Yes, there were several little changes carried out about that time."

"They seem to have been of a most interesting character—dummy bell-ropes, and ventilators which do not ventilate.

◆ Reading Check

What room is Holmes examining?

_____

_____

_____

_____

◆ Reading Strategy

What **evidence** does Holmes find that someone made special changes to the room?

_____

_____

_____

◆ Reading Strategy

In the bracketed passage, circle the two important pieces of **evidence** that Holmes finds above the bed. What significance do you think these clues might have?

_____

_____

_____

_____

_____

_____

_____

_____

_____

_____

_____

Mark the Text

_____

_____

_____

_____

In the bracketed passage, what **evidence** might Holmes be looking for that might connect the "saucer of milk" and the seat of the chair?

_____

_____

_____

_____

In the underlined passage, Holmes expresses an opinion that the worst kind of criminal is a "clever man." Do you agree or disagree with this idea? Explain why or why not.

_____

_____

_____

_____

_____

_____

_____

With your permission, Miss Stoner, we shall now carry our researches into the inner apartment."

Dr. Grimesby Roylott's chamber was larger than that of his stepdaughter, but was as plainly furnished. A camp bed, a small wooden shelf full of books, mostly of a technical character, an armchair beside the bed, a plain wooden chair against the wall, a round table, and a large iron safe were the principal things which met the eye. Holmes walked slowly round and examined each and all of them with the keenest interest.

"What's in here?" he asked, tapping the safe.

"My stepfather's business papers."

"Oh! you have seen inside, then?"

"Only once, some years ago. I remember that it was full of papers."

"There isn't a cat in it, for example?"

"No. What a strange idea!"

"Well, look at this!" He took up a small saucer of milk which stood on the top of it.

"No; we don't keep a cat. But there is a cheetah and a baboon."

"Ah, yes, of course! Well, a cheetah is just a big cat, and yet a saucer of milk does not go very far in satisfying its wants, I daresay. There is one point which I should wish to determine." He squatted down in front of the wooden chair and examined the seat of it with the greatest attention.

"Thank you. That is quite settled," said he, rising and putting his lens in his pocket. "Hello! Here is something interesting!"

The object which had caught his eye was a small dog lash hung on one corner of the bed. The lash, however, was curled upon itself and tied so as to make a loop of whipcord.

"What do you make of that, Watson?"

"It's a common enough lash. But I don't know why it should be tied."

"That is not quite so common, is it? Ah, me! it's a wicked world, and when a clever man turns his brains to crime it is the worst of all. I think that I have seen enough now, Miss Stoner, and with your permission we shall walk out upon the lawn."

I had never seen my friend's face so grim or his brow so dark as it was when we turned from the scene of this investigation. We had walked several times up and down the lawn, neither Miss Stoner nor myself liking to break in upon his thoughts before he roused himself from his reverie.

"It is very essential, Miss Stoner," said he, "that you should absolutely follow my advice in every respect."

Vocabulary Development: reverie (rev´ ər ē) *n.* daydream

"I shall most certainly do so."

"The matter is too serious for any hesitation. Your life may depend upon your compliance."[7]

"I assure you that I am in your hands."

"In the first place, both my friend and I must spend the night in your room."

Both Miss Stoner and I gazed at him in astonishment.

"Yes, it must be so. Let me explain. I believe that that is the village inn over there?"

"Yes, that is the Crown."

"Very good. Your windows would be visible from there?"

"Certainly."

"You must confine yourself to your room, on pretense of a headache, when your stepfather comes back. Then when you hear him retire for the night, you must open the shutters of your window, undo the hasp,[8] put your lamp there as a signal to us, and then withdraw quietly with everything which you are likely to want into the room which you used to occupy. I have no doubt that, in spite of the repairs, you could manage there for one night."

"Oh, yes, easily."

"The rest you will leave in our hands."

"But what will you do?"

"We shall spend the night in your room, and we shall investigate the cause of this noise which has disturbed you."

"I believe, Mr. Holmes, that you have already made up your mind," said Miss Stoner, laying her hand upon my companion's sleeve.

"Perhaps I have."

"Then, for pity's sake, tell me what was the cause of my sister's death."

"I should prefer to have clearer proofs before I speak."

"You can at least tell me whether my own thought is correct, and if she died from some sudden fright."

"No, I do not think so. I think that there was probably some more <u>tangible</u> cause. And now, Miss Stoner, we must leave you, for if Dr. Roylott returned and saw us our journey would be in vain. Goodbye, and be brave, for if you will do what I have told you, you may rest assured that we shall soon drive away the dangers that threaten you."

Sherlock Holmes and I had no difficulty in engaging a bedroom and sitting room at the Crown Inn. They were on the upper floor, and from our window we could command a

Vocabulary Development: **tangible** (tan´ jə bəl) *adj.* having form and substance; that can be touched or felt by touch

---

7. **compliance** (kəm plī´ əns) *n.* agreement to a request.
8. **hasp** *n.* hinged metal fastening of a window.

The Adventure of the Speckled Band **115**

In what way is the doctor's behavior in the underlined passage a piece of **evidence** in itself?

_____

_____

_____

_____

_____

_____

_____

_____

Circle the four pieces of **evidence** that Holmes mentions in the bracketed passage. What detail provides evidence that the bell-pull is related to the crime?

_____

_____

_____

What details about the room does Holmes point out to Watson?

_____

_____

_____

_____

view of the avenue gate, and of the inhabited wing of Stoke Moran Manor House. At dusk we saw Dr. Grimesby Roylott drive past, his huge form looming up beside the little figure of the lad who drove him. The boy had some slight difficulty in undoing the heavy iron gates, and we heard the hoarse roar of the doctor's voice and saw the fury with which he shook his clinched fists at him. The trap drove on, and a few minutes later we saw a sudden light spring up among the trees as the lamp was lit in one of the sitting rooms.

"Do you know, Watson," said Holmes as we sat together in the gathering darkness, "I have really some scruples as to taking you tonight. There is a distinct element of danger."

"Can I be of assistance?"

"Your presence might be invaluable."

"Then I shall certainly come."

"It is very kind of you."

"You speak of danger. You have evidently seen more in these rooms than was visible to me."

"No, but I fancy that I may have deduced a little more. I imagine that you saw all that I did."

"I saw nothing remarkable save the bell-rope, and what purpose that could answer I confess is more than I can imagine."

"You saw the ventilator, too?"

"Yes, but I do not think that it is such a very unusual thing to have a small opening between two rooms. It was so small that a rat could hardly pass through."

"I knew that we should find a ventilator before ever we came to Stoke Moran."

"My dear Holmes!"

"Oh, yes, I did. You remember in her statement she said that her sister could smell Dr. Roylott's cigar. Now, of course that suggested at once that there must be a communication between the two rooms. It could only be a small one, or it would have been remarked upon at the coroner's inquiry. I deduced a ventilator."

"But what harm can there be in that?"

"Well, there is at least a curious coincidence of dates. A ventilator is made, a cord is hung, and a lady who sleeps in the bed dies. Does not that strike you?"

"I cannot as yet see any connection."

"Did you observe anything very peculiar about that bed?"

"No."

"It was clamped to the floor. Did you ever see a bed fastened like that before?"

"I cannot say that I have."

"The lady could not move her bed. It must always be in the same relative position to the ventilator and to the rope—or so we may call it, since it was clearly never meant for a bell-pull."

"Holmes," I cried, "I seem to see dimly what you are hinting at. We are only just in time to prevent some subtle and horrible crime."

"Subtle enough and horrible enough. When a doctor does go wrong he is the first of criminals. He has nerve and he has knowledge. Palmer and Pritchard were among the heads of their profession. This man strikes even deeper, but I think, Watson, that we shall be able to strike deeper still. But we shall have horrors enough before the night is over; for goodness' sake let us have a quiet pipe and turn our minds for a few hours to something more cheerful."

About nine o'clock the light among the trees was extinguished, and all was dark in the direction of the Manor House. Two hours passed slowly away, and then, suddenly, just at the stroke of eleven, a single bright light shone out right in front of us.

"That is our signal," said Holmes, springing to his feet; "it comes from the middle window."

As we passed out he exchanged a few words with the landlord, explaining that we were going on a late visit to an acquaintance, and that it was possible that we might spend the night there. A moment later we were out on the dark road, a chill wind blowing in our faces, and one yellow light twinkling in front of us through the gloom to guide us on our somber errand.

There was little difficulty in entering the grounds; for unrepaired breaches gaped in the old park wall. Making our way among the trees, we reached the lawn, crossed it, and were about to enter through the window when out from a clump of laurel bushes there darted what seemed to be a hideous and distorted child, who threw itself upon the grass with writhing limbs and then ran swiftly across the lawn into the darkness.

"My God!" I whispered; "did you see it?"

Holmes was for the moment as startled as I. His hand closed like a vise upon my wrist in his agitation. Then he broke into a low laugh and put his lips to my ear.

"It is a nice household," he murmured. "That is the baboon."

I had forgotten the strange pets which the doctor affected. There was a cheetah, too; perhaps we might find it upon our shoulders at any moment. I confess that I felt easier in my mind when, after following Holmes's example and slipping off my shoes, I found myself inside the bedroom. My companion noiselessly closed the shutters, moved the lamp onto the table, and cast his eyes round the room. All was as we had seen it in the daytime. Then creeping up to me and making a trumpet of his hand, he whispered into my ear again so gently that it was all that I could do to distinguish

◆ **Literary Analysis**

How can you tell that the **plot**, or sequence of events, is reaching the point at which the **mystery's** outcome will be decided?

_____

_____

_____

_____

_____

_____

◆ **Literary Analysis**

The settings in a **mystery** contribute to the story's mounting tension, or suspense. In the bracketed passage, circle all the details that make the mood, or atmosphere, here seem tense or nervous. Describe the setting in your own words on the lines below.

Mark the Text

_____

_____

_____

_____

_____

◆ **Reading Check**

In what room are Holmes and Watson in the underlined passage, and how have they gotten in?

_____

_____

_____

_____

In what ways do Holmes and Watson prepare themselves as they wait in Helen Stoner's room?

_____
_____
_____
_____
_____

A **mystery** writer may use sensory language to describe settings and events so vividly that you almost feel you are there. In the bracketed passage, circle the descriptive details that appeal to your senses. To which senses—sight, smell, hearing, touch, or taste—do the descriptive details appeal?

_____
_____
_____
_____

What do Holmes and Watson hear after Holmes strikes at the bell-pull?

_____
_____

the words:

"The least sound would be fatal to our plans."

I nodded to show that I had heard.

"We must sit without light. He would see it through the ventilator."

I nodded again.

"Do not go asleep; your very life may depend upon it. Have your pistol ready in case we should need it. I will sit on the side of the bed, and you in that chair."

I took out my revolver and laid it on the corner of the table.

Holmes had brought up a long thin cane, and this he placed upon the bed beside him. By it he laid the box of matches and the stump of a candle. Then he turned down the lamp, and we were left in darkness.

How shall I ever forget that dreadful vigil? I could not hear a sound, not even the drawing of a breath, and yet I knew that my companion sat open-eyed, within a few feet of me, in the same state of nervous tension in which I was myself. The shutters cut off the least ray of light, and we waited in absolute darkness. From outside came the occasional cry of a night bird, and once at our very window a long-drawn catlike whine, which told us that the cheetah was indeed at liberty. Far away we could hear the deep tones of the parish clock, which boomed out every quarter of an hour. How long they seemed, those quarters! Twelve struck, and one and two and three, and still we sat waiting silently for whatever might befall.

Suddenly there was the momentary gleam of a light up in the direction of the ventilator, which vanished immediately, but was succeeded by a strong smell of burning oil and heated metal. Someone in the next room had lit a dark lantern.[9] I heard a gentle sound of movement, and then all was silent once more, though the smell grew stronger. For half an hour I sat with straining ears. Then suddenly another sound became audible—a very gentle, soothing sound, like that of a small jet of steam escaping continually from a kettle. The instant that we heard it, Holmes sprang from the bed, struck a match, and lashed furiously with his cane at the bell-pull.

"You see it, Watson?" he yelled. "You see it?"

But I saw nothing. At the moment when Holmes struck the light I heard a low, clear whistle, but the sudden glare flashing into my weary eyes made it impossible for me to tell what it was at which my friend lashed so savagely. I could, however, see that his face was deadly pale and filled with horror and loathing.

He had ceased to strike and was gazing up at the venti-

9. **dark lantern** lantern with a shutter that can hide the light.

lator when suddenly there broke from the silence of the night the most horrible cry to which I have ever listened. It swelled up louder and louder, a hoarse yell of pain and fear and anger all mingled in the one dreadful shriek. They say that away down in the village, and even in the distant parsonage, that cry raised the sleepers from their beds. It struck cold to our hearts, and I stood gazing at Holmes, and he at me, until the last echoes of it had died away into the silence from which it rose.

"What can it mean?" I gasped.

"It means that it is all over," Holmes answered. "And perhaps, after all, it is for the best. Take your pistol, and we will enter Dr. Roylott's room."

With a grave face he lit the lamp and led the way down the corridor. Twice he struck at the chamber door without any reply from within. Then he turned the handle and entered, I at his heels, with the cocked pistol in my hand.

It was a singular sight which met our eyes. On the table stood a dark lantern with the shutter half open, throwing a brilliant beam of light upon the iron safe, the door of which was ajar. Beside this table, on the wooden chair, sat Dr. Grimesby Roylott, clad in a long gray dressing gown, his bare ankles protruding beneath, and his feet thrust into red heelless Turkish slippers. Across his lap lay the short stock with the long lash which we had noticed during the day. His chin was cocked upward and his eyes were fixed in a dreadful, rigid stare at the corner of the ceiling. Round his brow he had a peculiar yellow band, with brownish speckles, which seemed to be bound tightly round his head. As we entered he made neither sound nor motion.

"The band! the speckled band!" whispered Holmes.

I took a step forward. In an instant his strange headgear began to move, and there reared itself from among his hair the squat diamond-shaped head and puffed neck of a loathsome serpent.

"It is a swamp adder!" cried Holmes; "the deadliest snake in India. He has died within ten seconds of being bitten. Violence does, in truth, recoil upon the violent, and the schemer falls into the pit which he digs for another. Let us thrust this creature back into its den, and we can then remove Miss Stoner to some place of shelter and let the county police know what has happened."

As he spoke he drew the dog whip swiftly from the dead man's lap, and throwing the noose round the reptile's neck he drew it from its horrid perch and, carrying it at arm's length, threw it into the iron safe, which he closed upon it.

Such are the true facts of the death of Dr. Grimesby Roylott, of Stoke Moran. It is not necessary that I should prolong a narrative which has already run to too great a

---

◆ Reading Check

Briefly summarize what happens in Helen Stoner's room from the time Holmes and Watson see the "gleam of light" to the time Watson gasps, "'What can it mean?'"

_____

_____

_____

_____

_____

_____

_____

_____

_____

_____

◆ Literary Analysis

In the underlined sentence, Holmes states a philosophical idea about violence. How does this climax of the **mystery**'s events support his idea?

_____

_____

_____

◆ Reading Check

What is the speckled band?

_____

How does Dr. Roylott die?

_____

_____

_____

What happens after Holmes and Watson find Dr. Roylott's body?

_____

_____

_____

_____

_____

_____

_____

_____

_____

_____

♦ Literary Analysis

The wrap-up, in which a detective explains his methods, often appears at the end of a **mystery story.** Underline details in Holmes's wrap-up that you were able to guess before they were revealed.

length by telling how we broke the sad news to the terrified girl, how we conveyed her by the morning train to the care of her good aunt at Harrow, of how the slow process of official inquiry came to the conclusion that the doctor met his fate while indiscreetly playing with a dangerous pet. The little which I had yet to learn of the case was told me by Sherlock Holmes as we traveled back next day.

"I had," said he, "come to an entirely erroneous conclusion which shows, my dear Watson, how dangerous it always is to reason from insufficient data. The presence of the gypsies, and the use of the word *band*, which was used by the poor girl, no doubt to explain the appearance which she had caught a hurried glimpse of by the light of her match, were sufficient to put me upon an entirely wrong scent. I can only claim the merit that I instantly reconsidered my position when, however, it became clear to me that whatever danger threatened an occupant of the room could not come either from the window or the door. My attention was speedily drawn, as I have already remarked to you, to this ventilator, and to the bell-rope which hung down to the bed. The discovery that this was a dummy, and that the bed was clamped to the floor, instantly gave rise to the suspicion that the rope was there as a bridge for something passing through the hole and coming to the bed. The idea of a snake instantly occurred to me, and when I coupled it with my knowledge that the doctor was furnished with a supply of creatures from India, I felt that I was probably on the right track. The idea of using a form of poison which could not possibly be discovered by any chemical test was just such a one as would occur to a clever and ruthless man who had had an Eastern training. The rapidity with which such a poison would take effect would also, from his point of view, be an advantage. It would be a sharp-eyed coroner, indeed, who could distinguish the two little dark punctures which would show where the poison fangs had done their work. Then I thought of the whistle. Of course he must recall the snake before the morning light revealed it to the victim. He had trained it, probably by the use of the milk which we saw, to return to him when summoned. He would put it through this ventilator at the hour that he thought best, with the certainty that it would crawl down the rope and land on the bed. It might or might not bite the occupant, perhaps she might escape every night for a week, but sooner or later she must fall a victim.

"I had come to these conclusions before ever I had entered his room. An inspection of his chair showed me that he had been in the habit of standing on it, which of course would be necessary in order that he should reach the ventilator. The sight of the safe, the saucer of milk, and the loop of whipcord were enough to finally dispel any doubts which may have remained. The metallic clang heard by Miss Stoner was obviously caused by her stepfather hastily closing the door of his safe upon its terrible occupant. Having once made up my mind, you know the steps which I took in order to put the matter to the proof. I heard the creature hiss as I have no doubt that you did also, and I instantly lit the light and attacked it."

"With the result of driving it through the ventilator."

"And also with the result of causing it to turn upon its master at the other side. Some of the blows of my cane came home and roused its snakish temper, so that it flew upon the first person it saw. In this way I am no doubt indirectly responsible for Dr. Grimesby Roylott's death, and I cannot say that it is likely to weigh very heavily upon my conscience."

◆ **Literary Analysis**

Who is the victor and who is the defeated in the **conflict** between the detective and the criminal in this **mystery**?

_____

_____

_____

_____

_____

_____

_____

Reader's Response: Would you like to be Sherlock Holmes's partner? Why or why not?

_____

_____

_____

_____

_____

_____

Thinking About the Skill: How did identifying evidence help you to understand the events in this mystery story?

_____

_____

_____

_____

_____

_____

A Glow in the Dark *from* Woodsong
Gary Paulsen

Summary

Gary Paulsen and his team of eight sled dogs are taking a journey in the Alaskan wilderness. After a rest in the afternoon, the dogs are eager to continue. Paulsen's head lamp will not work because of faulty wiring, but he decides to start the trip again at about one in the morning. In the dark, the glow of a strange light frightens the dogs into a sudden stop. Paulsen and the dogs creep forward. The dogs start to sing a death song, and Paulsen becomes very frightened. He is also curious, however. He and the dogs discover that the eerie green light comes from an old tree stump. Later, Paulsen learns the tree stump contains phosphorus, a natural substance that gives off light.

Visual Summary

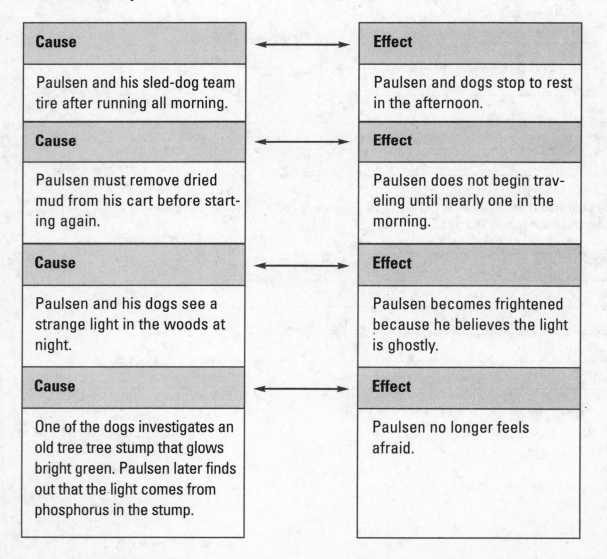

Cause		Effect
Paulsen and his sled-dog team tire after running all morning.	←→	Paulsen and dogs stop to rest in the afternoon.
Paulsen must remove dried mud from his cart before starting again.	←→	Paulsen does not begin traveling until nearly one in the morning.
Paulsen and his dogs see a strange light in the woods at night.	←→	Paulsen becomes frightened because he believes the light is ghostly.
One of the dogs investigates an old tree tree stump that glows bright green. Paulsen later finds out that the light comes from phosphorus in the stump.	←→	Paulsen no longer feels afraid.

A Glow in the Dark *from* Woodsong
Gary Paulsen

Gary Paulsen is an outdoorsman who has traveled by dogsled in north-ern Canada. In the following account, he describes coming upon some-thing strange that neither he nor his team of dogs has ever seen before.

There are night ghosts. Some people say that we can understand all things if we can know them, but there came a dark night in the fall when I thought that was wrong, and so did the dogs.

We had been running all morning and were tired; some of the dogs were young and could not sustain a long run. So we stopped in the middle of the afternoon when they seemed to want to rest. I made a fire, set up a gentle, peaceful camp, and went to sleep for four hours.

It hadn't snowed yet so we had been running with a three-wheel cart, which meant we had to run on logging roads and open areas. I had been hard pressed to find new country to run in to keep the young dogs from becoming bored and this logging trail was one we hadn't run. It had been rough going, with a lot of ruts and mud and the cart was a mess so I spent some time fixing it after I awakened, carving off the dried mud. The end result was we didn't get going again until close to one in the morning. This did not pose a prob-lem except that as soon as I hooked the dogs up and got them lined out—I was running an eight-dog team—my head lamp went out. I replaced the bulb and tried a new battery, but that didn't help—the internal wiring was bad. I thought briefly of sleeping again until daylight but the dogs were slamming into the harnesses, screaming to run, so I shrugged and jumped on the rig and untied it. Certainly, I thought, running without a head lamp would not be the worst thing I had ever done.

Immediately we blew into the darkness and the ride was madness. Without a lamp I could not tell when the rig was going to hit a rut or a puddle. It was cloudy and fairly warm—close to fifty—and had rained the night before. Without the moon or even starlight I had no idea where the puddles were until they splashed me—largely in the face—so I was soon dripping wet. Coupled with that, tree limbs I couldn't see hit at me as we passed, almost tearing me off the back of the rig. Inside an hour I wasn't sure if I was up, down, or sideways.

And the dogs stopped.

They weren't tired, not even a little, judging by the way they had been ripping through the night, but they stopped dead.

I had just taken a limb in the face and was temporarily blinded. All I knew was that they had stopped suddenly and that I had to jam down on the brakes to keep from running over them. It took me a couple of seconds to clear my eyes and when I did, I saw the light.

◆ **Activate Prior Knowledge**

Think about a time when your eyes played tricks on you, or when you could hardly believe what you saw. Briefly describe what you were looking at and what was unusual about it.

_____

_____

_____

_____

_____

_____

_____

_____

◆ **Literary Analysis**

The **tone** of a literary work is the writer's attitude about the subject. It might be serious, humorous, for-mal, mysterious, or something else. In the bracketed pas-sage, underline the words and phrases that create an informal, or casual, tone.

Mark the Text

◆ **Reading Check**

Where and when are Paulsen and his dogs running?

_____

_____

What happens to Paulsen's head-lamp?

_____

_____

What do the dogs and Paulsen see?

_____

_____

_____

_____

_____

◆ Reading Check

What do the dogs do that frightens Paulsen?

_____

_____

_____

Why does the dogs' behavior scare him?

_____

_____

_____

_____

◆ Reading Strategy

By reading ahead, you can some-times find words and phrases that **restate**, or say differently, what a word means. In the underlined passage, circle the words that restate the mean-ing of the word *diffused*.

In the first seconds I thought it was another person com-ing toward me. The light had an eerie green-yellow glow. It was quite bright and filled a whole part of the dark night ahead, down the trail. It seemed to be moving. I was in deep woods and couldn't think what a person would be doing there—there are no other teams where I train—but I was glad to see the light.

At first.

Then I realized the light was strange. It glowed and ebbed and seemed to fill too much space to be a regular light source. It was low to the ground, and wide.

I was still not frightened, and would probably not have become frightened except that the dogs suddenly started to sing.

I have already talked about some of their songs. Rain songs and first-snow songs and meat songs and come-back-and-stay-with-us songs and even puppy-training songs, but I had heard this song only once, when an old dog had died in the kennel. It was a death song.

And that frightened me.

They all sat. I could see them quite well in the glow from the light—the soft glow, the green glow, the ghost glow. It crept into my thinking without my knowing it: the ghost glow. Against my wishes I started thinking of all the things in my life that had scared me.

Ghosts and goblins and dark nights and snakes under the bed and sounds I didn't know and bodies I had found and graveyards under covered pale moons and death, death, death . . .

And they sang and sang. The cold song in the strange light. For a time I could do nothing but stand on the back of the wheeled rig and stare at the light with old, dusty terror.

But curiosity was stronger. My legs moved without my wanting them to move and my body followed them, alongside the team in the dark, holding to each dog like a security blan-ket until I reached the next one, moving closer to the light until I was at the front and there were no more dogs to hold.

The light had gotten brighter, seemed to pulse and flood back and forth, but I still could not see the source. I took another step, then another, trying to look around the corner, deeply feeling the distance from the dogs, the aloneness.

Two more steps, then one more, leaning to see around the corner and at last I saw it and when I did it was worse.

It was a form. Not human. A large, standing form glowing in the dark. The light came from within it, a cold-glowing green light with yellow edges that <u>diffused the shape, mak-ing it change and grow as I watched.</u>

Vocabulary Development: diffused (di fyo͞ozd´) *v.* spread out widely into different directions

I felt my heart slam up into my throat.

I couldn't move. I stared at the upright form and was sure it was a ghost, a being from the dead sent for me. I could not move and might not have ever moved except that the dogs had followed me, pulling the rig quietly until they were around my legs, peering ahead, and I looked down at them and had to laugh.

They were caught in the green light, curved around my legs staring at the standing form, ears cocked and heads turned sideways while they studied it. I took another short step forward and they all followed me, then another, and they stayed with me until we were right next to the form.

It was a stump.

A six-foot-tall, old rotten stump with the bark knocked off, glowing in the dark with a bright green glow. Impossible. I stood there with the dogs around my legs, smelling the stump and touching it with their noses. I found out later that it glowed because it had sucked phosphorus[1] from the ground up into the wood and held the light from day all night.

But that was later. There in the night I did not know this. Touching the stump, and feeling the cold light, I could not quite get rid of the fear until a black-and-white dog named Fonzie came up, smelled the stump, snorted, and relieved himself on it.

So much for ghosts.

---

1. **phosphorus** (fäs´ fə rəs) *n.* substance that gives off light after exposure to radiant energy.

Reader's Response: What might you have thought you were seeing if you saw the "green-yellow glow"?

_____

_____

_____

Thinking About the Skill: Give one or more examples of restatement in the text that helps you understand the meaning of a word, or the meaning of a word to Paulsen.

_____

_____

_____

How do Paulsen and the dogs use each other to be less afraid as they move toward the glow?

_____

_____

_____

_____

◆ Reading Check

What is glowing in the dark?

_____

_____

_____

_____

◆ Literary Analysis

In the bracketed passage, circle the words and phrases that tell you the writer's **tone** has turned humorous.

_____

_____

_____

_____

◆ Reading Check

What is the cause of the glow in the dark?

_____

_____

_____

_____

The Tell-Tale Heart
Edgar Allan Poe

Summary

The murderer himself tells this chilling story of how he kills an old man because he is disgusted by the man's filmy blue eye. First the murderer practices carefully opening the door to the old man's room every night for a week. On the eighth night, he enters the room and hears the beating of the old man's heart. The killer leaps upon his victim and kills him. The murderer then dismembers the corpse and hides the pieces under the floor boards of the room. When police arrive because of a neighbor's complaint of a shriek in the night, the murderer confidently lets them in to search the premises. The officers remain on the scene when the murderer begins to hear the dead man's heartbeat. The sound increases and upsets the murder so much that he confesses to his crime.

Visual Summary

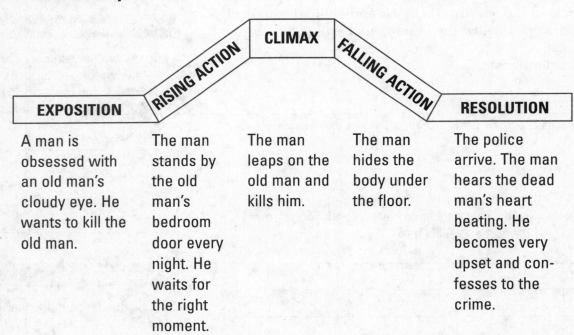

EXPOSITION
A man is obsessed with an old man's cloudy eye. He wants to kill the old man.

RISING ACTION
The man stands by the old man's bedroom door every night. He waits for the right moment.

CLIMAX
The man leaps on the old man and kills him.

FALLING ACTION
The man hides the body under the floor.

RESOLUTION
The police arrive. The man hears the dead man's heart beating. He becomes very upset and confesses to the crime.

The Tell-Tale Heart
Edgar Allan Poe

What goes through a killer's mind before and after a murder? Edgar Allen Poe, a master of horror stories, spins a scary tale of a murder from the killer's point of view. As you might expect, this is no ordinary murder and no ordinary murderer.

True!—nervous—very, very dreadfully nervous I had been and am; but why will you say that I am mad? The disease had sharpened my senses—not destroyed—not dulled them. Above all was the sense of hearing <u>acute</u>. I heard all things in the heaven and in the earth. I heard many things in hell. How, then, am I mad? Hearken![1] and observe how healthily—how calmly I can tell you the whole story.

It is impossible to say how first the idea entered my brain; but once conceived, it haunted me day and night. Object there was none. Passion there was none. I loved the old man. He had never wronged me. He had never given me insult. For his gold I had no desire. I think it was his eye! yes, it was this! One of his eyes resembled that of a vulture—a pale blue eye, with a film over it. Whenever it fell upon me, my blood ran cold; and so by degrees—very gradually—I made up my mind to take the life of the old man, and thus rid myself of the eye forever.

Now this is the point. You fancy me mad. Madmen know nothing. But you should have seen *me*. You should have seen how wisely I proceeded—with what caution— with what foresight—with what <u>dissimulation</u> I went to work! I was never kinder to the old man than during the whole week before I killed him. And every night, about midnight, I turned the latch of his door and opened it—oh, so gently! And then, when I had made an opening sufficient for my head, I put in a dark lantern, all closed, closed, so that no light shone out, and then I thrust in my head. Oh, you would have laughed to see how cunningly I thrust it in! I moved it slowly—very, very slowly, so that I might not disturb the old man's sleep. It took me an hour to place my whole head within the opening so far that I could see him as he lay upon his bed. Ha!—would a madman have been so wise as this? And then, when my head was well in the room, I undid the lantern cautiously—oh, so cautiously—cautiously (for the hinges creaked)—I undid it just so much that a single thin ray fell upon the vulture eye. And this I did for

---

Vocabulary Development: acute (ə kyo͞ot′) *adj.* sensitive
dissimulation (di sim′ yə lā′ shən) *n.* hiding of one's feelings or purposes

---

1. **Hearken** (här′ kən) *v.* listen.

Story Clue	My Prediction

Proved   ☐ True

☐ False

◆ **Literary Analysis**

How does the author build suspense into the **plot** in the bracketed passage?

_____

_____

_____

_____

◆ **Literary Analysis**

Is the **conflict** introduced into the **plot** an external struggle between two people, and external struggle between one person and a force of nature, or an internal struggle within one person? Explain.

_____

_____

_____

seven long nights—every night just at midnight—but I found the eye always closed; and so it was impossible to do the work; for it was not the old man who vexed me, but his evil eye. And every morning, when the day broke, I went boldly into the chamber, and spoke courageously to him, calling him by name in a hearty tone, and inquiring how he had passed the night. So you see he would have been a very <u>profound</u> old man, indeed, to suspect that every night, just at twelve, I looked in upon him while he slept.

<u>Upon the eighth night I was more than usually cautious in opening the door.</u> A watch's minute hand moves more quickly than did mine. Never, before that night, had I _felt_ the extent of my own powers—of my <u>sagacity</u>. I could scarcely contain my feelings of triumph. To think that there I was, opening the door, little by little, and he not even to dream of my secret deeds or thoughts. I fairly chuckled at the idea; and perhaps he heard me; for he moved on the bed suddenly, as if startled. Now you may think that I drew back—but no. His room was as black as pitch with the thick darkness (for the shutters were close fastened, through fear of robbers), and so I knew that he could not see the opening of the door, and I kept pushing it on steadily, steadily.

I had my head in, and was about to open the lantern, when my thumb slipped upon the tin fastening, and the old man sprang up in the bed, crying out—"Who's there?"

I kept quite still and said nothing. For a whole hour I did not move a muscle, and in the meantime I did not hear him lie down. He was still sitting up in the bed, listening;—just as I have done, night after night, hearkening to the death-watches[2] in the wall.

Presently I heard a slight groan, and I knew it was the groan of mortal terror. It was not a groan of pain or of grief—oh, no!—it was the low stifled sound that arises from the bottom of the soul when overcharged with awe. I knew the sound well. Many a night, just at midnight, when all the world slept, it has welled up from my own bosom, deepening, with its dreadful echo, the terrors that distracted me. I say I knew it well. I knew what the old man felt, and pitied him, although I chuckled at heart. I knew that he had been lying awake ever since the first slight noise, when he had turned in the bed. His fears had been ever since growing upon him. He had been trying to fancy them causeless, but

---

Vocabulary Development: profound (prō found´) _adj._ intellectually deep; getting to the bottom of the matter
sagacity (sə gas´ ə tē) _n._ high intelligence and sound judgment

---

2. **deathwatches** (deth´ woch´ əz) _n._ wood-boring beetles whose heads make a tapping sound superstitiously regarded as an omen of death.

could not. He had been saying to himself—"It is nothing but the wind in the chimney—it is only a mouse crossing the floor," or "it is merely a cricket which has made a single chirp." Yes, he has been trying to comfort himself with these suppositions: but he had found all in vain. *All in vain*; because Death, in approaching him, had stalked with his black shadow before him, and enveloped the victim. And it was the mournful influence of the unperceived shadow that caused him to feel—although he neither saw nor heard—to *feel* the presence of my head within the room.

When I had waited a long time, very patiently, without hearing him lie down, I resolved to open a little—a very, very little <u>crevice</u> in the lantern. So I opened it—you cannot imagine how stealthily, stealthily— until, at length, a single dim ray, like the thread of the spider, shot from out the crevice and fell upon the vulture eye.

It was open—wide, wide open—and I grew furious as I gazed upon it. I saw it with perfect distinctness—all a dull blue, with a hideous veil over it that chilled the very marrow in my bones; but I could see nothing else of the old man's face or person for I had directed the ray as if by instinct, precisely upon the spot.

And now—have I not told you that what you mistake for madness is but overacuteness of the senses?—now, I say, there came to my ears a low, dull, quick sound, such as a watch makes when enveloped in cotton. I knew *that* sound well, too. It was the beating of the old man's heart. It increased my fury, as the beating of a drum stimulates the soldier into courage.

But even yet I refrained and kept still. I scarcely breathed. I held the lantern motionless. I tried how steadily I could maintain the ray upon the eye. Meantime the hellish tattoo of the heart increased. It grew quicker and quicker, and louder and louder every instant. The old man's terror *must* have been extreme! It grew louder, I say, louder every moment!—do you mark me well? I have told you that I am nervous: so I am. And now at the dead hour of the night, amid the dreadful silence of that old house, so strange a noise as this excited me to uncontrollable terror. Yet, for some minutes longer I refrained and stood still. But the beating grew louder, louder! I thought the heart must burst. And now a new anxiety seized me—the sound would be heard by a neighbor! The old man's hour had come! With a loud yell, I threw open the lantern and leaped into the room. He shrieked once —once only. In an instant I dragged him to the floor, and pulled the heavy bed over him. I then smiled gaily, to find the deed so far done. But, for many minutes, the heart beat on with a muffled sound. This, however, did

Vocabulary Development: crevice (krev´ is) *n.* a narrow opening

◆ **Reading Check**

In the bracketed passage, Poe appeals to the reader's senses of sight, hearing, and touch. Circle images that appeal to each of these senses.

◆ **Reading Check**

What part of the old man's body troubled the narrator at first?

_____

_____

_____

_____

◆ **Reading Strategy**

Circle a sentence in the bracketed passage that helps you **predict** that the narrator is going to kill the old man very soon.

◆ **Reading Check**

Did the man die instantly? How do you know?

_____

_____

_____

_____

What event marks the **climax** of the **plot**? Explain.

_____

_____

_____

_____

_____

Predict whether the police will solve the crime or not. Write your prediction below. Later, go back and indicate whether your prediction proved true or false.

Story Clue	My Prediction

Proved   ☐ True
          ☐ False

What new **conflict** is being introduced into the **plot** beginning with the underlined sentence?

_____

_____

_____

_____

_____

not vex me; it would not be heard through the wall. At length it ceased. The old man was dead. I removed the bed and examined the corpse. Yes, he was stone, stone dead. I placed my hand upon the heart and held it there many minutes. There was no pulsation. He was stone dead. His eye would trouble me no more.

If still you think me mad, you will think so no longer when I describe the wise precautions I took for the concealment of the body. The night waned, and I worked hastily, but in silence. First of all I dismembered the corpse. I cut off the head and the arms and the legs.

I then took up three planks from the flooring of the chamber, and deposited all between the scantlings.[3] I then replaced the boards so cleverly, so cunningly, that no human eye—not even *his* —could have detected anything wrong. There was nothing to wash out—no stain of any kind—no blood-spot whatever. I had been too wary for that. A tub had caught all—ha! ha!

When I had made an end of these labors, it was four o'clock—still dark as midnight. As the bell sounded the hour, there came a knocking at the street door. I went down to open it with a light heart—for what had I *now* to fear? There entered three men, who introduced themselves, with perfect suavity, as officers of the police. A shriek had been heard by a neighbor during the night; suspicion of foul play had been aroused; information had been lodged at the police office, and they (the officers) had been deputed to search the premises.

I smiled—for *what* had I to fear? I bade the gentlemen welcome. The shriek, I said, was my own in a dream. The old man, I mentioned, was absent in the country. I took my visitors all over the house. I bade them search—search *well*. I led them, at length, to *his* chamber. I showed them his treasures, secure, undisturbed. In the enthusiasm of my confidence, I brought chairs into the room, and desired them *here* to rest from their fatigues, while I myself, in the wild audacity of my perfect triumph, placed my own seat upon the very spot beneath which reposed the corpse of the victim.

The officers were satisfied. My *manner* had convinced them. I was singularly at ease. They sat, and while I answered cheerily, they chatted of familiar things. But, ere long, I felt myself getting pale and wished them gone. My head ached, and I fancied a ringing in my ears: but still they sat and still chatted. The ringing became more distinct:—it continued and became more distinct: I talked more freely to get rid of the feeling: but it continued and gained definitiveness—until, at length, I found that the noise was *not* within my ears.

---

3. **scantlings** (skant′ liŋz) *n.* small beams or timbers.

No doubt I now grew *very* pale—but I talked more fluently, and with a heightened voice. Yet the sound increased—and what could I do? It was a *low, dull, quick sound—much such a sound as a watch makes when enveloped in cotton.* I gasped for breath—and yet the officers heard it not. I talked more quickly—more vehemently; but the noise steadily increased. I arose and argued about trifles, in a high key and with violent gesticulations; but the noise steadily increased. Why *would* they not be gone? I paced the floor to and fro with heavy strides, as if excited to fury by the observations of the men—but the noise steadily increased. Oh! what *could* I do? I foamed—I raved—I swore! I swung the chair upon which I had been sitting, and grated it upon the boards, but the noise arose over all, and continually increased. It grew louder—louder—*louder!* And still the men chatted pleasantly, and smiled. Was it possible they heard not?— no, no! They heard!—they suspected!— they *knew!* — they were making a mockery of my horror!—this I thought, and this I think. But anything was better than this agony! Anything was more tolerable than this derision! I could bear those hypocritical smiles no longer! I felt that I must scream or die!—and now again! hark! louder! louder! louder! *louder!*—

"Villains!" I shrieked, "dissemble[4] no more! I admit the deed!—tear up the planks!—here, here!—it is the beating of his hideous heart!"

Build Vocabulary: gesticulations (jes tik´ yo͞o lā´ shənz) *n.* energetic hand or arm movements
derision (di rizh´ ən) *n.* contempt; ridicule

---

4. **dissemble** (di sem´ bəl) *v.* conceal under a false appearance; to conceal the truth of one's true feelings or motives.

Reader's Response: : At which point of the story did you find the narrator the most frightening?

_____

_____

_____

Thinking About the Skill: Why is **making predictions** a good way to stay involved in a mystery or horror story?

_____

_____

_____

© Pearson Education, Inc.

◆ Literary Analysis

The **falling action** occurs quickly in this paragraph leading to the **conclusion**. Follow the events by circling each verb that follows the pronoun *I* in the bracketed passage.

◆ Reading Check

Why does the murderer confess in the end?

_____

_____

_____

_____

_____

_____

_____

_____

_____

_____

_____

_____

Hamadi
Naomi Shahib Nye

Summary

"Hamadi" is a story about discovering who you are with the help of a wise older person. Susan is a Palestinian American high school student living in Texas. She searches for ways to combine her family's Palestinian past with her American present. Susan enjoys the company of Hamadi, a strange but fascinating older friend of her family. Hamadi lives simply and cares mainly about books and ideas. Susan invites Hamadi to go out Christmas caroling with her, her friends, and her family. While caroling, her friend Tracy breaks down in tears over the loss of a boy she has a crush on. Hamadi turns out to be an unexpected source of comfort and wisdom.

Visual Summary

"Hamadi" is mainly about the character Hamadi and the effect he has on other people, especially Susan. The following diagram shows some of his unique traits.

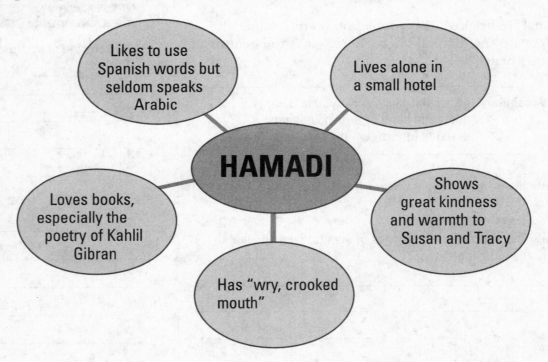

Likes to use Spanish words but seldom speaks Arabic

Lives alone in a small hotel

Loves books, especially the poetry of Kahlil Gibran

HAMADI

Shows great kindness and warmth to Susan and Tracy

Has "wry, crooked mouth"

Hamadi
Naomi Shihab Nye

Susan, a Palestinian American high school student, longs for a connection to her relatives living near Jerusalem and to her heritage. She finds this connection in Saleh Hamadi, an unusual family friend, whose wisdom and kind heart make her life richer.

Susan didn't really feel interested in Saleh Hamadi until she was a freshman in high school carrying a thousand questions around. Why this way? Why not another way? Who said so and why can't I say something else? Those <u>brittle</u> women at school in the counselor's office treated the world as if it were a yardstick and they had tight hold of both ends.

Sometimes Susan felt polite with them, sorting attendance cards during her free period, listening to them gab about fingernail polish and television. And other times she felt she could run out of the building yelling. That's when she daydreamed about Saleh Hamadi, who had nothing to do with any of it. Maybe she thought of him as escape, the way she used to think about the Sphinx at Giza[1] when she was younger. She would picture the golden Sphinx sitting quietly in the desert with sand blowing around its face, never changing its expression. She would think of its wry, slightly crooked mouth and how her grandmother looked a little like that as she waited for her bread to bake in the old village north of Jerusalem. Susan's family had lived in Jerusalem for three years before she was ten and drove out to see her grandmother every weekend. They would find her patting fresh dough between her hands, or pressing cakes of dough onto the black rocks in the *taboon*, the rounded old oven outdoors. Sometimes she moved her lips as she worked. Was she praying? Singing a secret song? Susan had never seen her grandmother rushing.

Now that she was fourteen, she took long walks in America with her father down by the drainage ditch at the end of their street. Pecan trees shaded the path. She tried to get him to tell stories about his childhood in Palestine. She didn't want him to forget anything. She helped her American mother complete tedious kitchen tasks without complaining—rolling grape leaves around their lemony rice stuffing, scrubbing carrots for the roaring juicer. Some evenings when

---

Vocabulary Development: brittle (brit´ əl) *adj.* stiff and unbending in manner; lacking warmth

---

1. **Sphinx** (sfiŋks) **at Giza** (gē´ zə) huge statue with the head of a man and the body of a lion, located near Cairo in northern Egypt.

◆ **Activate Prior Knowledge**

You have probably known an older adult to whom you looked for wisdom and advice. Briefly describe this person. Include some of his or her wise words if you can remember them.

_____

_____

_____

_____

◆ **Reading Strategy**

Try to **identify with the main character**, Susan, to understand her better. After reading the first two paragraphs, list two ways that you are similar to Susan and two ways that you are different from her.

Similar

1._____

_____

2._____

_____

Different

1._____

_____

2._____

_____

◆ **Reading Check**

Where do Susan's parents come from?

_____

_____

_____

_____

In the bracketed passage that began on page 133, find two ways that Susan's parents help preserve the family's Palestinian heritage. Circle or underline them.

◆ Literary Analysis

Hamadi is a **round character** with many different traits or qualities. Circle any traits in the following list that seem to fit Hamadi's character. Be prepared to explain your choices.

- quiet
- sentimental
- neat
- energetic
- smart
- greedy

◆ Reading Check

Why does speaking Arabic make Hamadi "feel too sad"?

_____

_____

_____

◆ Reading Check

Based on the underlined remark, does Susan's father think that Hamadi really lived with Gibran? Explain.

_____

_____

_____

_____

the soft Texas twilight pulled them all outside, she thought of her far-away grandmother and said, "Let's go see Saleh Hamadi. Wouldn't he like some of that cheese pie Mom made?" And they would wrap a slice of pie and drive downtown. Somehow he felt like a good substitute for a grandmother, even though he was a man.

Usually Hamadi was wearing a white shirt, shiny black tie, and a jacket that reminded Susan of the earth's surface just above the treeline on a mountain—thin, somehow purified. He would raise his hands high before giving advice.

"It is good to drink a tall glass of water every morning upon arising!" If anyone doubted this, he would shake his head. "Oh Susan, Susan, Susan," he would say.

He did not like to sit down, but he wanted everyone else to sit down. He made Susan sit on the wobbly chair beside the desk and he made her father or mother sit in the saggy center of the bed. He told them people should eat six small meals a day.

They visited him on the sixth floor of the Traveler's Hotel, where he had lived so long nobody could remember him ever traveling. Susan's father used to remind him of the apartments available over the Victory Cleaners, next to the park with the fizzy pink fountain, but Hamadi would shake his head, pinching kisses at his spartan room. "A white handkerchief spread across a tabletop, my two extra shoes lined by the wall, this spells 'home' to me, this says 'mi casa.' What more do I need?"

Hamadi liked to use Spanish words. They made him feel expansive, worldly. He'd learned them when he worked at the fruits and vegetables warehouse on Zarzamora Street, marking off crates of apples and avocados on a long white pad. Occasionally he would speak Arabic, his own first language, with Susan's father and uncles, but he said it made him feel too sad, as if his mother might step into the room at any minute, her arms laden with fresh mint leaves. He had come to the United States on a boat when he was eighteen years old and he had never been married. "I married books," he said. "I married the wide horizon."

"What is he to us?" Susan used to ask her father. "He's not a relative, right? How did we meet him to begin with?"

Susan's father couldn't remember. "I think we just drifted together. Maybe we met at your uncle Hani's house. Maybe that old Maronite priest who used to cry after every service introduced us. The priest once shared an apartment with Kahlil Gibran[2] in New York—so he said. And Saleh always says he stayed with Gibran when he first got off the boat. I'll bet that popular guy Gibran has had a lot of roommates he doesn't even know about."

2. **Kahlil Gibran** (kä lēl´ ji brän´) Lebanese novelist, poet, and artist who lived from 1883 to 1931; his most famous book is *The Prophet*.

Susan said, "Dad, he's dead."

"I know, I know," her father said.

Later Susan said, "Mr. Hamadi, did you really meet Kahlil Gibran? He's one of my favorite writers." Hamadi walked slowly to the window of his room and stared out. There wasn't much to look at down on the street—a bedraggled[3] flower shop, a boarded-up tavern with a hand-lettered sign tacked to the front, GONE TO FIND JESUS. Susan's father said the owners had really gone to Alabama.

Hamadi spoke patiently. "Yes, I met brother Gibran. And I meet him in my heart every day. When I was a young man—shocked by all the visions of the new world—the tall buildings—the wild traffic—the young people without shame—the proud mailboxes in their blue uniforms—I met him. And he has stayed with me every day of my life."

"But did you really meet him, like in person, or just in a book?"

He turned dramatically. "Make no such distinctions, my friend. Or your life will be a pod with only dried-up beans inside. Believe anything can happen."

Susan's father looked irritated, but Susan smiled. "I do," she said. "I believe that. I want fat beans. If I imagine something, it's true, too. Just a different kind of true."

Susan's father was twiddling with the knobs on the old-fashioned sink. "Don't they even give you hot water here? You don't mean to tell me you've been living without hot water?"

On Hamadi's rickety desk lay a row of different "Love" stamps issued by the post office.

"You must write a lot of letters," Susan said.

"No, no, I'm just focusing on that word," Hamadi said. "I particularly like the globe in the shape of a heart," he added.

"Why don't you take a trip back to his village in Lebanon?" Susan's father asked. "Maybe you still have relatives living there."

Hamadi looked pained. "'Remembrance is a form of meeting,' my brother Gibran says, and <u>I do believe I meet with my cousins every day.</u>"

"But aren't you curious? You've been gone so long! Wouldn't you like to find out what has happened to everybody and everything you knew as a boy?" Susan's father traveled back to Jerusalem once every year to see his family.

"I would not. In fact, I already know. <u>It is there and it is not there.</u> Would you like to share an orange with me?"

His long fingers, tenderly peeling. Once when Susan was younger, he'd given her a <u>lavish</u> ribbon off a holiday fruit basket and expected her to wear it on her head. In the car, Susan's father said, "Riddles. He talks in riddles. I don't

Vocabulary Development: lavish (lav´ ish) *adj.* showy

3. **bedraggled** (bē drag´ əld) *adj.* limp and dirty, as if dragged through mud.

◆ **Reading Strategy**

How does Susan's background influence her choice of a favorite writer?

_____

_____

_____

_____

◆ **Reading Strategy**

In the bracketed passage, what do Hamadi and Susan mean by "fat beans"?

_____

_____

_____

_____

Identify with the characters. Do you want fat beans in your life, too? Why or why not?

_____

_____

_____

_____

◆ **Reading Check**

How can you explain Hamadi's two underlined remarks in the bracketed passage?

_____

_____

_____

_____

_____

_____

◆ **Reading Check**

List three things that Susan and Tracy have in common.

1. _____

   _____

2. _____

   _____

3. _____

   _____

◆ **Reading Check**

How do Susan and Tracy differ in the way they think about Eddie?

_____

_____

_____

_____

_____

◆ **Reading Strategy**

Do you **identify** with what Susan says in the bracketed paragraph about having a boyfriend (or a girl-friend)? Explain.

_____

_____

_____

_____

_____

_____

know why I have patience with him." Susan stared at the people talking and laughing in the next car. She did not even exist in their world.

* * *

Susan carried *The Prophet* around on top of her English textbook and her Texas history. She and her friend Tracy read it out loud to one another at lunch. Tracy was a jun-ior—they'd met at the literary magazine meeting where Susan, the only freshman on the staff, got assigned to do proofreading. They never ate in the cafeteria; they sat out-side at picnic tables with sack lunches, whole wheat crack-ers and fresh peaches. Both of them had given up meat.

Tracy's eyes looked steamy. "You know that place where Gibran says, 'Hate is a dead thing. Who of you would be a tomb?'"

Susan nodded. Tracy continued. "Well, I hate someone. I'm trying not to, but I can't help it. I hate Debbie for liking Eddie and it's driving me nuts."

"Why shouldn't Debbie like Eddie?" Susan said. "*You* do."

Tracy put her head down on her arms. A gang of cheer-leaders walked by giggling. One of them flicked her finger in greeting.

"In fact, we *all* like Eddie," Susan said. "Remember, here in this book—wait and I'll find it—where Gibran says that loving teaches us the secrets of our hearts and that's the way we connect to all of Life's heart? You're not talking about liking or loving, you're talking about owning."

Tracy looked glum. "Sometimes you remind me of a minister."

Susan said, "Well, just talk to me someday when *I'm* depressed."

Susan didn't want a boyfriend. Everyone who had boyfriends or girlfriends all seemed to have troubles. Susan told people she had a boyfriend far away, on a farm in Missouri, but the truth was, boys still seemed like cousins to her. Or brothers. Or even girls.

A squirrel sat in the crook of a tree, eyeing their sand-wiches. When the end-of-lunch bell blared, Susan and Tracy jumped—it always seemed too soon. Squirrels were lucky; they didn't have to go to school.

* * *

Susan's father said her idea was ridiculous: to invite Saleh Hamadi to go Christmas caroling with the English

Club. "His English is archaic,[4] for one thing, and he won't know any of the songs."

"How could you live in America for years and not know 'Joy to the World' or 'Away in a Manger'?"

"Listen, I grew up right down the road from 'Oh Little Town of Bethlehem' and I still don't know a single verse."

"I want him. We need him. It's boring being with the same bunch of people all the time."

So they called Saleh and he said he would come—"thrilled" was the word he used. He wanted to ride the bus to their house, he didn't want anyone to pick him up. Her father muttered, "He'll probably forget to get off." Saleh thought "caroling" meant they were going out with a woman named Carol. He said, "Holiday spirit—I was just reading about it in the newspaper."

Susan said, "Dress warm."

Saleh replied, "Friend, my heart is warmed simply to hear your voice."

All that evening Susan felt light and bouncy. She decorated the coffee can they would use to collect donations to be sent to the children's hospital in Bethlehem. She had started doing this last year in middle school, when a singing group collected $100 and the hospital responded on exotic onion-skin stationery that they were "eternally grateful."

Her father shook his head. "You get something into your mind and it really takes over," he said. "Why do you like Hamadi so much all of a sudden? You could show half as much interest in your own uncles."

Susan laughed. Her uncles were dull. Her uncles shopped at the mall and watched TV. "Anyone who watches TV more than twelve minutes a week is uninteresting," she said.

Her father lifted an eyebrow.

"He's my surrogate grandmother," she said. "He says interesting things. He makes me think. Remember when I was little and he called me The Thinker? We have a connection." She added, "Listen, do you want to go too? It is not a big deal. And Mom has a *great* voice, why don't you both come?"

A minute later her mother was digging in the closet for neck scarves, and her father was digging in the drawer for flashlight batteries.

Saleh Hamadi arrived precisely on time, with flushed red cheeks and a sack of dates stuffed in his pocket. "We may need sustenance on our journey." Susan thought the older people seemed quite giddy as they drove down to the high school to meet the rest of the carolers. Strands of winking lights wrapped around their neighbors' drainpipes and trees. A giant Santa tipped his hat on Dr. Garcia's roof.

Her friends stood gathered in front of the school. Some

---

4. **archaic** (är kā´ ik) *adj.* old-fashioned; out-of-date.

◆ **Reading Strategy**

With whom do you agree more—Susan or her father—about inviting Hamadi to go caroling? Explain.

_____

_____

_____

_____

_____

_____

◆ **Literary Analysis**

What does the **indirect characterization** of Susan in the bracketed passage—her words and actions and what others say about her—reveal about her personality? Circle details in the passage that lead you to your answer.

_____

_____

_____

_____

_____

◆ **Reading Check**

How do you know that Susan's parents are excited about going caroling?

_____

_____

_____

_____

_____

were smoothing out song sheets that had been crammed in a drawer or cabinet for a whole year. Susan thought holidays were strange; they came, and you were supposed to feel ready for them. What if you could make up your own holidays as you went along? She had read about a woman who used to have parties to celebrate the arrival of fresh asparagus in the local market. Susan's friends might make holidays called Eddie Looked at Me Today and Smiled.

Two people were alleluia-ing in harmony. Saleh Hamadi went around the group formally introducing himself to each person and shaking hands. A few people laughed behind their hands when his back was turned. He had stepped out of a painting, or a newscast, with his outdated long overcoat, his clunky old men's shoes and elegant manners.

Susan spoke more loudly than usual. "I'm honored to introduce you to one of my best friends, Mr. Hamadi."

"Good evening to you," he pronounced musically, bowing a bit from the waist.

What could you say back but "Good evening, sir." His old-fashioned manners were contagious.

They sang at three houses which never opened their doors. They sang "We Wish You a Merry Christmas" each time they moved on. Lisa had a fine, clear soprano. Tracy could find the alto harmony to any line. Cameron and Elliot had more enthusiasm than accuracy. Lily, Rita, and Jeannette laughed every time they said a wrong word and fumbled to find their places again. Susan loved to see how her mother knew every word of every verse without looking at the paper, and her father kept his hands in his pockets and seemed more interested in examining people's mailboxes or yard displays than in trying to sing. And Saleh Hamadi—what language was he singing in? He didn't even seem to be pronouncing words, but humming deeply from his throat. Was he saying, "Om?" Speaking Arabic? Once he caught her looking and whispered, "That was an Aramaic word that just drifted into my mouth—the true language of the Bible, you know, the language Jesus Christ himself spoke."

By the fourth block their voices felt tuned up and friendly people came outside to listen. Trays of cookies were passed around and dollar bills stuffed into the little can. Thank you, thank you. Out of the dark from down the block, Susan noticed Eddie sprinting toward them with his coat flapping, unbuttoned. She shot a glance at Tracy, who pretended not to notice. "Hey, guys!" shouted Eddie. "The first time in my life I'm late and everyone else is on time! You could at least have left a note about which way you were going." Someone slapped him on the back. Saleh Hamadi, whom he had never seen before, was the only one who managed a reply. "Welcome, welcome to our cheery group!"

Eddie looked mystified. "Who is this guy?"

◆ Reading Strategy

Identify with Susan. Would you feel comfortable introducing Hamadi to your friends? Why or why not?

_____

_____

_____

_____

◆ Reading Check

What differences among the carolers does Susan observe?

_____

_____

_____

_____

_____

◆ Literary Analysis

Is Eddie a **round character** or a **flat character**?

_____

_____

What trait(s) does he seem to have?

_____

_____

_____

Susan whispered, "My friend."

Eddie approached Tracy, who read her song sheet intently just then, and stuck his face over her shoulder to whisper, "Hi." Tracy stared straight ahead into the air and whispered "Hi" vaguely, glumly. Susan shook her head. Couldn't Tracy act more cheerful at least?

They were walking again. They passed a string of blinking reindeer and a wooden snowman holding a painted candle. Ridiculous!

Eddie fell into step beside Tracy, murmuring so Susan couldn't hear him anymore. Saleh Hamadi was flinging his arms up high as he strode. Was he power walking? Did he even know what power walking was? Between houses, Susan's mother hummed obscure songs people never remembered: "What Child Is This?" and "The Friendly Beasts."

Lisa moved over to Eddie's other side. "I'm so *excited* about you and Debbie!" she said loudly. "Why didn't she come tonight?"

Eddie said, "She has a sore throat."

Tracy shrank up inside her coat.

Lisa chattered on. "James said we should make our reservations *now* for dinner at the Tower after the Sweetheart Dance, can you believe it? In December, making a reservation for February? But otherwise it might get booked up!"

Saleh Hamadi tuned into this conversation with interest; the Tower was downtown, in his neighborhood. He said, "This sounds like significant preliminary planning! Maybe you can be an international advisor someday." Susan's mother bellowed, "Joy to the World!" and voices followed her, stretching for notes. Susan's father was gazing off into the sky. Maybe he thought about all the refugees in camps in Palestine far from doorbells and shutters. Maybe he thought about the horizon beyond Jerusalem when he was a boy, how it seemed to be inviting him, "Come over, come over." Well, he'd come all the way to the other side of the world, and now he was doomed to live in two places at once. To Susan, immigrants seemed bigger than other people, and always slightly melancholy. They also seemed doubly interesting. Maybe someday Susan would meet one her own age.

Two thin streams of tears rolled down Tracy's face. Eddie had drifted to the other side of the group and was clowning with Cameron, doing a tap dance shuffle. "While fields and floods, rocks hills and plains, repeat the sounding joy, repeat the sounding joy . . ." Susan and Saleh Hamadi noticed her. Hamadi peered into Tracy's face, inquiring,

---

Vocabulary Development: refugees (ref´ yoo jēz´) *n.* people who flee from their homes in a time of trouble
melancholy (mel´ ən käl´ ē) *adj.* sad; depressed

◆ **Reading Strategy**

Identify with Tracy. How would you feel if you were in her position? Why?

_____

_____

_____

_____

_____

_____

_____

_____

◆ **Literary Analysis**

Which of the following is a **dynamic character**, who seems to change or grow during the story? Explain your choice.

- Susan's father
- Susan
- Tracy

_____

_____

_____

_____

_____

_____

_____

Note the **indirect characterization** of Hamadi in the bracketed passage by circling one thing he does and one thing he says. Then, on the lines below, write what this action and this speech reveal about him.

_____

_____

_____

_____

_____

_____

_____

_____

_____

_____

_____

_____

_____

_____

_____

_____

_____

"Why? Is it pain? Is it gratitude? We are such mysterious creatures, human beings!"

Tracy turned to him, pressing her face against the old wool of his coat, and wailed. The song ended. All eyes on Tracy, and this tall, courteous stranger who would never in a thousand years have felt comfortable stroking her hair. But he let her stand there, crying as Susan stepped up to stand firmly on the other side of Tracy, putting her arms around her friend. Hamadi said something Susan would remember years later, whenever she was sad herself, even after college, a creaky anthem sneaking back into her ear, "We go on. On and on. We don't stop where it hurts. We turn a corner. It is the reason why we are living. To turn a corner. Come, let's move."

Above them, in the heavens, stars lived out their lonely lives. People whispered, "What happened? What's wrong?" Half of them were already walking down the street.

Reader's Response: Would you like to know someone like Hamadi? Why or why not?

_____

_____

_____

Thinking About the Skill: How does **identifying with a character** help you understand him or her better?

_____

_____

_____

Tears of Autumn
Yoshiko Uchida

Summary

Hana Omiya is a shy Japanese woman from an old-fashioned Japanese family. Hana's uncle comes one day to tell the family that he is looking for a young woman to marry a Japanese man. The man is living in the United States, in Oakland, California. Hana realizes that this may be her chance to escape from the limits of her role as a youngest daughter. She tells her uncle that she might be interested in traveling to America to marry the man. Even though her uncle and her mother express doubts, Hana seems ready to make this big move in her life. The young man in Oakland sends her some letters, and she prepares for the long trip. After a long, hard boat journey, Hana arrives in the United States. Her husband-to-be is waiting for her. She is very nervous and a bit disappointed when she first sees him. But then Hana remembers why she came and looks forward to her new life.

Visual Summary

Set-up	Conflict	Resolution
• Hana lives with her mother and relatives in Japan. She longs to escape from the suffocating atmosphere of her home.	• Hana agrees to marry a man far away, in Oakland, California. She worries about whether she has made the right decision and whether she will like living in a new country.	• Hana follows through on her decision. She travels by boat to join the man and start a new life in the United States.

Tears of Autumn
Yoshiko Uchida

Hana goes halfway around the world to meet a husband she has seen only in an old photograph. Has she made the right decision? What will her new life be like?

Hana Omiya stood at the railing of the small ship that shuddered toward America in a <u>turbulent</u> November sea. She shivered as she pulled the folds of her silk kimono close to her throat and tightened the wool shawl about her shoulders.

She was thin and small, her dark eyes shadowed in her pale face, her black hair piled high in a pompadour that seemed too heavy for so slight a woman. She clung to the moist rail and breathed the damp salt air deep into her lungs. Her body seemed leaden and lifeless, as though it were simply the vehicle transporting her soul to a strange new life, and she longed with childlike intensity to be home again in Oka Village.

She longed to see the bright persimmon dotting the barren trees beside the thatched roofs, to see the fields of golden rice stretching to the mountains where only last fall she had gathered plum white mushrooms, and to see once more the maple trees lacing their flaming colors through the green pine. If only she could see a familiar face, eat a meal without retching, walk on solid ground, and stretch out at night on a *tatami* mat[1] instead of in a hard narrow bunk. She thought now of seeking the warm shelter of her bunk but could not bear to face the relentless smell of fish that penetrated the lower decks.

Why did I ever leave Japan? she wondered bitterly. Why did I ever listen to my uncle? And yet she knew it was she herself who had begun the chain of events that placed her on this heaving ship. It was she who had first planted in her uncle's mind the thought that she would make a good wife for Taro Takeda, the lonely man who had gone to America to make his fortune in Oakland, California.

It all began one day when her uncle had come to visit her mother.

"I must find a nice young bride," he had said, startling Hana with this blunt talk of marriage in her presence. She blushed and was ready to leave the room when her uncle quickly added, "My good friend Takeda has a son in America. I must find someone willing to travel to that far land."

Vocabulary Development: turbulent (tur´ byoo lənt) *adj.* full of commotion; wild

---

1. **tatami** (tə tä´ mē) **mat** *n.* floor mat woven of rice straw, traditionally used in Japanese homes.

This last remark was intended to indicate to Hana and her mother that he didn't consider this a suitable prospect for Hana, who was the youngest daughter of what once had been a fine family. Her father, until his death fifteen years ago, had been the largest landholder of the village and one of its last samurai.[2] They had once had many servants and field hands, but now all that was changed. Their money was gone. Hana's three older sisters had made good marriages, and the eldest remained in their home with her husband to carry on the Omiya name and perpetuate the homestead. Her other sisters had married merchants in Osaka and Nagoya and were living comfortably.

Now that Hana was twenty-one, finding a proper husband for her had taken on an urgency that produced an embarrassing secretive air over the entire matter. Usually, her mother didn't speak of it until they were lying side by side on their quilts at night. Then, under the protective cover of darkness, she would suggest one name and then another, hoping that Hana would indicate an interest in one of them.

Her uncle spoke freely of Taro Takeda only because he was so sure Hana would never consider him. "He is a conscientious, hardworking man who has been in the United States for almost ten years. He is thirty-one, operates a small shop, and rents some rooms above the shop where he lives." Her uncle rubbed his chin thoughtfully. "He could provide well for a wife," he added.

"Ah," Hana's mother said softly.

"You say he is successful in this business?" Hana's sister inquired.

"His father tells me he sells many things in his shop—clothing, stockings, needles, thread, and buttons—such things as that. He also sells bean paste, pickled radish, bean cake, and soy sauce. A wife of his would not go cold or hungry."

They all nodded, each of them picturing this merchant in varying degrees of success and <u>affluence</u>. There were many Japanese emigrating to America these days, and Hana had heard of the picture brides who went with nothing more than an exchange of photographs to bind them to a strange man.

"Taro San[3] is lonely," her uncle continued. "I want to find for him a fine young woman who is strong and brave enough to cross the ocean alone."

"It would certainly be a different kind of life," Hana's sister ventured, and for a moment, Hana thought she glimpsed a

---

Vocabulary Development: affluence (af´ loo əns) *n.* wealth; abundance

---

2. **samurai** (sam´ ə rī) *n.* Japanese army officer or member of the military class.
3. **San** (sän) Japanese term added to names, indicating respect.

◆ **Reading Strategy**

Asking yourself questions while you are reading can help you understand what is special about the people and events in a story. Ask yourself: Why is it so important for Hana and her sisters to make good marriages? Write your answer, based on what you have read in this paragraph and what you know from your own experience.

_____

_____

_____

_____

_____

_____

_____

◆ **Reading Strategy**

Ask yourself: Why might Hana consider Taro Takeda a proper husband for her? Circle possible answers in the bracketed passage of the text.

◆ **Reading Check**

Why does a wife for Taro need to be brave and strong?

_____

_____

_____

Use your experience to help answer the question: How would Hana's life be different in the U.S. from in her village in Japan? Write three differences on the lines below.

1. _____

_____

2. _____

_____

3. _____

_____

In what ways is Hana different from most other women in the time and place where this story is set?

_____

_____

_____

_____

_____

_____

longing ordinarily concealed behind her quiet, obedient face. In that same instant, Hana knew she wanted more for herself than her sisters had in their proper, arranged, and loveless marriages. She wanted to escape the smothering strictures of life in her village. She certainly was not going to marry a farmer and spend her life working beside him planting, weeding, and harvesting in the rice paddies until her back became bent from too many years of stooping and her skin was turned to brown leather by the sun and wind. Neither did she particularly relish the idea of marrying a merchant in a big city as her two sisters had done. Since her mother objected to her going to Tokyo to seek employment as a teacher, perhaps she would consent to a flight to America for what seemed a proper and respectable marriage.

Almost before she realized what she was doing, she spoke to her uncle. "Oji San, perhaps I should go to America to make this lonely man a good wife."

"You, Hana Chan?"[4] Her uncle observed her with startled curiosity. "You would go all alone to a foreign land so far away from your mother and family?"

"I would not allow it." Her mother spoke fiercely. Hana was her youngest and she had lavished upon her the attention and latitude that often befall the last child. How could she permit her to travel so far, even to marry the son of Takeda who was known to her brother?

But now, a notion that had seemed quite impossible a moment before was lodged in his receptive mind, and Hana's uncle grasped it with the pleasure that comes from an unexpected discovery.

"You know," he said looking at Hana, "it might be a very good life in America."

Hana felt a faint fluttering in her heart. Perhaps this lonely man in America was her means of escaping both the village and the encirclement of her family.

Her uncle spoke with increasing enthusiasm of sending Hana to become Taro's wife. And the husband of Hana's sister, who was head of their household, spoke with equal eagerness. Although he never said so, Hana guessed he would be pleased to be rid of her, the spirited younger sister who stirred up his placid life with what he considered radical ideas about life and the role of women. He often claimed that Hana had too much schooling for a girl. She had graduated from Women's High School in Kyoto, which gave her five more years of schooling than her older sister.

"It has addled her brain—all that learning from those books," he said when he tired of arguing with Hana.

A man's word carried much weight for Hana's mother. Pressed by the two men, she consulted her other daughters

4. **Chan** (chän) Japanese term added to children's names.

and their husbands. She discussed the matter carefully with her brother and asked the village priest. Finally, she agreed to an exchange of family histories and an investigation was begun into Taro Takeda's family, his education, and his health, so they would be assured there was no insanity or tuberculosis or police records concealed in his family's past. Soon Hana's uncle was devoting his energies entirely to serving as go-between for Hana's mother and Taro Takeda's father.

When at last an agreement to the marriage was almost reached, Taro wrote his first letter to Hana. It was brief and proper and gave no more clue to his character than the stiff formal portrait taken at his graduation from middle school. Hana's uncle had given her the picture with apologies from his parents, because it was the only photo they had of him and it was not a flattering likeness.

Hana hid the letter and photograph in the sleeve of her kimono and took them to the outhouse to study in private. Squinting in the dim light and trying to ignore the foul odor, she read and reread Taro's letter, trying to find the real man somewhere in the sparse unbending prose.

By the time he sent her money for her steamship tickets, she had received ten more letters, but none revealed much more of the man than the first. In none did he disclose his loneliness or his need, but Hana understood this. In fact, she would have recoiled from a man who bared his intimate thoughts to her so soon. After all, they would have a lifetime together to get to know one another.

So it was that Hana had left her family and sailed alone to America with a small hope trembling inside of her. Tomorrow, at last, the ship would dock in San Francisco and she would meet face to face the man she was soon to marry. Hana was overcome with excitement at the thought of being in America, and terrified of the meeting about to take place. What would she say to Taro Takeda when they first met, and for all the days and years after?

Hana wondered about the flat above the shop. Perhaps it would be luxuriously furnished with the finest of brocades and lacquers,[5] and perhaps there would be a servant, although he had not mentioned it. She worried whether she would be able to manage on the meager English she had learned at Women's High School. The overwhelming anxiety for the day to come and the violent rolling of the ship were more than Hana could bear. Shuddering in the face of the wind, she leaned over the railing and became violently and wretchedly ill.

By five the next morning, Hana was up and dressed in her finest purple silk kimono and coat. She could not eat the bean

---

◆ **Reading Check**

What information about themselves do Hana and Taro share first?

_____

_____

_____

◆ **Literary Analysis**

In which **setting** does Hana study Taro's letter and photograph?

_____

Why do you think the author chose this setting?

_____

_____

_____

◆ **Reading Strategy**

Use the text and your experience to answer the question: Would I feel the same or different from Hana as I prepare to land in America? Circle details about Hana's feelings in the text to help you develop your answer.

_____

_____

_____

_____

_____

---

5. **brocades** (brō′ kādz′) **and lacquers** (lak′ ərz) *n.* Brocades are rich cloths with raised designs; lacquers are highly polished, decorative pieces of wood.

Find three details in this paragraph that began on page 145 that reflect Hana's Japanese culture?

1. _____

2. _____

3. _____

Circle **setting** details in the bracketed passage that add to or reflect Hana's feelings of worry as she prepares to land.

Mark THE Text

Why is Hana kept for two days on Angel Island?

_____

_____

_____

_____

How do **setting** details in the underlined sentence reflect Hana's feelings as the launch lands?

_____

_____

_____

_____

soup and rice that appeared for breakfast and took only a few bites of the yellow pickled radish. Her bags, which had scarcely been touched since she boarded the ship, were easily packed, for all they contained were her kimonos and some of her favorite books. The large willow basket, tightly secured by a rope, remained under the bunk, untouched since her uncle had placed it there.

She had not befriended the other women in her cabin, for they had lain in their bunks for most of the voyage, too sick to be company to anyone. Each morning Hana had fled the closeness of the sleeping quarters and spent most of the day huddled in a corner of the deck, listening to the lonely songs of some Russians also traveling to an alien land.

As the ship approached land, Hana hurried up to the deck to look out at the gray expanse of ocean and sky, eager for a first glimpse of her new homeland.

"We won't be docking until almost noon," one of the deck-hands told her.

Hana nodded, "I can wait," she answered, but the last hours seemed the longest.

When she set foot on American soil at last, it was not in the city of San Francisco as she had expected, but on Angel Island, where all third-class passengers were taken. She spent two miserable days and nights waiting, as the immigrants were questioned by officials, examined for trachoma[6] and tuberculosis, and tested for hookworm.[7] It was a bewildering, degrading beginning, and Hana was sick with anxiety, wondering if she would ever be released.

On the third day, a Japanese messenger from San Francisco appeared with a letter for her from Taro. He had written it the day of her arrival, but it had not reached her for two days.

Taro welcomed her to America, and told her that the bearer of the letter would inform Taro when she was to be released so he could be at the pier to meet her.

The letter eased her anxiety for a while, but as soon as she was released and boarded the launch for San Francisco, new fears rose up to smother her with a feeling almost of dread. The early morning mist had become a light chilling rain, and on the pier black umbrellas bobbed here and there, making the task of recognition even harder. Hana searched desperately for a face that resembled the photo she had studied so long and hard. Suppose he hadn't come. What would she do then?

Hana took a deep breath, lifted her head and walked slowly from the launch. The moment she was on the pier, a man in a

---

Vocabulary Development: degrading (dē grād′ iŋ) *adj.* insulting; dishonorable

---

6. **trachoma** (trə kō′ mə) *n.* contagious infection of the eyes.
7. **hookworm** (hoͦk′ wʉrm′) *n.* disease caused by hookworms, small worms that attach themselves to the intestines.

black coat, wearing a derby and carrying an umbrella, came quickly to her side. He was of slight build, not much taller than she, and his face was sallow and pale. He bowed stiffly and murmured, "You have had a long trip, Miss Omiya. I hope you are well."

Hana caught her breath. "You are Takeda San?" she asked.

He removed his hat and Hana was further startled to see that he was already turning bald.

"You are Takeda San?" she asked again. He looked older than thirty-one.

"I am afraid I no longer resemble the early photo my parents gave you. I am sorry."

Hana had not meant to begin like this. It was not going well.

"No, no," she said quickly. "It is just that I . . . that is, I am terribly nervous. . . ." Hana stopped abruptly, too flustered to go on.

"I understand," Taro said gently. "You will feel better when you meet my friends and have some tea. Mr. and Mrs. Toda are expecting you in Oakland. You will be staying with them until . . ." He couldn't bring himself to mention the marriage just yet and Hana was grateful he hadn't.

He quickly made arrangements to have her baggage sent to Oakland, then led her carefully along the rain-slick pier toward the streetcar that would take them to the ferry.

Hana shuddered at the sight of another boat, and as they climbed to its upper deck she felt a queasy tightening of her stomach.

"I hope it will not rock too much," she said anxiously. "Is it many hours to your city?"

Taro laughed for the first time since their meeting, revealing the gold fillings of his teeth. "Oakland is just across the bay," he explained. "We will be there in twenty minutes."

Raising a hand to cover her mouth, Hana laughed with him and suddenly felt better. I am in America now, she thought, and this is the man I came to marry. Then she sat down carefully beside Taro, so no part of their clothing touched.

© Pearson Education, Inc.

◆ **Reading Strategy**

What **question** would you ask about Hana's first meeting with Taro? Write the question and its answer below.

_____

_____

_____

◆ **Reading Strategy**

How does Taro make Hana feel more comfortable being in America? Circle details in the bracketed passage to help you answer the question.

Mark the Text

_____

_____

_____

_____

◆ **Reading Check**

What is significant about the last sentence in the story?

_____

_____

_____

_____

Reader's Response: If you were Hana, would you feel you had made a mistake in coming to the United States? Why or why not?

_____

_____

Thinking About the Skill: How does asking questions as you read help you stay involved with a story?

_____

_____

Animal Craftsmen

Bruce Brooks

Summary

Bruce Brooks, the writer of this essay, uses personal experience to remind readers that animals can create amazing things. When he is a child, Brooks admires something strange in a barn. He discovers that it is a wasp's nest. The nest is built in such a complicated way that he assumes it was made by humans. When he learns that the wasps themselves built the nest, he is even more awed. Brooks then thinks about other animals that can craft delicate designs. He knows that the designs can survive in a variety of conditions. He tries to imagine these animal structures from the animal's point of view. The nests, webs, or tunnels that the animals create become more wondrous to him.

Visual Summary

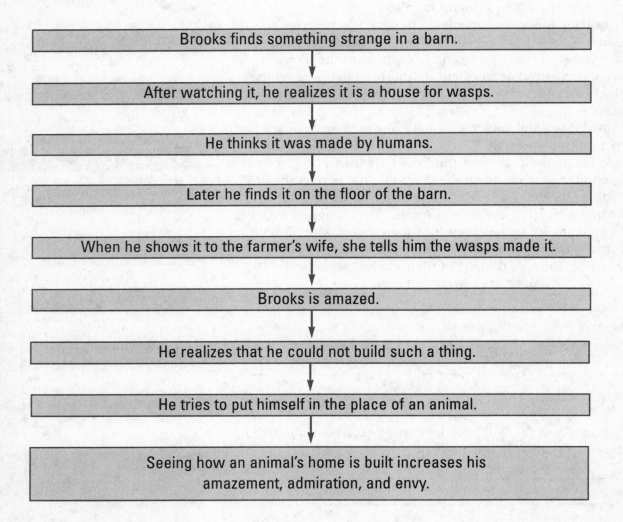

Brooks finds something strange in a barn.

↓

After watching it, he realizes it is a house for wasps.

↓

He thinks it was made by humans.

↓

Later he finds it on the floor of the barn.

↓

When he shows it to the farmer's wife, she tells him the wasps made it.

↓

Brooks is amazed.

↓

He realizes that he could not build such a thing.

↓

He tries to put himself in the place of an animal.

↓

Seeing how an animal's home is built increases his amazement, admiration, and envy.

Animal Craftsmen
Bruce Brooks

In this essay, the author relates how he first became interested in the building skills of animals.

One evening, when I was about five, I climbed up a ladder on the outside of a rickety old tobacco barn at sunset. The barn was part of a small farm near the home of a country relative my mother and I visited periodically; though we did not really know the farm's family, I was allowed to roam, poke around, and conduct sudden studies of anything small and harmless. On this evening, as on most of my jaunts, I was not looking for anything; I was simply climbing with an open mind. But as I balanced on the next-to-the-top rung and inhaled the spicy stink of the tobacco drying inside, I *did* find something under the eaves[1]—something very strange.

It appeared to be a kind of gray paper sphere, suspended from the dark planks by a thin stalk, like an apple made of ashes hanging on its stem. I studied it closely in the clear light. I saw that the bottom was a little ragged, and open. I could not tell if it had been torn, or if it had been made that way on purpose—for it was clear to me, as I studied it, that this thing had been *made*. This was no fruit or fungus.[2] Its shape, rough but trim; its intricately[3] colored surface with subtle swirls of gray and tan; and most of all the uncanny adhesiveness with which the perfectly tapered stem stuck against the rotten old pine boards—all of these features gave evidence of some intentional design. The troubling thing was figuring out who had designed it, and why.

I assumed the designer was a human being: someone from the farm, someone wise and skilled in a craft that had so far escaped my curiosity. Even when I saw wasps entering and leaving the thing (during a vigil I kept every evening for two weeks), it did not occur to me that the wasps might have fashioned it for themselves. I assumed it was a man-made "wasp house" placed there expressly for the purpose of attracting a family of wasps, much as the "martin hotel," a giant birdhouse on a pole near the farmhouse, was maintained to shelter migrant[4] purple martins who returned every spring. I didn't ask myself why anyone would want to give wasps a bivouac;[5] it seemed no more odd than attracting birds.

As I grew less wary of the wasps (and they grew less wary of me), and as my confidence on the ladder improved, I moved to the upper rung and peered through the sphere's

---

1. **eaves** (ēvz) *n.* lower edges of a roof.
2. **fungus** (fuŋ´ gəs) *n.* one of a group of plants such as mushrooms, yeasts, and molds.
3. **intricately** (in´ tri kit lē) *adv.* in a complex, highly detailed way.
4. **migrant** (mī´ grənt) *adj.* moving from one region to another with the changing seasons.
5. **bivouac** (biv´ wak´) *n.* temporary shelter.

◆ **Activate Prior Knowledge**

Have you ever seen animals working, or seen something animals have built (for example, an ant hill or bird's nest)? Describe what you saw and how you felt about it.

_____

_____

_____

_____

_____

_____

_____

_____

_____

_____

_____

◆ **Reading Check**

What does Brooks assume about the designer of the "wasp house"?

_____

_____

_____

_____

Why do you think he assumes this?

_____

_____

_____

_____

A **reflective essay** is a short non-fiction work about an idea or topic. In this type of essay, the writer expresses his or her thoughts about the subject. What role does the writer's imagination play in this reflective essay?

_____

_____

_____

_____

_____

Evaluate the author's presentation of his discovery. Why does he take the reader through each step of it?

_____

_____

_____

_____

_____

After finding it gone, what does Brooks assume has happened to the "sphere"?

_____

_____

_____

Where does he find it?

_____

_____

_____

bottom. I could see that the paper swirled in layers around some secret center the wasps inhabited, and I marveled at the delicate hands of the craftsman who had devised such tiny apertures[6] for their protection.

I left the area in the late summer, and in my imagination I took the strange structure with me. I envisioned unwrapping it, and in the middle finding—what? A tiny room full of bits of wool for sleeping, and countless manufactured pellets of scientifically determined wasp food? A glowing blue jewel that drew the wasps at twilight, and gave them a cool infusion of energy as they clung to it overnight? My most definite idea was that the wasps lived in a small block of fine cedar the craftsman had drilled full of holes, into which they slipped snugly, rather like the bunks aboard submarines in World War II movies.

As it turned out, I got the chance to discover that my idea of the cedar block had not been wrong by much. We visited our relative again in the winter. We arrived at night, but first thing in the morning I made straight for the farm and its barn. The shadows under the eaves were too dense to let me spot the sphere from far off. I stepped on the bottom rung of the ladder—slick with frost—and climbed carefully up. My hands and feet kept slipping, so my eyes stayed on the rung ahead, and it was not until I was secure at the top that I could look up. The sphere was gone.

I was crushed. That object had fascinated me like nothing I had come across in my life; I had even grown to love wasps because of it. I sagged on the ladder and watched my breath eddy[7] around the blank eaves. I'm afraid I pitied myself more than the apparently homeless wasps.

But then something snapped me out of my sense of loss: I recalled that I had watched the farmer taking in the purple martin hotel every November, after the birds left. From its spruce appearance when he brought it out in March, it was clear he had cleaned it and repainted it and kept it out of the weather. Of course he would do the same thing for *this* house, which was even more fragile. I had never mentioned the wasp dwelling to anyone, but now I decided I would go to the farm, introduce myself, and inquire about it. Perhaps I would even be permitted to handle it, or, best of all, learn how to make one myself.

I scrambled down the ladder, leaping from the third rung and landing in the frosty salad of tobacco leaves and windswept grass that collected at the foot of the barn wall. I looked down and saw that my left boot had, by no more than an inch, just missed crushing the very thing I was rushing off to seek. There, lying dry and separate on the leaves, was the wasp house.

I looked up. Yes. I was standing directly beneath the spot

---

6. **apertures** (ap´ ər chərz) *n.* openings.
7. **eddy** (ed´ ē) *v.* move in a circular motion.

where the sphere had hung—it was a straight fall. I picked up the wasp house, gave it a shake to see if any insects were inside, and, discovering none, took it home.

My awe of the craftsman grew as I unwrapped the layers of the nest. Such beautiful paper! It was much tougher than any I had encountered, and it held a curve (something my experimental paper airplanes never did), but it was very light, too. The secret at the center of the swirl turned out to be a neatly made fan of tiny cells, all of the same size and shape, reminding me of the heart of a sunflower that had lost its seeds to birds. The fan hung from the sphere's ceiling by a stem the thickness of a pencil lead.

The rest of the story is a little embarrassing. More impressed than ever, I decided to pay homage to the creator of this habitable sculpture. I went boldly to the farmhouse. The farmer's wife answered my knock. I showed her the nest and asked to speak with the person in the house who had made it. She blinked and frowned. I had to repeat my question twice before she understood what I believed my mission to be; then, with a gentle laugh, she dispelled my illusion about an ingenious old papersmith fond of wasps. The nest, she explained, had been made entirely by the insects themselves, and wasn't that amazing?

Well, of course it was. It still is. I needn't have been so embarrassed—the structures that animals build, and the sense of design they display, *should* always astound us. On my way home from the farmhouse, in my own defense I kept thinking, "But *I* couldn't build anything like this! Nobody could!"

The most natural thing in the world for us to do, when we are confronted with a piece of animal architecture, is to figure out if we could possibly make it or live in it. Who hasn't peered into the dark end of a mysterious hole in the woods and thought, "It must be pretty weird to live in there!" or looked up at a hawk's nest atop a huge sycamore and shuddered at the thought of waking up every morning with nothing but a few twigs preventing a hundred-foot fall. How, we wonder, do those twigs stay together, and withstand the wind so high?

It is a human tendency always to regard animals first in terms of ourselves. Seeing the defensive courage of a mother bear whose cubs are threatened, or the cooperative determination of a string of ants dismantling a stray chunk of cake, we naturally use our own behavior as reference for our empathy. We put ourselves in the same situation and express the animal's action in feelings—and words—that apply to the way people do things.

Sometimes this is useful. But sometimes it is misleading. Attributing human-like intentions to an animal can keep us from looking at the *animal's* sense of itself in its surroundings—its immediate and future needs, its physical and mental

In a **reflective essay,** the writer usually reflects on, or thinks about, emotions and reactions, as well as events. What do the emotions and reactions expressed so far in this essay tell you about the young Brooks and his interest in nature?

_____

_____

_____

_____

◆ Reading Check

Why is Brooks embarrassed?

_____

_____

_____

_____

◆ Reading Strategy

Underline the main point in the bracketed paragraph. Then, **evaluate the author's presentation** of his idea. How effectively do Brooks's examples illustrate this idea?

_____

_____

_____

_____

_____

Rewrite in your own words what the author means in the underlined sentence.

_____

_____

_____

_____

_____

_____

_____

_____

In this **reflective essay,** what are the writer's thoughts that grow out of the story of the wasp's nest?

_____

_____

_____

_____

_____

_____

_____

_____

_____

_____

_____

capabilities, its genetic[8] instincts. Most animals, for example, use their five senses in ways that human beings cannot possibly understand or express. How can a forty-two-year-old nearsighted biologist have any real idea what a two-week-old barn owl sees in the dark? How can a sixteen-year-old who lives in the Arizona desert identify with the muscular jumps improvised by a waterfall-leaping salmon in Alaska? There's nothing wrong with trying to empathize with an animal, but we shouldn't forget that ultimately animals live *animal* lives.

Animal structures let us have it both ways—we can be struck with a strange wonder, and we can empathize right away, too. Seeing a vast spiderweb, taut and glistening between two bushes, it's easy to think, "I have no idea how that is done; the engineering is awesome." But it is just as easy to imagine climbing across the bright strands, springing from one to the next as if the web were a new Epcot attraction, the Invisible Flying Flexible Space Orb. That a clear artifact of an animal's wits and agility[9] stands right there in front of us—that we can touch it, look at it from different angles, sometimes take it home—inspires our imagination as only a strange reality can. We needn't move into a molehill to experience a life of darkness and digging; our creative wonder takes us down there in a second, without even getting our hands dirty.

But what if we discover some of the mechanics of how the web is made? Once we see how the spider works (or the humming bird, or the bee), is the engineering no longer awesome? This would be too bad: we don't want to lose our sense of wonder just because we gain understanding.

And we certainly do *not* lose it. In fact, seeing how an animal makes its nest or egg case or food storage vaults has the effect of increasing our amazement. The builder's energy, concentration, and athletic adroitness are qualities we can readily admire and envy. Even more startling is the recognition that the animal is working from a precise design in its head, a design that is exactly replicated time after time. This knowledge of architecture—knowing where to build, what materials to use, how to put them together—remains one of the most intriguing mysteries of animal behavior. And the more *we* develop that same knowledge, the more we appreciate the instincts and intelligence of the animals.

---

8. genetic (jə net´ ik) *adj.* inherited biologically.
9. agility (ə jil´ ə tē) *n.* ability to move quickly and easily.

Reader's Response: What subject in nature amazes or inspires you so much that you could write a reflective essay about it?

_____

_____

Baseball

Lionel G. García

Summary

This autobiographical narrative, or story about the writer's own life, shows how children use their imagination to create their own world. The writer recalls a version of baseball that he and his childhood friends played. The children's baseball was like a traditional game in several ways. For example, they had a pitcher and a batter. However, they made up their own baseball rules, too. They did not play with a regular bat; they batted with a stick. They did not have three bases; they had one. Instead of running directly to home plate, the batter ran to avoid being hit by a thrown ball. Often, the batter ran all the way into town. Although the children ignored many baseball rules, they enjoyed playing their own game.

Visual Summary

Outfielder

Outfielder   **Outfielder**

First Baseman

Outfielder   First Base

Pitcher

Home Plate

Batter

Catcher

◆ Activate Prior Knowledge

What does it feel like to play a group sport or game?

_____

_____

_____

_____

_____

_____

_____

◆ Literary Analysis

Autobiographical writing is narrative writing about the author's own life. What do the first four paragraphs tell you about García's background?

_____

_____

_____

_____

_____

◆ Reading Check

Whose rules did García and his friends follow when they played baseball?

_____

_____

_____

_____

_____

Baseball
Lionel G. García

We loved to play baseball. We would take the old mesquite[1] stick and the old ball across the street to the parochial[2] school grounds to play a game. Father Zavala enjoyed watching us. We could hear him laugh mightily from the screened porch at the rear of the rectory[3] where he sat.

The way we played baseball was to rotate positions after every out. First base, the only base we used, was located where one would normally find second base. This made the batter have to run past the pitcher and a long way to first baseman, increasing the odds of getting thrown out. The pitcher stood in line with the batter, and with first base, and could stand as close or as far from the batter as he or she wanted. Aside from the pitcher, the batter and the first baseman, we had a catcher. All the rest of us would stand in the outfield. After an out, the catcher would come up to bat. The pitcher took the position of catcher, and the first baseman moved up to be the pitcher. Those in the outfield were left to their own <u>devices</u>. I don't remember ever getting to bat.

There was one exception to the rotation scheme. I don't know who thought of this, but whoever caught the ball on the fly would go directly to be the batter. This was not a popular thing to do. You could expect to have the ball thrown at you on the next pitch.

There was no set distance for first base. First base was wherever Matías or Juan or Cota tossed a stone. They were the law. The distance could be long or short depending on how soon we thought we were going to be called in to eat. The size of the stone marking the base mattered more than the distance from home plate to first base. If we hadn't been called in to eat by dusk, first base was hard to find. Sometimes someone would kick the stone farther away and arguments erupted.

When the batter hit the ball in the air and it was caught that was an out. So far so good. But if the ball hit the ground, the fielder had two choices. One, in keeping with the standard rules of the game, the ball could be thrown to the first baseman and, if caught before the batter arrived at the base, that was an out. But the second, more interesting option allowed the fielder, ball in hand, to take off running after the batter. When close enough, the fielder would throw the ball at the batter. If the batter was hit before reaching

---

Vocabulary Development: devices (di vīs´ ez) *n.* techniques or means for working things out

---

1. **mesquite** (mes´ kēt´) *n.* thorny shrub of North America.
2. **parochial** (pə rō´ kē əl) *adj.* supported by a church.
3. **rectory** (rek´ tər ē) *n.* residence for priests.

first base, the batter was out. But if the batter <u>evaded</u> being hit with the ball, he or she could either run to first base or run back to home plate. All the while, everyone was chasing the batter, picking up the ball and throwing it at him or her. To complicate matters, on the way to home plate the batter had the choice of running anywhere possible to avoid getting hit. For example, the batter could run to hide behind the hackberry trees at the parochial school grounds, going from tree to tree until he or she could make it safely back to home plate. Many a time we would wind up playing the game past Father Zavala and in front of the rectory half a block away. Or we could be seen running after the batter several blocks down the street toward town, trying to hit the batter with the ball. One time we wound up all the way across town before we cornered Juan against a fence, held him down, and hit him with the ball. Afterwards, we all fell laughing in a pile on top of each other, exhausted from the run through town.

The old codgers, the old shiftless men who spent their day talking at the street corners, never caught on to what we were doing. They would halt their idle conversation just long enough to watch us run by them, hollering and throwing the old ball at the batter.

It was the only kind of baseball game Father Zavala had ever seen. What a wonderful game it must have been for him to see us hit the ball, run to a rock, then run for our lives down the street. He loved the game, shouting from the screened porch at us, pushing us on. And then all of a sudden we were gone, running after the batter. What a game! In what enormous stadium would it be played to allow such freedom over such an expanse of ground.

My uncle Adolfo, who had pitched for the Yankees and the Cardinals in the majors, had given us the ball several years before. Once when he returned for a visit, he saw us playing from across the street and walked over to ask us what we were doing.

"Playing baseball," we answered as though we thought he should know better. After all, he was the professional baseball player.

He walked away shaking his head. "What a waste of a good ball," we heard him say, marveling at our ignorance.

Vocabulary Development: evaded (ē vād´ əd) *v.* avoided

Reader's Response: Would you like to play baseball with García and his friends? Why or why not?

_____

_____

♦ **Reading Strategy**

Authors write for many reasons— to make you think, laugh, or cry; to explain or persuade; or to share their experiences in an interesting way. What do all the details about the game's "rules" help you to **understand** about **the author's purpose**?

_____

_____

_____

_____

_____

♦ **Stop to Reflect**

What are the most obvious differences between this game and regular baseball?

_____

_____

_____

_____

♦ **Literary Analysis**

Why do you think García includes the reactions of Father Zavala, Uncle Adolfo, and the old men in his **autobiographical narrative**?

_____

_____

_____

_____

_____

_____

_____

_____

_____

Forest Fire

Anaïs Nin

Summary

The author of this selection describes a terrifying forest fire. The fire rages in the mountains near the community of Sierra Madre, California. Despite the courageous efforts of firefighters, the fire grows. As the fire advances, smoke fills the air. Trees are turned into skeletons in one minute. Animals such as coyotes and deer become confused and frightened. Residents are told to prepare to leave for their own safety, and they begin to pack. A week after the fire has ended, other related problems begin. Heavy rains cause floods and mudslides in the area. As the author observes all that happens in nature, she understands that nature is both peaceful and dangerous. She appreciates both characteristics.

Visual Summary

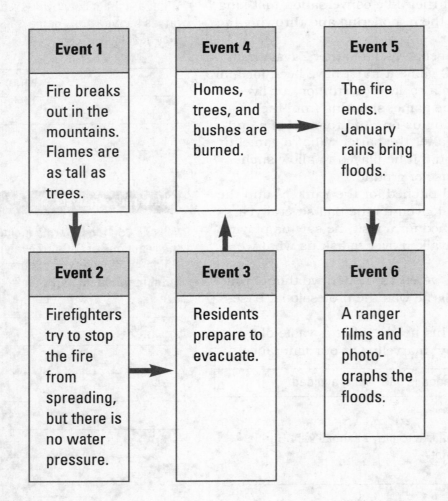

Event 1

Fire breaks out in the mountains. Flames are as tall as trees.

Event 2

Firefighters try to stop the fire from spreading, but there is no water pressure.

Event 3

Residents prepare to evacuate.

Event 4

Homes, trees, and bushes are burned.

Event 5

The fire ends. January rains bring floods.

Event 6

A ranger films and photographs the floods.

Forest Fire
Anaïs Nin

The author describes a wildfire in Angeles National Forest in southern California.

A man rushed in to announce he had seen smoke on Monrovia Peak.[1] As I looked out of the window I saw the two mountains facing the house on fire. The entire rim burning wildly in the night. The flames, driven by hot Santa Ana winds[2] from the desert, were as tall as the tallest trees, the sky already tinted coral, and the crackling noise of burning trees, the ashes and the smoke were already increasing. The fire raced along, sometimes descending behind the mountain where I could only see the glow, sometimes descending toward us. I thought of the foresters in danger. I made coffee for the weary men who came down occasionally with horses they had led out, or with old people from the isolated cabins. They were covered with soot from their battle with the flames.

At six o'clock the fire was on our left side and rushing toward Mount Wilson. <u>Evacuees</u> from the cabins began to arrive and had to be given blankets and hot coffee. The streets were blocked with fire engines readying to fight the fire if it touched the houses. Policemen and firemen and guards turned away the sightseers. Some were relatives concerned over the fate of the foresters, or the pack station family. The policemen lighted flares, which gave the scene a theatrical, tragic air. The red lights on the police cars twinkled alarmingly. More fire engines arrived. Ashes fell, and the roar of the fire was now like thunder.

We were told to ready ourselves for evacuation. I packed the diaries. The saddest spectacle, beside that of the men fighting the fire as they would a war, were the animals, rabbits, coyotes, mountain lions, deer, driven by the fire to the edge of the mountain, taking a look at the crowd of people and panicking, choosing rather to rush back into the fire.

The fire now was like a ring around Sierra Madre,[3] every mountain was burning. People living at the foot of the mountain were packing their cars. I rushed next door to the

---

Vocabulary Development: evacuees (ē vak´ yoo ēz´) *n.* people who leave a place, especially because of danger

---

1. **Monrovia** (mən rō´ vē ə) **Peak** mountain in the San Gabriel Mountains of southwest California.
2. **Santa** (san´ tə) **Ana** (an´ ə) **winds** hot desert winds from the east or northeast in southern California.
3. **Sierra** (sē er´ ə) **Madre** (mä´ drā) community northeast of Los Angeles in the foothills of the San Gabriel Mountains.

◆ **Activate Prior Knowledge**

Describe a time when you witnessed an interesting or frightening natural event, such as a storm or an earthquake. What lesson did it teach you?

_____

_____

_____

_____

_____

_____

◆ **Reading Strategy**

A good way to get the most from your reading is to **set a purpose** before you read. After reading the first paragraph of this essay, what purpose do you have for reading the rest?

_____

_____

_____

◆ **Reading Check**

What is the setting—the time and place—of the fire?

_____

_____

_____

_____

_____

_____

In a **descriptive essay,** a writer uses descriptive details and figurative language—metaphors, similes, and personification—to create vivid images for the reader. In the bracketed passage, circle phrases in which Nin compares the fire to something else. How do these comparisons help you understand what she saw and felt?

_____

_____

_____

_____

_____

From whose point of view do fire and human beings look like "two forms of death"?

_____

_____

What does this comparison reveal about the author's ideas about animals and the natural world?

_____

_____

_____

_____

Why is the fire so hard to put out?

_____

_____

_____

Campion children, who had been left with a baby-sitter, and got them into the car. It was impossible to save all the horses. We parked the car on the field below us. I called up the Campions, who were out for the evening, and reassured them. The baby-sitter dressed the children warmly. I made more coffee. I answered frantic telephone calls.

All night the fire engines sprayed water over the houses. But the fire grew immense, angry, and rushing at a speed I could not believe. It would rush along and suddenly leap over a road, a trail, like a monster, devouring all in its path. The firefighters cut breaks in the heavy brush, but when the wind was strong enough, the fire leaped across them. At dawn one arm of the fire reached the back of our houses but was finally contained.

But high above and all around, the fire was burning, more vivid than the sun, throwing spirals of smoke in the air like the smoke from a volcano. Thirty-three cabins burned, and twelve thousand acres of forest still burning endangered countless homes below the fire. The fire was burning to the back of us now, and a rain of ashes began to fall and continued for days. The smell of the burn in the air, acid and pungent and <u>tenacious</u>. The dragon tongues of flames devouring, the flames leaping, the roar of destruction and <u>dissolution</u>, the eyes of the panicked animals, caught between fire and human beings, between two forms of death. They chose the fire. It was as if the fire had come from the bowels of the earth, like that of a fiery volcano, it was so powerful, so swift, and so <u>ravaging</u>. I saw trees become skeletons in one minute, I saw trees fall, I saw bushes turned to ashes in a second, I saw weary, ash-covered men, looking like men returned from war, some with burns, others overcome by smoke.

The men were rushing from one spot to another watching for recrudescence.[4] Some started backfiring up the mountain so that the ascending flames could counteract the descending ones.

As the flames reached the cities below, hundreds of roofs burst into flame at once. There was no water pressure because all the fire hydrants were turned on at the same time, and the fire departments were helpless to save more than a few of the burning homes.

Vocabulary Development: tenacious (tə nā′ shəs) *adj.* holding on firmly
dissolution (dis′ ə lōō′ shən) *n.* the act of breaking down and crumbling
ravaging (rav′ ij iŋ) *adj.* severely damaging

---

4. **recrudescence** (rē′ krōō des′ əns) *n.* fresh outbreak of something that has been inactive.

The blaring loudspeakers of passing police cars warned us to prepare to evacuate in case the wind changed and drove the fire in our direction. What did I wish to save? I thought only of the diaries. I appeared on the porch carrying a huge stack of diary volumes, preparing to pack them in the car. A reporter for the Pasadena *Star News* was taking pictures of the evacuation. He came up, very annoyed with me. "Hey, lady, next time could you bring out something more important than all those old papers? Carry some clothes on the next trip. We gotta have human interest in these pictures!"

A week later, the danger was over.

Gray ashy days.

In Sierra Madre, following the fire, the January rains brought floods. People are sandbagging their homes. At four a.m. the streets are covered with mud. The bare, burnt, naked mountains cannot hold the rains and slide down bringing rocks and mud. One of the rangers must now take photographs and movies of the disaster. He asks if I will help by holding an umbrella over the cameras. I put on my raincoat and he lends me hip boots which look to me like seven-league boots.

We drive a little way up the road. At the third curve it is impassable. A river is rushing across the road. The ranger takes pictures while I hold the umbrella over the camera. It is terrifying to see the muddied waters and rocks, the mountain disintegrating. When we are ready to return, the road before us is covered by large rocks but the ranger pushes on as if the truck were a jeep and forces it through. The edge of the road is being carried away.

I am laughing and scared too. The ranger is at ease in nature, and without fear. It is a wild moment of danger. It is easy to love nature in its peaceful and consoling moments, but one must love it in its furies too, in its despairs and wildness, especially when the damage is caused by us.

Reader's Response: If firefighters asked you to evacuate your home, what would you wish to save?

_____

_____

Thinking About the Skill: Did you change or extend your purpose for reading this essay? If so, explain how and why.

_____

_____

◆ **Literary Analysis**

The papers Nin is holding are the volumes of her diary—her most important literary work. Why do you think she includes this reporter's comments in her **descriptive essay**?

_____

_____

_____

_____

◆ **Reading Check**

What second natural disaster occurs as a result of the fire?

_____

_____

◆ **Literary Analysis**

In the bracketed paragraph, underline the conclusion Nin draws from the events her **essay** describes. Rewrite this idea in your own words.

_____

_____

_____

_____

Who does Nin blame for the fire's damage, and why?

_____

_____

_____

_____

_____

The Trouble with Television
Robert MacNeil

Summary

In "The Trouble with Television," well-known broadcast journalist Robert MacNeil sharply criticizes television. He realizes that television is a powerful medium, but he thinks that it discourages concentration. He states that television appeals to viewers with short attention spans. For this reason, television presents incomplete information and simple solutions to complex problems. MacNeil also believes that television contributes to functional illiteracy, or the problem of Americans who cannot read well enough to function well daily. He urges everyone to examine the potentially negative influence that television has on American society.

Visual Summary

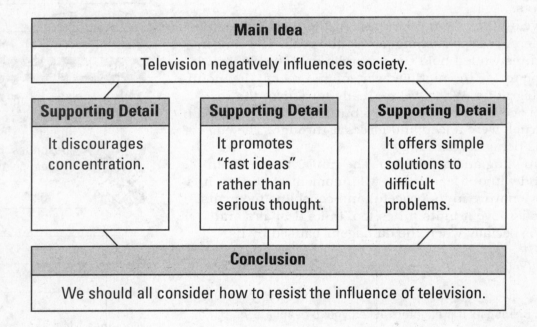

Main Idea

Television negatively influences society.

Supporting Detail

It discourages concentration.

Supporting Detail

It promotes "fast ideas" rather than serious thought.

Supporting Detail

It offers simple solutions to difficult problems.

Conclusion

We should all consider how to resist the influence of television.

The Trouble with Television
Robert MacNeil

Former broadcast journalist Robert MacNeil presents a persuasive case to prove his point that television has had a negative effect on American society. In his view, television threatens to undermine our language, literacy, imagination, tolerance for effort, and particularly our ability to handle complexity.

It is difficult to escape the influence of television. If you fit the statistical averages, by the age of 20 you will have been exposed to at least 20,000 hours of television. You can add 10,000 hours for each decade you have lived after the age of 20. The only things Americans do more than watch television are work and sleep.

Calculate for a moment what could be done with even a part of those hours. Five thousand hours, I am told, are what a typical college undergraduate spends working on a bachelor's degree. In 10,000 hours you could have learned enough to become an astronomer or engineer. You could have learned several languages fluently. If it appealed to you, you could be reading Homer[1] in the original Greek or Dostoevski[2] in Russian. If it didn't, you could have walked around the world and written a book about it.

The trouble with television is that it discourages concentration. Almost anything interesting and rewarding in life requires some constructive, consistently applied effort. The dullest, the least gifted of us can achieve things that seem miraculous to those who never concentrate on anything. But television encourages us to apply no effort. It sells us instant gratification. It <u>diverts</u> us only to divert, to make the time pass without pain.

Television's variety becomes a narcotic,[3] not a stimulus.[4] Its serial, kaleidoscopic[5] exposures force us to follow its lead. The viewer is on a perpetual guided tour: thirty minutes at the museum, thirty at the cathedral, then back on the bus to the next attraction—except on television, typically, the spans allotted are on the order of minutes or seconds, and the chosen delights are more often car crashes and people killing one

---

Vocabulary Development: diverts (dī vʉrts′) *v.* distracts

---

1. **Homer** (hō′ mər) Greek epic poet of the eighth century B.C.
2. **Dostoevski** (dôs′ tô yef′ skē) Fyodor (fyô′ dôr) Dostoevski (1821–1881); Russian novelist.
3. **narcotic** (när kät′ ik) *n.* something that has a soothing effect.
4. **stimulus** (stim′ yə ləs) *n.* something that rouses to action.
5. **kaleidoscopic** (kə lī′ də skäp′ ik) *adj.* constantly changing.

◆ **Activate Prior Knowledge**

Think about your experiences with television—how often you watch it and what effect television has on you. On the lines below, complete the statement: "The trouble with television is . . . ."

_____

_____

_____

_____

◆ **Reading Check**

About how much television does MacNeil say the typical American watches?

_____

_____

_____

_____

◆ **Literary Analysis**

Persuasive techniques are methods a writer uses to influence a reader's reaction to a persuasive message. For example, a writer might support main ideas with facts or quotations, use words that stir an emotional reaction, or repeat key ideas or phrases. What persuasive techniques does MacNeil use in the beginning of this essay?

_____

_____

_____

_____

According to MacNeil, what is the main goal of most television programming? Underline the part of this paragraph where he states it.

Mark the Text

_____

_____

_____

_____

_____

_____

_____

_____

◆ Reading Strategy

When you **evaluate a writer's logic**, or reasoning, you make a judgment about the sense of the argument. Does the reasoning in the last sentence of the bracketed passage seem logical to you? Why or why not?

_____

_____

_____

_____

_____

_____

_____

_____

_____

_____

another. In short, a lot of television usurps one of the most precious of all human gifts, the ability to focus your attention yourself, rather than just passively surrender it.

Capturing your attention—and holding it—is the prime motive of most television programming and enhances its role as a profitable advertising vehicle. Programmers live in constant fear of losing anyone's attention—anyone's. The surest way to avoid doing so is to keep everything brief, not to strain the attention of anyone but instead to provide constant stimulation through variety, novelty, action and movement. Quite simply, television operates on the appeal to the short attention span.

It is simply the easiest way out. But it has come to be regarded as a given, as inherent[6] in the medium[7] itself: as an imperative, as though General Sarnoff, or one of the other august pioneers of video, had bequeathed to us tablets of stone commanding that nothing in television shall ever require more than a few moments' concentration.

In its place that is fine. Who can quarrel with a medium that so brilliantly packages escapist entertainment as a mass-marketing tool? But I see its values now pervading this nation and its life. It has become fashionable to think that, like fast food, fast ideas are the way to get to a fast-moving, impatient public.

In the case of news, this practice, in my view, results in inefficient communication. I question how much of television's nightly news effort is really absorbable and understandable.

Much of it is what has been aptly described as "machine gunning with scraps." I think its technique fights coherence.[8] I think it tends to make things ultimately boring and dismissable (unless they are accompanied by horrifying pictures) because almost anything is boring and dismissable if you know almost nothing about it.

I believe that TV's appeal to the short attention span is not only inefficient communication but decivilizing as well. Consider the casual assumptions that television tends to cultivate: that complexity must be avoided, that visual stimulation is a substitute for thought, that verbal precision is an anachronism.[9] It may be old-fashioned, but I was taught that thought is words, arranged in grammatically precise ways.

Vocabulary Development: usurps (yo͞o sʉrps´) v. takes over
august (ô gust´) adj. honored
pervading (pər vād´ iŋ) v. spreading throughout

---

6. **inherent** (in hir´ ənt) adj. natural.
7. **medium** (mē´ dē əm) n. means of communication.
8. **coherence** (kō hir´ əns) n. the quality of being connected in an understandable way.
9. **anachronism** (ə nak´ rə niz´ əm) n. anything that seems to be out of its proper time in history; in other words, something that is no longer used or understood.

There is a crisis of literacy in this country. One study estimates that some 30 million adult Americans are "functionally illiterate" and cannot read or write well enough to answer a want ad or understand the instructions on a medicine bottle.

Literacy may not be an inalienable human right, but it is one that the highly literate Founding Fathers might not have found unreasonable or even unattainable. We are not only not attaining it as a nation, statistically speaking, but we are falling further and further short of attaining it. And, while I would not be so simplistic as to suggest that television is the cause, I believe it contributes and is an influence.

Everything about this nation—the structure of the society, its forms of family organization, its economy, its place in the world—has become more complex, not less. Yet its dominating communications instrument, its principal form of national linkage, is one that sells neat resolutions to human problems that usually have no neat resolutions. It is all symbolized in my mind by the hugely successful art form that television has made central to the culture, the thirty-second commercial: the tiny drama of the earnest housewife who finds happiness in choosing the right toothpaste.

When before in human history has so much humanity collectively surrendered so much of its leisure to one toy, one mass diversion? When before has virtually an entire nation surrendered itself wholesale to a medium for selling?

Some years ago Yale University law professor Charles L. Black, Jr. wrote: ". . . forced feeding on trivial fare is not itself a trivial matter." I think this society is being force fed with trivial fare, and I fear that the effects on our habits of mind, our language, our tolerance for effort, and our appetite for complexity are only dimly perceived. If I am wrong, we will have done no harm to look at the issue skeptically and critically, to consider how we should be resisting it. I hope you will join with me in doing so.

Reader's Response: Is television a bad influence, or a valuable resource? Explain.

_____

_____

_____

Thinking About the Skill: Why do you think it is a good idea to evaluate the writer's logic in an essay such as this?

_____

_____

_____

◆ **Reading Check**

To what growing crisis in the United States does MacNeil believe television contributes?

_____

_____

_____

_____

_____

◆ **Literary Analysis**

Underline the words in the bracketed paragraph that, in your opinion, have the strongest **emotional impact**. What effect do these words have on the reader?

Mark the Text

_____

_____

_____

_____

_____

◆ **Reading Check**

What is the biggest trouble with television, according to MacNeil?

_____

_____

_____

_____

_____

_____

_____

_____

The Diary of Anne Frank

Frances Goodrich and Albert Hackett

Act 1, Scenes 1–3

Summary

Scene 1

At the end of World War II, Mr. Frank returns to Amsterdam, to the cramped attic above his old business. There, Miep and Mr. Kraler helped him and seven other Jews to hide for two years from the Nazis. He tells Miep he is leaving Amsterdam. Then he holds his daughter's diary. Her offstage voice takes him back to the days of the family's time in hiding.

Scene 2

Fear and lack of privacy create strains for the two families in hiding, the Franks and the Van Daans. Anne is thirteen years old and beginning to resent her mother's bossiness. She develops a crush on sixteen-year-old Peter Van Daan.

Scene 3

Two months have passed. Peter and Anne continue to study hard and flirt occasionally. Peter still seems awkward around Anne, who is much more confident and mature than he is. Tensions mount among the two families in the cramped quarters. Anne and Mr. Van Daan argue over what he claims is her lack of respect for adults. One day Anne dances around the apartment. She accidentally knocks a glass of milk on Mrs. Van Daan's coat and makes her very angry. Mr. Kraler, a non-Jew who is helping to hide the families, comes to deliver supplies. He brings another Jewish man who needs a hiding place—Mr. Dussel, a dentist. Dussel brings bad news about the mass arrests of Jews all over Denmark, including Anne's best friend, Jopie. Dussel ends up rooming with Anne. He is a stiff and proper man. He does not get along well with Anne, who has free and open ways.

Visual Summary

The main units of a play are called **acts.** A play can consist of one act or several acts. Acts are often divided into **scenes.** This selection consists of the first three scenes of Act I of *The Diary of Anne Frank*.

Scene I	Scene II	Scene III
After World War II, Mr. Frank returns to an attic where his family hid from the Nazis during the war. Miep shows him Anne's diary. He begins to think back to those terrible days.	Tensions begin to arise among two families hiding in the attic: the Franks and the Van Daans. Anne develops a crush on Peter.	Two months pass. Anne argues with Mr. Van Daan. She begins to resent her mother. The families take in Mr. Dussel. He brings bad news about the Jews of Amsterdam.

The Diary of Anne Frank
Frances Goodrich and Albert Hackett

Act 1, Scene 1

During World War II, the German army took over many countries in Europe, including Holland. The Germans passed laws against Jews living in these countries and shipped many Jews off to prison camps where they were killed. This play is about two Jewish families who are hiding from the Germans in a small apartment in Holland during World War II.

CHARACTERS (in order of appearance)

Mr. Frank, Anne's father, a German Jew living in Holland

Miep, young Dutch woman who used to work for Mr. Frank

Mrs. Van Daan, Dutch Jewish woman

Mr. Van Daan, Dutch Jewish man, an acquaintance of Mr. Frank

Peter Van Daan, sixteen-year-old Dutch Jewish boy

Mrs. Frank, Anne's mother

Margot Frank, Anne's eighteen-year-old sister

Anne Frank, thirteen-year-old Jewish girl living in Holland

Mr. Kraler, Dutch man who used to work for Mr. Frank

Mr. Dussel, Dutch Jewish man, a former dentist

[The scene remains the same throughout the play. It is the top floor of a warehouse and office building in Amsterdam, Holland. The sharply peaked roof of the building is outlined against a sea of other rooftops, stretching away into the distance. Nearby is the belfry[1] of a church tower, the Westertoren, whose carillon[2] rings out the hours. Occasionally faint sounds float up from below: the voices of children playing in the street, the tramp of marching feet, a boat whistle from the canal.

The three rooms of the top floor and a small attic space above are exposed to our view. The largest of the rooms is in the center, with two small rooms, slightly raised, on either side. On the right is a bathroom, out of sight. A narrow steep flight of stairs at the back leads up to the attic. The rooms are sparsely furnished with a few chairs, cots, a table or two. The windows are painted over, or covered with makeshift blackout curtains.[3] In the main room there is a sink, a gas ring for cooking and a woodburning stove for warmth.

The room on the left is hardly more than a closet. There is a skylight in the sloping ceiling. Directly under this room is a

---

1. **belfry** (bel′ frē) *n.* the part of a tower that holds the bells.
2. **carillon** (kar′ ə län′) *n.* a set of stationary bells, each producing one note of the scale.
3. **blackout curtains** draperies that conceal all lights that might otherwise be visible to enemy air raiders at night.

◆ **Activate Prior Knowledge**

List at least three things you know about what happened in Europe during World War II.

1. _____

_____

_____

_____

2. _____

_____

_____

_____

3. _____

_____

_____

_____

◆ **Literary Analysis**

The **stage directions** in the bracketed passage help you picture how the stage looks to the audience. How many rooms are there?

_____

_____

What furniture is visible on stage?

_____

_____

_____

_____

_____

Knowing the **historical context**—the time period in which the play is set—can help you understand characters' feelings and actions. As the underlined passage indicates, the play opens in November 1945, soon after World War II has ended in Europe. Why might that time period be significant?

_____

_____

_____

_____

Using the **stage directions,** picture what Mr. Frank is like. List at least five adjectives that describe his age, his personality, his health, and his feelings.

_____

_____

_____

_____

_____

_____

Why can't Mr. Frank stay in Amsterdam?

_____

_____

_____

_____

small steep stairwell, with steps leading down to a door. This is the only entrance from the building below. When the door is opened we see that it has been concealed on the outer side by a bookcase attached to it.

The curtain rises on an empty stage. It is late afternoon, November 1945.

The rooms are dusty, the curtains in rags. Chairs and tables are overturned.

The door at the foot of the small stairwell swings open. MR. FRANK comes up the steps into view. He is a gentle, cultured European in his middle years. There is still a trace of a German accent in his speech.

He stands looking slowly around, making a supreme effort at self-control. He is weak, ill. His clothes are threadbare.

After a second he drops his rucksack[4] on the couch and moves slowly about. He opens the door to one of the smaller rooms, and then abruptly closes it again, turning away. He goes to the window at the back, looking off at the Westertoren as its carillon strikes the hour of six, then he moves restlessly on.

From the street below we hear the sound of a barrel organ[5] and children's voices at play. There is a many-colored scarf hanging from a nail. MR. FRANK takes it, putting it around his neck. As he starts back for his rucksack, his eye is caught by something lying on the floor. It is a woman's white glove. He holds it in his hand and suddenly all of his self-control is gone. He breaks down, crying.

We hear footsteps on the stairs. MIEP GIES comes up, looking for MR. FRANK. MIEP is a Dutch girl of about twenty-two. She wears a coat and hat, ready to go home. She is pregnant. Her attitude toward MR. FRANK is protective, compassionate.]

> **MIEP.** Are you all right, Mr. Frank?
> **MR. FRANK.** [Quickly controlling himself] Yes, Miep, yes.
> **MIEP.** Everyone in the office has gone home . . . It's after six. [Then pleading] Don't stay up here, Mr. Frank. What's the use of torturing yourself like this?
> **MR. FRANK.** I've come to say good-bye . . . I'm leaving here, Miep.
> **MIEP.** What do you mean? Where are you going? Where?
> **MR. FRANK.** I don't know yet. I haven't decided.
> **MIEP.** Mr. Frank, you can't leave here! This is your home! Amsterdam is your home. Your business is here, waiting for you . . . You're needed here . . . Now that the war is over, there are things that . . .
> **MR. FRANK.** I can't stay in Amsterdam, Miep. It has too many memories for me. Everywhere there's something . . . the house we lived in . . . the

4. **rucksack** (ruk′ sak′) *n.* knapsack or backpack.
5. **barrel organ** *n.* mechanical musical instrument played by turning a crank.

school . . . that street organ playing out there . . . I'm not the person you used to know, Miep. I'm a bitter old man. *[Breaking off]* Forgive me. I shouldn't speak to you like this . . . after all that you did for us . . . the suffering . . .

MIEP. No. No. It wasn't suffering. You can't say we suffered. *[As she speaks, she straightens a chair which is overturned.]*

MR. FRANK. I know what you went through, you and Mr. Kraler. I'll remember it as long as I live. *[He gives one last look around.]* Come, Miep. *[He starts for the steps, then remembers his rucksack, going back to get it.]*

MIEP. *[Hurrying up to a cupboard]* Mr. Frank, did you see? There are some of your papers here. *[She brings a bundle of papers to him.]* We found them in a heap of rubbish on the floor after . . . after you left.

MR. FRANK. Burn them. *[He opens his rucksack to put the glove in it.]*

MIEP. But, Mr. Frank, there are letters, notes . . .

MR. FRANK. Burn them. All of them.

MIEP. Burn this? *[She hands him a paperbound notebook.]*

MR. FRANK. *[Quietly]* Anne's diary. *[He opens the diary and begins to read.]* "Monday, the sixth of July, nineteen forty-two." *[To MIEP]* Nineteen forty-two. Is it possible, Miep? . . . Only three years ago. *[As he continues his reading, he sits down on the couch.]* "Dear Diary, since you and I are going to be great friends, I will start by telling you about myself. My name is Anne Frank. I am thirteen years old. I was born in Germany the twelfth of June, nineteen twenty-nine. As my family is Jewish, we emigrated to Holland when Hitler came to power."

[As MR. FRANK reads on, another voice joins his, as if coming from the air. It is ANNE'S VOICE.]

MR. FRANK AND ANNE. "My father started a business, importing spice and herbs. Things went well for us until nineteen forty. Then the war came, and the Dutch capitulation,[6] followed by the arrival of the Germans. Then things got very bad for the Jews."

[MR. FRANK'S voice dies out. ANNE'S VOICE continues alone. The lights dim slowly to darkness. The curtain falls on the scene.]

6. **capitulation** (kə pich′ ə lā′ shən) *n.* surrender.

◆ **Reading Check**

What kinds of things do you think Miep did for Mr. Frank and his family? As you read ahead in the play you will find out whether your answer is correct.

_____

_____

_____

_____

◆ **Reading Strategy**

The bracketed passage provides more important details about the historical context. Circle details in the passage that help you answer the following questions:

Mark the Text

1. When was Anne born? _____

_____

2. Why did her family move to Holland?

_____

_____

_____

_____

3. When did things get bad for Jews in Holland and why?

_____

_____

_____

_____

_____

_____

_____

Analyze the historical context.
How were the lives of Jews in Holland affected under German occupation during the early 1940s? Circle several examples noted in the bracketed passage. Then, write your answers below.

_____

_____

_____

_____

_____

_____

_____

_____

_____

_____

_____

_____

ANNE'S VOICE. You could not do this and you could not do that. They forced Father out of his business. We had to wear yellow stars.[7] I had to turn in my bike. I couldn't go to a Dutch school any more. I couldn't go to the movies, or ride in an automobile, or even on a streetcar, and a million other things. But somehow we children still managed to have fun. Yesterday Father told me we were going into hiding. Where, he wouldn't say. At five o'clock this morning Mother woke me and told me to hurry and get dressed. I was to put on as many clothes as I could. It would look too suspicious if we walked along carrying suitcases. It wasn't until we were on our way that I learned where we were going. Our hiding place was to be upstairs in the building where Father used to have his business. Three other people were coming in with us . . . the Van Daans and their son Peter . . . Father knew the Van Daans but we had never met them . . .

[During the last lines the curtain rises on the scene. The lights dim on. ANNE'S VOICE _fades out.]_

---

7. **yellow stars** Stars of David, which are six-pointed stars that are symbols of Judaism. The Nazis ordered all Jews to wear them sewn to their clothing so that Jews could be easily identified.

Reader's Response: What do you think would be the biggest problem about going into hiding for a long time?

_____

_____

_____

Thinking About the Skill: How does recognizing the historical context of a play or story help you better understand what is happening?

_____

_____

_____

The Diary of Anne Frank
Frances Goodrich and Albert Hackett

Act 1, Scene 2

When seven people are in hiding together in a tiny apartment, everyone must follow rules and avoid disagreements. That isn't always easy, as the families in the play discover.

[*It is early morning, July 1942. The rooms are bare, as before, but they are now clean and orderly.*

MR. VAN DAAN, *a tall, portly[1] man in his late forties, is in the main room, pacing up and down, nervously smoking a cigarette. His clothes and overcoat are expensive and well cut.*

MRS. VAN DAAN *sits on the couch, clutching her possessions, a hatbox, bags, etc. She is a pretty woman in her early forties. She wears a fur coat over her other clothes.*

PETER VAN DAAN *is standing at the window of the room on the right, looking down at the street below. He is a shy, awkward boy of sixteen. He wears a cap, a raincoat, and long Dutch trousers, like "plus fours."[2] At his feet is a black case, a carrier for his cat. The yellow Star of David is <u>conspicuous</u> on all of their clothes.*]

 MRS. VAN DAAN. [*Rising, nervous, excited*] Something's happened to them! I know it!

 MR. VAN DAAN. Now, Kerli!

 MRS. VAN DAAN. Mr. Frank said they'd be here at seven o'clock. He said . . .

 MR. VAN DAAN. They have two miles to walk. You can't expect . . .

 MRS. VAN DAAN. They've been picked up. That's what's happened. They've been taken . . .

[MR. VAN DAAN *indicates that he hears someone coming.*]

 MR. VAN DAAN. You see?

[PETER *takes up his carrier and his schoolbag, etc., and goes into the main room as* MR. FRANK *comes up the stairwell from below.* MR. FRANK *looks much younger now. His movements are brisk, his manner confident. He wears an overcoat and carries his hat and a small cardboard box. He crosses to the* VAN DAANS, *shaking hands with each of them.*]

 MR. FRANK. Mrs. Van Daan, Mr. Van Daan, Peter. [*Then, in explanation of their lateness*] There were too many of the Green Police[3] on the streets . . . we had to take the long way around.

[*Up the steps come* MARGOT FRANK, MRS. FRANK, MIEP (*not*

Vocabulary Development: conspicuous (kən spik´ yōō əs) *adj.* noticeable

---

1. **portly** (pôrt´ lē) *adj.* large, heavy, and dignified.
2. **plus fours** *n.* loose knickers worn for active sports.
3. **Green Police** Nazi police, who wore green uniforms.

◆ **Reading Review**

Complete the sentences below to review what you read in Scene 1 of the play. Look back if you need help filling in the details:
The play is set in the country of

_____

during and right after

_____.

Two families of _____ people are in hiding hoping to escape being captured and killed by the _____ army.

◆ **Literary Analysis**

In the boxes below, list information about each of the Van Daans that you learn from the bracketed **stage directions**—such as their age, appearance, and personality. Underline details in the stage directions that help you fill in the boxes.

Mr. Van Daan

[ ]

Mrs. Van Daan

[ ]

Peter Van Daan

[ ]

_____

_____

The **stage directions** in the bracketed passage help you visualize what Anne's personality is like even before she speaks. Circle details about Anne's personality in the text. Then, on the lines below, list three adjectives you would use to describe Anne.

1._____

2._____

3._____

Why are Miep and Mr. Kraler able to move around Amsterdam to obtain food, drugs, and ration books for the Franks and the Van Daans?

_____

_____

_____

Think of the **historical context**. In the underlined sentence, Mr. Frank says they won't be living "according to regulations." What do you think the regulations were for Jews in Amsterdam in 1942?

_____

_____

_____

pregnant now) and MR. KRALER. All of them carry bags, packages, and so forth. The Star of David is conspicuous on all of the FRANKS' clothing. MARGOT is eighteen, beautiful, quiet, shy. MRS. FRANK is a young mother, gently bred, reserved. She, like MR. FRANK, has a slight German accent. MR. KRALER is a Dutchman, dependable, kindly.

As MR. KRALER and MIEP go upstage to put down their parcels, MRS. FRANK turns back to call ANNE.]

    MRS. FRANK. Anne?

[ANNE comes running up the stairs. She is thirteen, quick in her movements, interested in everything, <u>mercurial</u> in her emotions. She wears a cape, long wool socks and carries a schoolbag.]

    MR. FRANK. [Introducing them] My wife, Edith. Mr. and
        Mrs. Van Daan . . . their son, Peter . . . my daughters,
        Margot and Anne.

[MRS. FRANK hurries over, shaking hands with them.]

    [ANNE gives a polite little curtsy as she shakes MR. VAN DAAN's hand. Then she immediately starts off on a tour of investigation of her new home, going upstairs to the attic room. MIEP and MR. KRALER are putting the various things they have brought on the shelves.]

    MR. KRALER. I'm sorry there is still so much confusion.

    MR. FRANK. Please. Don't think of it. After all, we'll have
        plenty of <u>leisure</u> to arrange everything ourselves.

    MIEP. [To MRS. FRANK] We put the stores of food you sent
        in here. Your drugs are here . . . soap, linen here.

    MRS. FRANK. Thank you, Miep.

    MIEP. I made up the beds . . . the way Mr. Frank and Mr.
        Kraler said. [She starts out.] Forgive me. I have to
        hurry. I've got to go to the other side of town to get
        some ration books[4] for you.

    MRS. VAN DAAN. Ration books? If they see our names on
        ration books, they'll know we're here.

    MR. KRALER. There isn't anything . . .

    MIEP. Don't worry. Your names won't be on them. [As she
        hurries out] I'll be up later.

    MR. FRANK. Thank you, Miep.

    MRS. FRANK. [To MR. KRALER] It's illegal, then, the ration
        books? We've never done anything illegal.

    MR. FRANK. <u>We won't be living here exactly according to
        regulations.</u>

[As MR. KRALER reassures MRS. FRANK, he takes various small

Vocabulary Development: mercurial (mər kyoor′ ē əl) *adj.* quick or
                      changeable in behavior
             leisure (lezh′ ər) *n.* free and unoccupied time

---

4. **ration books** (rash′ ən books) *n.* books of stamps given to ensure the even distribution of scarce items, especially in wartime. Stamps as well as money must be given to obtain an item that is scarce.

things, such as matches, soap, etc., from his pockets, handing them to her.]

MR. KRALER. This isn't the black market,[5] Mrs. Frank. This is what we call the white market . . . helping all of the hundreds and hundreds who are hiding out in Amsterdam.

[The carillon is heard playing the quarter-hour before eight. MR. KRALER looks at his watch. ANNE stops at the window as she comes down the stairs.]

ANNE. It's the Westertoren!

MR. KRALER. I must go. I must be out of here and downstairs in the office before the workmen get here. *[He starts for the stairs leading out.]* Miep or I, or both of us, will be up each day to bring you food and news and find out what your needs are. Tomorrow I'll get you a better bolt for the door at the foot of the stairs. It needs a bolt that you can throw yourself and open only at our signal. *[To MR. FRANK]* Oh . . . You'll tell them about the noise?

MR. FRANK. I'll tell them.

MR. KRALER. Good-bye then for the moment. I'll come up again, after the workmen leave.

MR. FRANK. Good-bye, Mr. Kraler.

MRS. FRANK. *[Shaking his hand]* How can we thank you?

[The others murmur their good-byes.]

MR. KRALER. I never thought I'd live to see the day when a man like Mr. Frank would have to go into hiding. When you think—

[He breaks off, going out. MR. FRANK follows him down the steps, bolting the door after him. In the interval before he returns, PETER goes over to MARGOT, shaking hands with her. As MR. FRANK comes back up the steps, MRS. FRANK questions him anxiously.]

MRS. FRANK. What did he mean, about the noise?

MR. FRANK. First let us take off some of these clothes.

[They all start to take off garment after garment. On each of their coats, sweaters, blouses, suits, dresses, is another yellow Star of David. MR. and MRS. FRANK are underdressed quite simply. The others wear several things, sweaters, extra dresses, bathrobes, aprons, nightgowns, etc.]

MR. VAN DAAN. It's a wonder we weren't arrested, walking along the streets . . . Petronella with a fur coat in July . . . and that cat of Peter's crying all the way.

ANNE. A cat?

[Finally, as they have all removed their surplus clothes, they look to MR. FRANK, waiting for him to speak.]

MR. FRANK. Now. About the noise. While the men are in the building below, we must have complete quiet. Every sound can be heard down there, not only in the

---

5. **black market** illegal way of buying scarce items without ration stamps.

◆ **Reading Check**

Why is Mr. Kraler helping the Franks and the Van Daans?

Mark the Text

Underline a sentence in the bracketed passage that helps explain his motive.

_____

_____

_____

_____

_____

_____

_____

◆ **Reading Check**

Why are the characters wearing so much clothing? Why didn't they pack their clothes in suitcases and bring them to the apartment? Reread to find where Anne explained the reason earlier in the play. Then, write the answer below.

_____

_____

_____

_____

_____

Notice the **staging** described in the bracketed stage directions. What different feelings does the sound of marching feet create in the characters?

_____

_____

_____

How might they convey those feelings to the audience?

_____

_____

_____

Which of Mr. Frank's rules do you think would be the hardest for you to follow? Why?

_____

_____

_____

_____

_____

Why did Mr. Frank decide to help the Van Daans hide? Look for the answer in the bracketed passage.

_____

_____

_____

_____

_____

workrooms, but in the offices too. The men come at about eight-thirty, and leave at about five-thirty. So, to be perfectly safe, from eight in the morning until six in the evening we must move only when it is necessary, and then in stockinged feet. We must not speak above a whisper. We must not run any water. We cannot use the sink, or even, forgive me, the w.c.[6] The pipes go down through the workrooms. It would be heard. No trash . . .

[MR. FRANK _stops abruptly as he hears the sound of marching feet from the street below. Everyone is motionless, paralyzed with fear._ MR. FRANK _goes quietly into the room on the right to look down out of the window._ ANNE _runs after him, peering out with him. The tramping feet pass without stopping. The tension is relieved._ MR. FRANK, _followed by_ ANNE, _returns to the main room and resumes his instructions to the group._]

. . . No trash must ever be thrown out which might reveal that someone is living up here . . . not even a potato paring. We must burn everything in the stove at night. This is the way we must live until it is over, if we are to survive.

[_There is silence for a second._]

MRS. FRANK. Until it is over.

MR. FRANK. [_Reassuringly_] After six we can move about . . . we can talk and laugh and have our supper and read and play games . . . just as we would at home. [_He looks at his watch._] And now I think it would be wise if we all went to our rooms, and were settled before eight o'clock. Mrs. Van Daan, you and your husband will be upstairs. I regret that there's no place up there for Peter. But he will be here, near us. This will be our common room, where we'll meet to talk and eat and read, like one family.

MR. VAN DAAN. And where do you and Mrs. Frank sleep?

MR. FRANK. This room is also our bedroom.

MRS. VAN DAAN. That isn't right. We'll sleep here and you take the room upstairs.

MR. VAN DAAN. It's your place.

MR. FRANK. Please. I've thought this out for weeks. It's the best arrangement. The only arrangement.

MRS. VAN DAAN. [_To_ MR. FRANK] Never, never can we thank you. [_Then to_ MRS. FRANK] I don't know what would have happened to us, if it hadn't been for Mr. Frank.

MR. FRANK. You don't know how your husband helped me when I came to this country . . . knowing no one . . . not able to speak the language. I can never repay him for that. [_Going to_ VAN DAAN] May I help you with your things?

MR. VAN DAAN. No. No. [_To_ MRS. VAN DAAN] Come along, liefje.[7]

---

6. **w.c.** water closet; bathroom.
7. **liefje** (lēf´ hyə) Dutch for "little love."

MRS. VAN DAAN. You'll be all right, Peter? You're not afraid?

PETER. *[Embarrassed]* Please, Mother.

[They start up the stairs to the attic room above. MR. FRANK *turns to* MRS. FRANK.*]*

MR. FRANK. You too must have some rest, Edith. You didn't close your eyes last night. Nor you, Margot.

ANNE. I slept, Father. Wasn't that funny? I knew it was the last night in my own bed, and yet I slept soundly.

MR. FRANK. I'm glad, Anne. Now you'll be able to help me straighten things in here. *[To* MRS. FRANK *and* MARGOT*]* Come with me . . . You and Margot rest in this room for the time being.

[He picks up their clothes, starting for the room on the right.]

MRS. FRANK. You're sure . . . ? I could help . . . And Anne hasn't had her milk . . .

MR. FRANK. I'll give it to her. *[To* ANNE *and* PETER*]* Anne, Peter . . . it's best that you take off your shoes now, before you forget.

[He leads the way to the room, followed by MARGOT.*]*

MRS. FRANK. You're sure you're not tired, Anne?

ANNE. I feel fine. I'm going to help Father.

MRS. FRANK. Peter, I'm glad you are to be with us.

PETER. Yes, Mrs. Frank.

*[*MRS. FRANK *goes to join* MR. FRANK *and* MARGOT.*]*

[During the following scene MR. FRANK *helps* MARGOT *and* MRS. FRANK *to hang up their clothes. Then he persuades them both to lie down and rest. The* VAN DAANS *in their room above settle themselves. In the main room* ANNE *and* PETER *remove their shoes.* PETER *takes his cat out of the carrier.]*

ANNE. What's your cat's name?

PETER. Mouschi.

ANNE. Mouschi! Mouschi! Mouschi! *[She picks up the cat, walking away with it. To* PETER*]* I love cats. I have one . . . a darling little cat. But they made me leave her behind. I left some food and a note for the neighbors to take care of her . . . I'm going to miss her terribly. What is yours? A him or a her?

PETER. He's a tom. He doesn't like strangers. *[He takes the cat from her, putting it back in its carrier.]*

ANNE. *[Unabashed]* Then I'll have to stop being a stranger, won't I? Where did you go to school?

PETER. Jewish Secondary.

ANNE. But that's where Margot and I go! I never saw you around.

PETER. I used to see you . . . sometimes . . .

ANNE. You did?

PETER. . . . In the school yard. You were always in the

Vocabulary Development: unabashed (un ə basht´) *adj.* unashamed

---

© Pearson Education, Inc. The Diary of Anne Frank, Act 1, Scene 2 **173**

◆ **Reading Check**

Why didn't Mrs. Frank and Margot sleep the night before?

_____

_____

_____

◆ **Literary Analysis**

Notice the **staging** of the play in the bracketed stage directions. Underline and number five separate actions going on at almost the same time on the stage.

Mark the Text!

◆ **Reading Check**

How do Anne and Peter reveal what they are like in the bracketed dialogue here and on the next page? List two words or phrases to describe Anne and two to describe Peter.

Anne:

1. _____

2. _____

Peter:

1. _____

2. _____

Think of the **historical context**. Why did the Germans require that Anne and Peter wear the yellow star on their clothing?

_____

_____

_____

_____

How did wearing the yellow star probably make Jews like Peter and Anne feel?

_____

_____

_____

_____

_____

In the **staging** of this play, unlike in some others, most of the actors are on stage, resting or doing something all of the time. What extra meaning is conveyed by having the actors always in sight of the audience?

_____

_____

_____

_____

_____

_____

_____

middle of a bunch of kids.

[*He takes a penknife from his pocket.*]

ANNE. Why didn't you ever come over?

PETER. I'm sort of a lone wolf. [*He starts to rip off his Star of David.*]

ANNE. What are you doing?

PETER. Taking it off.

ANNE. But you can't do that. They'll arrest you if you go out without your star.

[*He tosses his knife on the table.*]

PETER. Who's going out?

ANNE. Why, of course! You're right! Of course we don't need them any more. [*She picks up his knife and starts to take her star off.*] I wonder what our friends will think when we don't show up today?

PETER. I didn't have any dates with anyone.

ANNE. Oh, I did. I had a date with Jopie to go and play ping-pong at her house. Do you know Jopie de Waal?

PETER. No.

ANNE. Jopie's my best friend. I wonder what she'll think when she telephones and there's no answer? . . . Probably she'll go over to the house . . . I wonder what she'll think . . . we left everything as if we'd suddenly been called away . . . breakfast dishes in the sink . . . beds not made . . . [*As she pulls off her star, the cloth underneath shows clearly the color and form of the star.*] Look! It's still there!

[PETER *goes over to the stove with his star.*]

What're you going to do with yours?

PETER. Burn it.

ANNE. [*She starts to throw hers in, and cannot.*] It's funny, I can't throw mine away. I don't know why.

PETER. You can't throw . . . ? Something they branded you with . . . ? That they made you wear so they could spit on you?

ANNE. I know. I know. But after all, it *is* the Star of David, isn't it?

[*In the bedroom, right,* MARGOT *and* MRS. FRANK *are lying down.* MR. FRANK *starts quietly out.*]

PETER. Maybe it's different for a girl.

[MR. FRANK *comes into the main room.*]

MR. FRANK. Forgive me, Peter. Now let me see. We must find a bed for your cat. [*He goes to a cupboard.*] I'm glad you brought your cat. Anne was feeling so badly about hers. [*Getting a used small washtub*] Here we are. Will it be comfortable in that?

PETER. [*Gathering up his things*] Thanks.

MR. FRANK. [*Opening the door of the room on the left*] And here is your room. But I warn you, Peter, you can't grow any more. Not an inch, or you'll have to sleep with your feet out of the skylight. Are you hungry?

PETER. No.

MR. FRANK. We have some bread and butter.

PETER. No, thank you.

MR. FRANK. You can have it for luncheon then. And tonight we will have a real supper . . . our first supper together.

PETER. Thanks. Thanks. *[He goes into his room. During the following scene he arranges his possessions in his new room.]*

MR. FRANK. That's a nice boy, Peter.

ANNE. He's awfully shy, isn't he?

MR. FRANK. You'll like him, I know.

ANNE. I certainly hope so, since he's the only boy I'm likely to see for months and months.

[MR. FRANK sits down, taking off his shoes.]

MR. FRANK. Annele,[8] there's a box there. Will you open it? *[He indicates a carton on the couch. ANNE brings it to the center table. In the street below there is the sound of children playing.]*

ANNE. *[As she opens the carton]* You know the way I'm going to think of it here? I'm going to think of it as a boarding house. A very peculiar summer boarding house, like the one that we—*[She breaks off as she pulls out some photographs.]* Father! My movie stars! I was wondering where they were! I was looking for them this morning . . . and Queen Wilhelmina![9] How wonderful!

MR. FRANK. There's something more. Go on. Look further. *[He goes over to the sink, pouring a glass of milk from a thermos bottle.]*

ANNE. *[Pulling out a pasteboard-bound book]* A diary! *[She throws her arms around her father.]* I've never had a diary. And I've always longed for one. *[She looks around the room.]* Pencil, pencil, pencil, pencil. *[She starts down the stairs.]* I'm going down to the office to get a pencil.

MR. FRANK. Anne! No! *[He goes after her, catching her by the arm and pulling her back.]*

ANNE. *[Startled]* But there's no one in the building now.

MR. FRANK. It doesn't matter. I don't want you ever to go beyond that door.

ANNE. *[Sobered]* Never . . . ? Not even at nighttime, when everyone is gone? Or on Sundays? Can't I go down to listen to the radio?

MR. FRANK. Never. I am sorry, Anneke.[10] It isn't safe. No, you must never go beyond that door. *[For the first time ANNE realizes what "going into hiding" means.]*

---

8. **Annele** (än´ ə lə) nickname for "Anne."
9. **Queen Wilhelmina** (wil´ hel mē´ nə) queen of the Netherlands from 1890 to 1948.
10. **Anneke** (än´ ə kə) nickname for "Anne."

How does Mr. Frank help Anne get rid of her feelings of panic?

_____

_____

_____

_____

_____

_____

◆ **Literary Analysis**

The **staging** helps the audience tell which characters already seem calm and which seem nervous about living in the small apartment. Underline clues in the bracketed stage directions, and then fill in the chart below:

Calm Characters	Nervous Characters

ANNE. I see.

MR. FRANK. It'll be hard, I know. But always remember this, Anneke. There are no walls, there are no bolts, no locks that anyone can put on your mind. Miep will bring us books. We will read history, poetry, mythology. *[He gives her the glass of milk.]* Here's your milk. *[With his arm about her, they go over to the couch, sitting down side by side.]* As a matter of fact, between us, Anne, being here has certain advantages for you. For instance, you remember the battle you had with your mother the other day on the subject of overshoes? You said you'd rather die than wear over-shoes? But in the end you had to wear them? Well now, you see, for as long as we are here you will never have to wear overshoes! Isn't that good? And the coat that you inherited from Margot, you won't have to wear that any more. And the piano! You won't have to practice on the piano. I tell you, this is going to be a fine life for you!

[ANNE's panic is gone. PETER appears in the doorway of his room, with a saucer in his hand. He is carrying his cat.]

PETER. I . . . I . . . I thought I'd better get some water for Mouschi before . . .

MR. FRANK. Of course.

[As he starts toward the sink the carillon begins to chime the hour of eight. He tiptoes to the window at the back and looks down at the street below. He turns to PETER, indicating in pantomime that it is too late. PETER starts back for his room. He steps on a creaking board. The three of them are frozen for a minute in fear. As PETER starts away again, ANNE tiptoes over to him and pours some of the milk from her glass into the saucer for the cat. PETER squats on the floor, putting the milk before the cat. MR. FRANK gives ANNE his fountain pen, and then goes into the room at the right. For a second ANNE watches the cat, then she goes over to the center table, and opens her diary.

In the room at the right, MRS. FRANK has sat up quickly at the sound of the carillon. MR. FRANK comes in and sits down beside her on the settee, his arm comfortingly around her.

Upstairs, in the attic room, MR. and MRS. VAN DAAN have hung their clothes in the closet and are now seated on the iron bed. MRS. VAN DAAN leans back exhausted. MR. VAN DAAN fans her with a newspaper.

ANNE starts to write in her diary. The lights dim out, the curtain falls.

In the darkness ANNE's VOICE comes to us again, faintly at first, and then with growing strength.]

ANNE'S VOICE. I expect I should be describing what it feels like to go into hiding. But I really don't know yet myself. I only know it's funny never to be able to go outdoors . . . never to breathe fresh air . . . never to run and shout and jump. It's the silence in the nights that frightens me most. Every time I hear a creak in the house, or a step on the street outside, I'm sure they're coming for us. The days aren't so bad. At least we know that Miep and Mr. Kraler are down there below us in the office. Our protectors, we call them. I asked Father what would happen to them if the Nazis found out they were hiding us. Pim (Anne's nickname for her father) said that they would suffer the same fate that we would . . . Imagine! They know this, and yet when they come up here, they're always cheerful and gay as if there were nothing in the world to bother them . . . Friday, the twenty-first of August, nineteen forty-two. Today I'm going to tell you our general news. Mother is unbearable. She insists on treating me like a baby, which I loathe. Otherwise things are going better. The weather is . . .

[As ANNE'S VOICE *is fading out, the curtain rises on the scene.*]

◆ **Stop to Reflect**

Briefly summarize what has happened so far in the play. Then predict what you think will happen in the next scene. Underline clues that Anne's diary entry provides.

_____

_____

_____

_____

_____

_____

_____

_____

_____

_____

_____

Reader's Response: Would you like to have Anne for a friend? Explain.

_____

_____

_____

Thinking About the Skill: What useful clues do the **stage directions** provide for understanding what characters are like?

_____

_____

_____

In Scene 2, Mr. Frank set out some key rules for how the fugitives would have to live in the apartment. List three of those rules below. Look back if you need help remembering.

1. _____

_____

2. _____

_____

3. _____

_____

Circle **stage directions** in the bracketed passage that show how different characters act when they are released from being quiet. What do the actions reveal about the personalities of Margot, Mrs. Van Daan, Peter, and Anne? Write a word or phrase to complete each sentence below.

Margot seems

_____

_____

Mrs. Van Daan seems

_____

_____

Peter seems

_____

_____

Anne seems

_____

_____

The Diary of Anne Frank
Frances Goodrich and Albert Hackett

Act 1, Scene 3

Living so close together in the cramped apartment, the fugitives are slowly getting on each other's nerves. There is only one way life could get more annoying—if someone else moved into the apartment, too.

[*It is a little after six o'clock in the evening, two months later.* MARGOT *is in the bedroom at the right, studying.* MR. VAN DAAN *is lying down in the attic room above.*

The rest of the "family" is in the main room. ANNE *and* PETER *sit opposite each other at the center table, where they have been doing their lessons.* MRS. FRANK *is on the couch.* MRS. VAN DAAN *is seated with her fur coat, on which she has been sewing, in her lap. None of them are wearing their shoes.*

Their eyes are on MR. FRANK, *waiting for him to give them the signal which will release them from their day-long quiet.* MR. FRANK, *his shoes in his hand, stands looking down out of the window at the back, watching to be sure that all of the workmen have left the building below.*

After a few seconds of motionless silence, MR. FRANK *turns from the window.*]

MR. FRANK. [*Quietly, to the group*] It's safe now. The last workman has left.

[*There is an immediate stir of relief.*]

ANNE. [*Her pent-up energy explodes.*] WHEE!

MR. FRANK. [*Startled, amused*] Anne!

MRS. VAN DAAN. I'm first for the w.c.

[*She hurries off to the bathroom.* MRS. FRANK *puts on her shoes and starts up to the sink to prepare supper.* ANNE *sneaks* PETER's *shoes from under the table and hides them behind her back.* MR. FRANK *goes in to* MARGOT's *room.*]

MR. FRANK. [*To* MARGOT] Six o'clock. School's over.

[MARGOT *gets up, stretching.* MR. FRANK *sits down to put on his shoes. In the main room* PETER *tries to find his.*]

PETER. [*To* ANNE] Have you seen my shoes?

ANNE. [*Innocently*] Your shoes?

PETER. You've taken them, haven't you?

ANNE. I don't know what you're talking about.

PETER. You're going to be sorry!

ANNE. Am I?

[PETER *goes after her.* ANNE, *with his shoes in her hand, runs from him, dodging behind her mother.*]

MRS. FRANK. [*Protesting*] Anne, dear!

PETER. Wait till I get you!

ANNE. I'm waiting!

[PETER *makes a lunge for her. They both fall to the floor.* PETER *pins her down, wrestling with her to get the shoes.*]

Don't! Don't! Peter, stop it. Ouch!

MRS. FRANK. Anne! . . . Peter!

[Suddenly PETER *becomes self-conscious. He grabs his shoes roughly and starts for his room.]*

    ANNE. *[Following him]* Peter, where are you going? Come dance with me.

    PETER. I tell you I don't know how.

    ANNE. I'll teach you.

    PETER. I'm going to give Mouschi his dinner.

    ANNE. Can I watch?

    PETER. He doesn't like people around while he eats.

    ANNE. Peter, please.

    PETER. No! *[He goes into his room.* ANNE *slams his door after him.]*

    MRS. FRANK. Anne, dear, I think you shouldn't play like that with Peter. It's not dignified.

    ANNE. Who cares if it's dignified? I don't want to be dignified.

*[*MR. FRANK *and* MARGOT *come from the room on the right.* MARGOT *goes to help her mother.* MR. FRANK *starts for the center table to correct* MARGOT's *school papers.]*

    MRS. FRANK. *[To* ANNE*]* You complain that I don't treat you like a grownup. But when I do, you resent it.

    ANNE. I only want some fun . . . someone to laugh and clown with . . . After you've sat still all day and hardly moved, you've got to have some fun. I don't know what's the matter with that boy.

    MR. FRANK. He isn't used to girls. Give him a little time.

    ANNE. Time? Isn't two months time? I could cry. *[Catching hold of* MARGOT*]* Come on, Margot . . . dance with me. Come on, please.

    MARGOT. I have to help with supper.

    ANNE. You know we're going to forget how to dance . . . When we get out we won't remember a thing.

[She starts to sing and dance by herself. MR. FRANK *takes her in his arms, waltzing with her.* MRS. VAN DAAN *comes in from the bathroom.]*

    MRS. VAN DAAN. Next? *[She looks around as she starts putting on her shoes.]* Where's Peter?

    ANNE. *[As they are dancing]* Where would he be!

    MRS. VAN DAAN. He hasn't finished his lessons, has he? His father'll kill him if he catches him in there with that cat and his work not done.

*[*MR. FRANK *and* ANNE *finish their dance. They bow to each other with extravagant formality.]*

    Anne, get him out of there, will you?

    ANNE. *[At* PETER's *door]* Peter? Peter?

    PETER. *[Opening the door a crack]* What is it?

    ANNE. Your mother says to come out.

    PETER. I'm giving Mouschi his dinner.

How has the relationship between Anne and Peter changed since Scene 2?

_____

_____

_____

_____

_____

_____

_____

◆ **Reading Check**

Notice Anne's underlined remark. What does dancing mean to Anne? Why is she worried about forgetting how to dance?

_____

_____

_____

_____

_____

◆ **Reading Check**

Which family has a closer relationship—the Franks or the Van Daans? Explain.

_____

_____

_____

_____

_____

_____

_____

_____

_____

Notice the **staging** described in the bracketed stage directions. Underline a description of one sound, one facial expression, and one character action that help show the pressure the characters are under and how they react to pressure.

In what ways is Peter like a cat?

_____

_____

_____

In what ways is Anne like a duck?

_____

_____

_____

MRS. VAN DAAN. You know what your father says. *[She sits on the couch, sewing on the lining of her fur coat.]*

PETER. For heaven's sake, I haven't even looked at him since lunch.

MRS. VAN DAAN. I'm just telling you, that's all.

ANNE. I'll feed him.

PETER. I don't want you in there.

MRS. VAN DAAN. Peter!

PETER. *[To ANNE]* Then give him his dinner and come right out, you hear?

[He comes back to the table. ANNE shuts the door of PETER's room after her and disappears behind the curtain covering his closet.]

MRS. VAN DAAN. *[To PETER]* Now is that any way to talk to your little girl friend?

PETER. Mother . . . for heaven's sake . . . will you please stop saying that?

MRS. VAN DAAN. Look at him blush! Look at him!

PETER. Please! I'm not . . . anyway . . . let me alone, will you?

MRS. VAN DAAN. He acts like it was something to be ashamed of. It's nothing to be ashamed of, to have a little girl friend.

PETER. You're crazy. She's only thirteen.

MRS. VAN DAAN. So what? And you're sixteen. Just perfect. Your father's ten years older than I am. *[To MR. FRANK]* I warn you, Mr. Frank, if this war lasts much longer, we're going to be related and then . . .

MR. FRANK. Mazeltov![1]

MRS. FRANK. *[Deliberately changing the conversation]* I wonder where Miep is. She's usually so prompt.

[Suddenly everything else is forgotten as they hear the sound of an automobile coming to a screeching stop in the street below. They are tense, motionless in their terror. The car starts away. A wave of relief sweeps over them. They pick up their occupations again. ANNE flings open the door of PETER's room, making a dramatic entrance. She is dressed in PETER's clothes. PETER looks at her in fury. The others are amused.]

ANNE. Good evening, everyone. Forgive me if I don't stay. *[She jumps up on a chair.]* I have a friend waiting for me in there. My friend Tom. Tom Cat. Some people say that we look alike. But Tom has the most beautiful whiskers, and I have only a little fuzz. I am hoping . . . in time . . .

PETER. All right, Mrs. Quack Quack!

ANNE. *[Outraged—jumping down]* Peter!

PETER. I heard about you . . . How you talked so much in class they called you Mrs. Quack Quack. How Mr. Smitter made you write a composition . . . "'Quack, quack,' said Mrs. Quack Quack."

---

1. **Mazeltov** (mä´ zəl tōv´) "good luck" or "congratulations" in Hebrew and Yiddish.

ANNE. Well, go on. Tell them the rest. How it was so good he read it out loud to the class and then read it to all his other classes!

PETER. Quack! Quack! Quack . . . Quack . . . Quack . . .

[ANNE pulls off the coat and trousers.]

ANNE. You are the most intolerable, <u>insufferable</u> boy I've ever met!

[She throws the clothes down the stairwell. PETER goes down after them.]

PETER. Quack, quack, quack!

MRS. VAN DAAN. *[To ANNE]* That's right, Anneke! Give it to him!

ANNE. With all the boys in the world . . . Why I had to get locked up with one like you! . . .

PETER. Quack, quack, quack, and from now on stay out of my room!

[As PETER passes her, ANNE puts out her foot, tripping him. He picks himself up, and goes on into his room.]

MRS. FRANK. *[Quietly]* Anne, dear . . . your hair. *[She feels ANNE's forehead.]* You're warm. Are you feeling all right?

ANNE. Please, Mother. *[She goes over to the center table, slipping into her shoes.]*

MRS. FRANK. *[Following her]* You haven't a fever, have you?

ANNE. *[Pulling away]* No. No.

MRS. FRANK. <u>You know we can't call a doctor here, ever.</u> There's only one thing to do . . . watch carefully. Prevent an illness before it comes. Let me see your tongue.

ANNE. Mother, this is perfectly absurd.

MRS. FRANK. Anne, dear, don't be such a baby. Let me see your tongue. *[As ANNE refuses, MRS. FRANK appeals to MR. FRANK]* Otto . . . ?

MR. FRANK. You hear your mother, Anne.

[ANNE flicks out her tongue for a second, then turns away.]

MRS. FRANK. Come on—open up! *[As ANNE opens her mouth very wide]* You seem all right . . . but perhaps an aspirin . . .

MRS. VAN DAAN. For heaven's sake, don't give that child any pills. I waited for fifteen minutes this morning for her to come out of the w.c.

ANNE. I was washing my hair!

MR. FRANK. I think there's nothing the matter with our Anne that a ride on her bike, or a visit with her friend Jopie de Waal wouldn't cure. Isn't that so, Anne?

◆ **Literary Analysis**

What do the **stage directions** in the bracketed passage reveal about the personalities of Anne and Peter?

_____

_____

_____

_____

_____

_____

_____

◆ **Reading Strategy**

Analyze the effect of the historical context of the underlined sentence. Why can't the people in the apartment call a doctor? What is going on in the world outside the apartment?

_____

_____

_____

_____

_____

◆ **Reading Check**

What does Mr. Frank think will "cure" Anne?

_____

_____

_____

Vocabulary Development: insufferable (in suf′ ər ə bəl) *adj.* unbearable

What other reminder of the **historical context** is presented in the underlined stage directions?

_____

_____

_____

_____

_____

_____

_____

Which of the Frank daughters is a more serious student? How do you know?

_____

_____

_____

_____

_____

_____

_____

What does the fur coat mean to Mrs. Van Daan?

_____

_____

_____

_____

[MR. VAN DAAN *comes down into the room. From outside we hear faint sounds of bombers going over and a burst of ack-ack.[2]*]

MR. VAN DAAN. Miep not come yet?

MRS. VAN DAAN. The workmen just left, a little while ago.

MR. VAN DAAN. What's for dinner tonight?

MRS. VAN DAAN. Beans.

MR. VAN DAAN. Not again!

MRS. VAN DAAN. Poor Putti! I know. But what can we do? That's all that Miep brought us.

[MR. VAN DAAN *starts to pace, his hands behind his back.* ANNE *follows behind him, imitating him.*]

ANNE. We are now in what is known as the "bean cycle." Beans boiled, beans en casserole, beans with strings, beans without strings . . .

[PETER *has come out of his room. He slides into his place at the table, becoming immediately absorbed in his studies.*]

MR. VAN DAAN. [*To* PETER] I saw you . . . in there, playing with your cat.

MRS. VAN DAAN. He just went in for a second, putting his coat away. He's been out here all the time, doing his lessons.

MR. FRANK. [*Looking up from the papers*] Anne, you got an excellent in your history paper today . . . and very good in Latin.

ANNE. [*Sitting beside him*] How about algebra?

MR. FRANK. I'll have to make a confession. Up until now I've managed to stay ahead of you in algebra. Today you caught up with me. We'll leave it to Margot to correct.

ANNE. Isn't algebra *vile*, Pim!

MR. FRANK. Vile!

MARGOT. [*To* MR. FRANK] How did I do?

ANNE. [*Getting up*] Excellent, excellent, excellent, excellent!

MR. FRANK. [*To* MARGOT] You should have used the subjunctive[3] here . . .

MARGOT. Should I? . . . I thought . . . look here . . . I didn't use it here . . .

[*The two become absorbed in the papers.*]

ANNE. Mrs. Van Daan, may I try on your coat?

MRS. FRANK. No, Anne.

MRS. VAN DAAN. [*Giving it to* ANNE] It's all right . . . but careful with it. [ANNE *puts it on and struts with it.*] My father gave me that the year before he died. He always bought the best that money could buy.

ANNE. Mrs. Van Daan, did you have a lot of boy friends before you were married?

MRS. FRANK. Anne, that's a personal question. It's not courteous to ask personal questions.

---

2. **ack-ack** (ak′ ak′) *n.* slang for an antiaircraft gun's fire.
3. **subjunctive** (səb juŋk′ tiv) *n.* a particular form of a verb.

MRS. VAN DAAN. Oh I don't mind. *[To ANNE]* Our house was always swarming with boys. When I was a girl we had . . .

MR. VAN DAAN. Oh, no. Not again!

MRS. VAN DAAN. *[Good-humored]* Shut up!

[Without a pause, to ANNE, MR. VAN DAAN mimics MRS. VAN DAAN, speaking the first few words in unison with her.]

One summer we had a big house in Hilversum. The boys came buzzing round like bees around a jam pot. And when I was sixteen! . . . We were wearing our skirts very short those days and I had good-looking legs. *[She pulls up her skirt, going to MR. FRANK.]* I still have 'em. I may not be as pretty as I used to be, but I still have my legs. How about it, Mr. Frank?

MR. VAN DAAN. All right. All right. We see them.

MRS. VAN DAAN. I'm not asking you. I'm asking Mr. Frank.

PETER. Mother, for heaven's sake.

MRS. VAN DAAN. Oh, I embarrass you, do I? Well, I just hope the girl you marry has as good. *[Then to ANNE]* My father used to worry about me, with so many boys hanging round. He told me, if any of them gets fresh, you say to him . . . "Remember, Mr. So-and-So, remember I'm a lady."

ANNE. "Remember, Mr. So-and-So, remember I'm a lady."

[She gives MRS. VAN DAAN her coat.]

MR. VAN DAAN. Look at you, talking that way in front of her! Don't you know she puts it all down in that diary?

MRS. VAN DAAN. So, if she does? I'm only telling the truth!

[ANNE stretches out, putting her ear to the floor, listening to what is going on below. The sound of the bombers fades away.]

MRS. FRANK. *[Setting the table]* Would you mind, Peter, if I moved you over to the couch?

ANNE. *[Listening]* Miep must have the radio on.

[PETER picks up his papers, going over to the couch beside MRS. VAN DAAN.]

MR. VAN DAAN. *[Accusingly, to PETER]* Haven't you finished yet?

PETER. No.

MR. VAN DAAN. You ought to be ashamed of yourself.

PETER. All right. All right. I'm a dunce. I'm a hopeless case. Why do I go on?

MRS. VAN DAAN. You're not hopeless. Don't talk that way. It's just that you haven't anyone to help you, like the girls have. *[To MR. FRANK]* Maybe you could help him, Mr. Frank?

MR. FRANK. I'm sure that his father . . . ?

MR. VAN DAAN. Not me. I can't do anything with him. He won't listen to me. You go ahead . . . if you want.

MR. FRANK. *[Going to PETER]* What about it, Peter? Shall we make our school coeducational?

◆ Literary Analysis

When Mr. Van Daan says, "Not again!" and Mrs. Van Daan says, "Shut up!" are they angry at each other? Circle two details in the **stage directions** in the bracketed passage that help you answer the question.

_____

_____

_____

_____

_____

◆ Reading Check

Based on her words and actions, what is Mrs. Van Daan like? List three words or phrases to describe her.

1._____

_____

_____

2._____

_____

_____

3._____

_____

_____

◆ **Literary Analysis**

Underline the **stage directions** in the bracketed passage. Then, answer the question: What do Mrs. Van Daan's actions reveal about her character?

_____

_____

_____

_____

_____

◆ **Reading Check**

Is the tone in the bracketed conversation between Mr. Van Daan and Mrs. Van Daan different from the tone of their dialogue on page 183? Why do you think so?

_____

_____

_____

◆ **Literary Analysis**

According to the underlined **stage directions**, in what way does Anne act differently during the Van Daans's argument than her mother or sister?

_____

_____

_____

MRS. VAN DAAN. [_Kissing_ MR. FRANK] You're an angel, Mr. Frank. An angel. I don't know why I didn't meet you before I met that one there. Here, sit down, Mr. Frank . . . [_She forces him down on the couch beside_ PETER.] Now, Peter, you listen to Mr. Frank.

MR. FRANK. It might be better for us to go into Peter's room.

[PETER _jumps up eagerly, leading the way._]

MRS. VAN DAAN. That's right. You go in there, Peter. You listen to Mr. Frank. Mr. Frank is a highly educated man.

[As MR. FRANK _is about to follow_ PETER _into his room,_ MRS. FRANK _stops him and wipes the lipstick from his lips. Then she closes the door after them._]

ANNE. [_On the floor, listening_] Shh! I can hear a man's voice talking.

MR. VAN DAAN. [_To_ ANNE] Isn't it bad enough here without your sprawling all over the place?

[ANNE _sits up._]

MRS. VAN DAAN. [_To_ MR. VAN DAAN] If you didn't smoke so much, you wouldn't be so bad-tempered.

MR. VAN DAAN. Am I smoking? Do you see me smoking?

MRS. VAN DAAN. Don't tell me you've used up all those cigarettes.

MR. VAN DAAN. One package. Miep only brought me one package.

MRS. VAN DAAN. It's a filthy habit anyway. It's a good time to break yourself.

MR. VAN DAAN. Oh, stop it, please.

MRS. VAN DAAN. You're smoking up all our money. You know that, don't you?

MR. VAN DAAN. Will you shut up?

[_During this,_ MRS. FRANK _and_ MARGOT _have studiously kept their eyes down. But_ ANNE, _seated on the floor, has been following the discussion interestedly._ MR. VAN DAAN _turns to see her staring up at him._]

And what are you staring at?

ANNE. I never heard grownups quarrel before. I thought only children quarreled.

MR. VAN DAAN. This isn't a quarrel! It's a discussion. And I never heard children so rude before.

ANNE. [_Rising, indignantly_] I, rude!

MR. VAN DAAN. Yes!

MRS. FRANK. [_Quickly_] Anne, will you get me my knitting?

[ANNE _goes to get it._]

I must remember, when Miep comes, to ask her to bring me some more wool.

MARGOT. [_Going to her room_] I need some hairpins and some soap. I made a list. [_She goes into her bedroom to get the list._]

MRS. FRANK. [_To_ ANNE] Have you some library books for Miep when she comes?

ANNE. It's a wonder that Miep has a life of her own, the way we make her run errands for us. Please, Miep, get me some starch. Please take my hair out and have it cut. Tell me all the latest news, Miep. [*She goes over, kneeling on the couch beside* MRS. VAN DAAN] Did you know she was engaged? His name is Dirk, and Miep's afraid the Nazis will ship him off to Germany to work in one of their war plants. That's what they're doing with some of the young Dutchmen . . . they pick them up off the streets—

MR. VAN DAAN. [*Interrupting*] Don't you ever get tired of talking? Suppose you try keeping still for five minutes. Just five minutes.

[*He starts to pace again. Again* ANNE *follows him, mimicking him.* MRS. FRANK *jumps up and takes her by the arm up to the sink, and gives her a glass of milk.*]

MRS. FRANK. Come here, Anne. It's time for your glass of milk.

MR. VAN DAAN. Talk, talk, talk. I never heard such a child. Where is my . . . ? Every evening it's the same talk, talk, talk. [*He looks around.*] Where is my . . . ?

MRS. VAN DAAN. What're you looking for?

MR. VAN DAAN. My pipe. Have you seen my pipe?

MRS. VAN DAAN. What good's a pipe? You haven't got any tobacco.

MR. VAN DAAN. At least I'll have something to hold in my mouth! [*Opening* MARGOT's *bedroom door*] Margot, have you seen my pipe?

MARGOT. It was on the table last night.

[ANNE *puts her glass of milk on the table and picks up his pipe, hiding it behind her back.*]

MR. VAN DAAN. I know. I know. Anne, did you see my pipe? . . . Anne!

MRS. FRANK. Anne, Mr. Van Daan is speaking to you.

ANNE. Am I allowed to talk now?

MR. VAN DAAN. You're the most aggravating . . . The trouble with you is, you've been spoiled. What you need is a good old-fashioned spanking.

ANNE. [*Mimicking* MRS. VAN DAAN] "Remember, Mr. So-and-So, remember I'm a lady." [*She thrusts the pipe into his mouth, then picks up her glass of milk.*]

MR. VAN DAAN. [*Restraining himself with difficulty*] Why aren't you nice and quiet like your sister Margot? Why do you have to show off all the time? Let me give you a little advice, young lady. Men don't like that kind of thing in a girl. You know that? A man likes a girl who'll listen to him once in a while . . . a domestic girl, who'll keep her house shining for her husband . . . who loves to cook and sew and . . .

ANNE. I'd cut my throat first! I'd open my veins! I'm going to be remarkable! I'm going to Paris . . .

◆ **Reading Strategy**

Be aware of the **historical context**. How do the Germans seem to treat even non-Jewish Dutch people? How do you think the Dutch feel about the Germans?

_____

_____

_____

_____

_____

_____

_____

_____

◆ **Literary Analysis**

Use the **stage directions** in the bracketed passage to help you imagine how Mr. Van Daan and Anne speak their lines. Write two words or phrases to describe the tone of each speaker.

Mr. Van Daan

1._____

2._____

Anne

1._____

2._____

_____

How does Mrs. Frank feel that Anne should act around the Van Daans? List three words or phrases to describe ways of acting that Mrs. Frank would consider appropriate.

1. _____

_____

2. _____

_____

3. _____

_____

◆ **Literary Analysis**

In the underlined sentences, Mrs. Frank says Anne is "self-willed." Underline several **stage directions** in this part of the play that help the audience picture Anne as being self-willed.

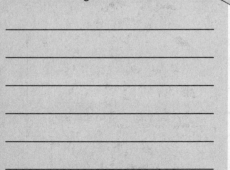

_____

_____

_____

_____

_____

MR. VAN DAAN. *[Scoffingly]* Paris!

ANNE. . . . to study music and art.

MR. VAN DAAN. Yeah! Yeah!

ANNE. I'm going to be a famous dancer or singer . . . or something wonderful.

[She makes a wide gesture, spilling the glass of milk on the fur coat in MRS. VAN DAAN's lap. MARGOT rushes quickly over with a towel. ANNE tries to brush the milk off with her skirt.]

MRS. VAN DAAN. Now look what you've done . . . you clumsy little fool! My beautiful fur coat my father gave me . . .

ANNE. I'm so sorry.

MRS. VAN DAAN. What do you care? It isn't yours . . . So go on, ruin it! Do you know what that coat cost? Do you? And now look at it! Look at it!

ANNE. I'm very, very sorry.

MRS. VAN DAAN. I could kill you for this. I could just kill you!

[MRS. VAN DAAN goes up the stairs, clutching the coat. MR. VAN DAAN starts after her.]

MR. VAN DAAN. Petronella . . . Liefje! Liefje! . . . Come back . . . the supper . . . come back!

MRS. FRANK. Anne, you must not behave in that way.

ANNE. It was an accident. Anyone can have an accident.

MRS. FRANK. I don't mean that. I mean the answering back. You must not answer back. They are our guests. We must always show the greatest courtesy to them. We're all living under terrible tension.

[She stops as MARGOT indicates that MR. VAN DAAN can hear. When he is gone, she continues.]

That's why we must control ourselves . . . You don't hear Margot getting into arguments with them, do you? Watch Margot. She's always courteous with them. Never familiar. She keeps her distance. And they respect her for it. Try to be like Margot.

ANNE. And have them walk all over me, the way they do her? No, thanks!

MRS. FRANK. I'm not afraid that anyone is going to walk all over you, Anne. I'm afraid for other people, that you'll walk on them. I don't know what happens to you, Anne. <u>You are wild, self-willed. If I had ever talked to my mother as you talk to me . . .</u>

ANNE. Things have changed. People aren't like that any more. "Yes, Mother." "No, Mother." "Anything you say, Mother." I've got to fight things out for myself! Make something of myself!

MRS. FRANK. It isn't necessary to fight to do it. Margot doesn't fight, and isn't she . . . ?

ANNE. *[Violently rebellious]* Margot! Margot! Margot! That's all I hear from everyone . . . how wonderful Margot is

. . . "Why aren't you like Margot?"

MARGOT. *[Protesting]* Oh, come on, Anne, don't be so . . .

ANNE. *[Paying no attention]* Everything she does is right, and everything I do is wrong! I'm the goat around here! . . . You're all against me! . . . And you worst of all!

[She rushes off into her room and throws herself down on the settee, stifling her sobs. MRS. FRANK sighs and starts toward the stove.]

MRS. FRANK. *[To MARGOT]* Let's put the soup on the stove . . . if there's anyone who cares to eat. Margot, will you take the bread out?

[MARGOT gets the bread from the cupboard.]

I don't know how we can go on living this way . . . I can't say a word to Anne . . . she flies at me . . .

MARGOT. You know Anne. In half an hour she'll be out here, laughing and joking.

MRS. FRANK. And . . . *[She makes a motion upwards, indicating the VAN DAANS.]* . . . I told your father it wouldn't work . . . but no . . . no . . . he had to ask them, he said . . . he owed it to him, he said. Well, he knows now that I was right! These quarrels! . . . This bickering!

MARGOT. *[With a warning look]* Shush. Shush.

[The buzzer for the door sounds. MRS. FRANK gasps, startled.]

MRS. FRANK. Every time I hear that sound, my heart stops!

MARGOT. *[Starting for PETER's door]* It's Miep. *[She knocks at the door.]* Father?

[MR. FRANK comes quickly from PETER's room.]

MR. FRANK. Thank you, Margot. *[As he goes down the steps to open the outer door]* Has everyone his list?

MARGOT. I'll get my books. *[Giving her mother a list]* Here's your list.

[MARGOT goes into her and ANNE's bedroom on the right. ANNE sits up, hiding her tears, as MARGOT comes in.]

Miep's here.

[MARGOT picks up her books and goes back. ANNE hurries over to the mirror, smoothing her hair.]

MR. VAN DAAN. *[Coming down the stairs]* Is it Miep?

MARGOT. Yes. Father's gone down to let her in.

MR. VAN DAAN. At last I'll have some cigarettes!

MRS. FRANK. *[To MR. VAN DAAN]* I can't tell you how unhappy I am about Mrs. Van Daan's coat. Anne should never have touched it.

MR. VAN DAAN. She'll be all right.

MRS. FRANK. Is there anything I can do?

MR. VAN DAAN. Don't worry.

◆ **Literary Analysis**

How can you tell from the bracketed **stage directions** that Mrs. Frank is used to Anne's emotional outbursts?

_____

_____

_____

_____

◆ **Reading Strategy**

Analyze the historical context of the underlined remark. Why does the door buzzer make Mrs. Frank afraid?

_____

_____

_____

◆ **Reading Check**

Why are all of the people in the apartment so excited when they think that Miep is here?

_____

_____

_____

_____

◆ Literary Analysis

According to the **staging**, what is the mood of Mr. Frank and Mr. Kraler when they enter the room? How does that mood differ from the tone of the lines delivered by the other characters in the bracketed passage?

_____

_____

_____

◆ Stop to Reflect

Note Mr. Frank's underlined remark. How does the line make you feel? What do you think is going to happen? Write your prediction below. Then read ahead to see whether your guess is right.

_____

_____

_____

_____

◆ Reading Strategy

Analyze the historical context to answer the question: What kind of trouble is Mr. Dussel in?

_____

_____

_____

_____

[He turns to meet MIEP. *But it is not* MIEP *who comes up the steps. It is* MR. KRALER, *followed by* MR. FRANK. *Their faces are grave.* ANNE *comes from the bedroom.* PETER *comes from his room.]*

MRS. FRANK. Mr. Kraler!

MR. VAN DAAN. How are you, Mr. Kraler?

MARGOT. This is a surprise.

MRS. FRANK. When Mr. Kraler comes, the sun begins to shine.

MR. VAN DAAN. Miep is coming?

MR. KRALER. Not tonight.

*[*MR. KRALER *goes to* MARGOT *and* MRS. FRANK *and* ANNE, *shaking hands with them.]*

MRS. FRANK. Wouldn't you like a cup of coffee? . . . Or, better still, will you have supper with us?

MR. FRANK. Mr. Kraler has something to talk over with us. <u>Something has happened, he says, which demands an immediate decision.</u>

MRS. FRANK. *[Fearful]* What is it?

*[*MR. KRALER *sits down on the couch. As he talks he takes bread, cabbages, milk, etc., from his briefcase, giving them to* MARGOT *and* ANNE *to put away.]*

MR. KRALER. Usually, when I come up here, I try to bring you some bit of good news. What's the use of telling you the bad news when there's nothing that you can do about it? But today something has happened . . . Dirk . . . Miep's Dirk, you know, came to me just now. He tells me that he has a Jewish friend living near him. A dentist. He says he's in trouble. He begged me, could I do anything for this man? Could I find him a hiding place? . . . So I've come to you . . . I know it's a terrible thing to ask of you, living as you are, but would you take him in with you?

MR. FRANK. Of course we will.

MR. KRALER. *[Rising]* It'll be just for a night or two . . . until I find some other place. This happened so suddenly that I didn't know where to turn.

MR. FRANK. Where is he?

MR. KRALER. Downstairs in the office.

MR. FRANK. Good. Bring him up.

MR. KRALER. His name is Dussel . . . Jan Dussel.

MR. FRANK. Dussel . . . I think I know him.

MR. KRALER. I'll get him.

[He goes quickly down the steps and out. MR. FRANK *suddenly becomes conscious of the others.]*

MR. FRANK. Forgive me. I spoke without consulting you. But I knew you'd feel as I do.

MR. VAN DAAN. There's no reason for you to consult anyone. This is your place. You have a right to do exactly as you please. The only thing I feel . . . there's so little food as it is . . . and to take in another person . . .

[PETER *turns away, ashamed of his father.*]

MR. FRANK. We can stretch the food a little. It's only for a few days.

MR. VAN DAAN. You want to make a bet?

MRS. FRANK. I think it's fine to have him. But, Otto, where are you going to put him? Where?

PETER. He can have my bed. I can sleep on the floor. I wouldn't mind.

MR. FRANK. That's good of you, Peter. But your room's too small . . . even for *you.*

ANNE. I have a much better idea. I'll come in here with you and Mother, and Margot can take Peter's room and Peter can go in our room with Mr. Dussel.

MARGOT. That's right. We could do that.

MR. FRANK. No, Margot. You mustn't sleep in that room . . . neither you nor Anne. Mouschi has caught some rats in there. Peter's brave. He doesn't mind.

ANNE. Then how about *this*? I'll come in here with you and Mother, and Mr. Dussel can have my bed.

MRS. FRANK. No. No. *No!* Margot will come in here with us and he can have her bed. It's the only way. Margot, bring your things in here. Help her, Anne.

[MARGOT *hurries into her room to get her things.*]

ANNE. [*To her mother*] Why Margot? Why can't I come in here?

MRS. FRANK. Because it wouldn't be proper for Margot to sleep with a . . . Please, Anne. Don't argue. Please.

[ANNE *starts slowly away.*]

MR. FRANK. [*To* ANNE] You don't mind sharing your room with Mr. Dussel, do you, Anne?

ANNE. No. No, of course not.

MR. FRANK. Good.

[ANNE *goes off into her bedroom, helping* MARGOT. MR. FRANK *starts to search in the cupboards.*]

Where's the cognac?

MRS. FRANK. It's there. But, Otto, I was saving it in case of illness.

MR. FRANK. I think we couldn't find a better time to use it. Peter, will you get five glasses for me?

[PETER *goes for the glasses.* MARGOT *comes out of her bedroom, carrying her possessions, which she hangs behind a curtain in the main room.* MR. FRANK *finds the cognac and pours it into the five glasses that* PETER *brings him.* MR. VAN DAAN *stands looking on sourly.* MRS. VAN DAAN *comes downstairs and looks around at all the bustle.*]

MRS. VAN DAAN. What's happening? What's going on?

MR. VAN DAAN. Someone's moving in with us.

MRS. VAN DAAN. In here? You're joking.

© Pearson Education, Inc.

The Diary of Anne Frank, Act 1, Scene 3   **189**

◆ Reading Check

Do you agree more with Mr. Frank or Mr. Van Daan about whether to take in Mr. Dussel? Explain.

_____

_____

_____

_____

◆ Reading Check

What do Peter, Margot, and Anne reveal about themselves in the bracketed passage by their efforts to make room for Mr. Dussel in the apartment?

_____

_____

_____

_____

_____

◆ Literary Analysis

Notice the **staging** of the play in the bracketed stage directions.
Underline and number five separate actions going on at almost the same time on the stage.

Mark the Text

Based on the description of Mr. Dussel in the bracketed **stage directions,** do you think he will fit in well in the apartment? Why or why not?

_____

_____

_____

_____

_____

Be aware of the **historical context.** Underline Mr. Kraler's remarks that show that he and other Dutch people are opposed to the Germans and their laws against the Jews.

Why is Mr. Dussel surprised to see Mr. Frank?

_____

_____

_____

_____

MARGOT. It's only for a night or two . . . until Mr. Kraler finds him another place.

MR. VAN DAAN. Yeah! Yeah!

[MR. FRANK *hurries over as* MR. KRALER *and* DUSSEL *come up.* DUSSEL *is a man in his late fifties,* meticulous, *finicky . . . bewildered now. He wears a raincoat. He carries a briefcase, stuffed full, and a small medicine case.*]

MR. FRANK. Come in, Mr. Dussel.

MR. KRALER. This is Mr. Frank.

DUSSEL. Mr. Otto Frank?

MR. FRANK. Yes. Let me take your things.

[*He takes the hat and briefcase, but* DUSSEL *clings to his medicine case.*]

This is my wife, Edith . . . Mr. and Mrs. Van Daan . . . their son, Peter . . . and my daughters, Margot and Anne.

[DUSSEL *shakes hands with everyone.*]

MR. KRALER. Thank you, Mr. Frank. Thank you all. Mr. Dussel, I leave you in good hands. Oh . . . Dirk's coat.

[DUSSEL *hurriedly takes off the raincoat, giving it to* MR. KRALER. *Underneath is his white dentist's jacket, with a yellow Star of David on it.*]

DUSSEL. [*To* MR. KRALER] What can I say to thank you . . . ?

MRS. FRANK. [*To* DUSSEL] Mr. Kraler and Miep . . . They're our life line. Without them we couldn't live.

MR. KRALER. Please. Please. You make us seem very heroic. It isn't that at all. We simply don't like the Nazis. [*To* MR. FRANK, *who offers him a drink*] No, thanks. [*Then going on*] We don't like their methods. We don't like . . .

MR. FRANK. [*Smiling*] I know. I know. "No one's going to tell us Dutchmen what to do with our Jews!"

MR. KRALER. [*To* DUSSEL] Pay no attention to Mr. Frank. I'll be up tomorrow to see that they're treating you right. [*To* MR. FRANK] Don't trouble to come down again. Peter will bolt the door after me, won't you, Peter?

PETER. Yes, sir.

MR. FRANK. Thank you, Peter. I'll do it.

MR. KRALER. Good night. Good night.

GROUP. Good night, Mr. Kraler. We'll see you tomorrow, etc., etc.

[MR. KRALER *goes out with* MR. FRANK, MRS. FRANK *gives each one of the "grownups" a glass of cognac.*]

MRS. FRANK. Please, Mr. Dussel, sit down.

[MR. DUSSEL *sinks into a chair.* MRS. FRANK *gives him a glass of cognac.*]

DUSSEL. I'm dreaming. I know it. I can't believe my eyes. Mr. Otto Frank here! [*To* MRS. FRANK] You're not in Switzerland then? A woman told me . . . She said

---

Vocabulary Development: meticulous (mə tik´ yo͞o ləs) *adj.* extremely careful about details

she'd gone to your house . . . the door was open, everything was in disorder, dishes in the sink. She said she found a piece of paper in the wastebasket with an address scribbled on it . . . an address in Zurich. She said you must have escaped to Zurich.

ANNE. Father put that there purposely . . . just so people would think that very thing!

DUSSEL. And you've been *here* all the time?

MRS. FRANK. All the time . . . ever since July.

[ANNE *speaks to her father as he comes back.*]

ANNE. It worked, Pim . . . the address you left! Mr. Dussel says that people believe we escaped to Switzerland.

MR. FRANK. I'm glad. . . . And now let's have a little drink to welcome Mr. Dussel.

[*Before they can drink,* MR. DUSSEL *bolts his drink.* MR. FRANK *smiles and raises his glass.*]

To Mr. Dussel. Welcome. We're very honored to have you with us.

MRS. FRANK. To Mr. Dussel, welcome.

[*The* VAN DAANS *murmur a welcome. The "grownups" drink.*]

MRS. VAN DAAN. Um. That was good.

MR. VAN DAAN. Did Mr. Kraler warn you that you won't get much to eat here? You can imagine . . . three ration books among the seven of us . . . and now you make eight.

[PETER *walks away, humiliated. Outside a street organ is heard dimly.*]

DUSSEL. [*Rising*] Mr. Van Daan, you don't realize what is happening outside that you should warn me of a thing like that. You don't realize what's going on . . .

[*As* MR. VAN DAAN *starts his characteristic pacing,* DUSSEL *turns to speak to the others.*]

Right here in Amsterdam every day hundreds of Jews disappear . . . They surround a block and search house by house. Children come home from school to find their parents gone. Hundreds are being deported . . . people that you and I know . . . the Hallensteins . . . the Wessels . . .

MRS. FRANK. [*In tears*] Oh, no. No!

DUSSEL. They get their call-up notice . . . come to the Jewish theater on such and such a day and hour . . . bring only what you can carry in a rucksack. And if you refuse the call-up notice, then they come and drag you from your home and ship you off to Mauthausen.[4] The death camp!

MRS. FRANK. We didn't know that things had got so much worse.

DUSSEL. Forgive me for speaking so.

4. **Mauthausen** (mou tou´ zən) village in Austria that was the site of a Nazi concentration camp.

Notice Anne's underlined remark. Why did Mr. Frank want everyone to think the family had escaped to Switzerland?

_____

_____

_____

_____

_____

_____

_____

_____

_____

Analyze the historical context. What information does Mr. Dussel provide about what is happening to Jews outside in Amsterdam?

_____

_____

_____

_____

_____

_____

_____

_____

_____

_____

_____

_____

How does the playwright use **staging** to show that Anne is more emotional than the rest of her family?

_____

_____

_____

_____

_____

_____

_____

Analyze the effect of the historical context. Mr. Dussel considers himself more Dutch than Jewish. How do the Germans feel about him, however? What does the bracketed speech reveal?

_____

_____

_____

_____

_____

_____

_____

_____

_____

_____

_____

_____

ANNE. *[Coming to* DUSSEL*]* Do you know the de Waals? . . . What's become of them? Their daughter Jopie and I are in the same class. Jopie's my best friend.

DUSSEL. They are gone.

ANNE. Gone?

DUSSEL. With all the others.

ANNE. Oh, no. Not Jopie!

[She turns away, in tears. MRS. FRANK *motions to* MARGOT *to comfort her.* MARGOT *goes to* ANNE, *putting her arms comfortingly around her.]*

MRS. VAN DAAN. There were some people called Wagner. They lived near us . . . ?

MR. FRANK. *[Interrupting, with a glance at* ANNE*]* I think we should put this off until later. We all have many questions we want to ask . . . But I'm sure that Mr. Dussel would like to get settled before supper.

DUSSEL. Thank you. I would. I brought very little with me.

MR. FRANK. *[Giving him his hat and briefcase]* I'm sorry we can't give you a room alone. But I hope you won't be too uncomfortable. We've had to make strict rules here . . . a schedule of hours . . . We'll tell you after supper. Anne, would you like to take Mr. Dussel to his room?

ANNE. *[Controlling her tears]* If you'll come with me, Mr. Dussel? *[She starts for her room.]*

DUSSEL. *[Shaking hands with each in turn]* Forgive me if I haven't really expressed my gratitude to all of you. This has been such a shock to me. I'd always thought of myself as Dutch. I was born in Holland. My father was born in Holland, and my grandfather. And now . . . after all these years . . . *[He breaks off.]* If you'll excuse me.

*[*DUSSEL *gives a little bow and hurries off after* ANNE. MR. FRANK *and the others are subdued.]*

ANNE. *[Turning on the light]* Well, here we are.

*[*DUSSEL *looks around the room. In the main room* MARGOT *speaks to her mother.]*

MARGOT. The news sounds pretty bad, doesn't it? It's so different from what Mr. Kraler tells us. Mr. Kraler says things are improving.

MR. VAN DAAN. I like it better the way Kraler tells it.

[They resume their occupations, quietly. PETER *goes off into his room. In* ANNE's *room,* ANNE *turns to* DUSSEL.*]*

ANNE. You're going to share the room with me.

DUSSEL. I'm a man who's always lived alone. I haven't had to adjust myself to others. I hope you'll bear with me until I learn.

ANNE. Let me help you. *[She takes his briefcase.]* Do you always live all alone? Have you no family at all?

DUSSEL. No one. *[He opens his medicine case and spreads his bottles on the dressing table.]*

ANNE. How dreadful. You must be terribly lonely.

DUSSEL. I'm used to it.

ANNE. I don't think I could ever get used to it. Didn't you even have a pet? A cat, or a dog?

DUSSEL. I have an allergy for fur-bearing animals. They give me asthma.

ANNE. Oh, dear. Peter has a cat.

DUSSEL. Here? He has it here?

ANNE. Yes. But we hardly ever see it. He keeps it in his room all the time. I'm sure it will be all right.

DUSSEL. Let us hope so. *[He takes some pills to fortify himself.]*

ANNE. That's Margot's bed, where you're going to sleep. I sleep on the sofa there. *[Indicating the clothes hooks on the wall]* We cleared these off for your things. *[She goes over to the window.]* The best part about this room . . . you can look down and see a bit of the street and the canal. There's a houseboat . . . you can see the end of it . . . a bargeman lives there with his family . . . They have a baby and he's just beginning to walk and I'm so afraid he's going to fall into the canal some day. I watch him. . . .

DUSSEL. *[Interrupting]* Your father spoke of a schedule.

ANNE. *[Coming away from the window]* Oh, yes. It's mostly about the times we have to be quiet. And times for the w.c. You can use it now if you like.

DUSSEL. *[Stiffly]* No, thank you.

ANNE. I suppose you think it's awful, my talking about a thing like that. But you don't know how important it can get to be, especially when you're frightened . . . About this room, the way Margot and I did . . . she had it to herself in the afternoons for studying, reading . . . lessons, you know . . . and I took the mornings. Would that be all right with you?

DUSSEL. I'm not at my best in the morning.

ANNE. You stay here in the mornings then. I'll take the room in the afternoons.

DUSSEL. Tell me, when you're in here, what happens to me? Where am I spending my time? In there, with all the people?

ANNE. Yes.

DUSSEL. I see. I see.

ANNE. We have supper at half past six.

DUSSEL. *[Going over to the sofa]* Then, if you don't mind . . . I like to lie down quietly for ten minutes before eating. I find it helps the digestion.

ANNE. Of course. I hope I'm not going to be too much of a bother to you. I seem to be able to get everyone's back up.

[DUSSEL lies down on the sofa, curled up, his back to her.]

© Pearson Education, Inc.

◆ **Literary Analysis**

Imagine the **staging** of the dialogue between Anne and Mr. Dussel. Which character will probably speak quickly and excitedly? Which will probably speak sadly and nervously?

_____

_____

_____

◆ **Literary Analysis**

Circle **stage directions** in the bracketed passage that show that Mr. Dussel is nervous and proper.

◆ **Reading Check**

In the underlined sentence, Mr. Dussel says he gets along well with children. Do you think that is true? Explain.

_____

_____

_____

Summarize how life in the apartment has changed from Scene 2 to Scene 3. Predict what you think may happen in the rest of the play.

_____

_____

_____

_____

_____

_____

_____

_____

_____

_____

_____

DUSSEL. I always get along very well with children. My patients all bring their children to me, because they know I get on well with them. So don't you worry about that.

[ANNE *leans over him, taking his hand and shaking it gratefully.*]

ANNE. Thank you. Thank you, Mr. Dussel.

[*The lights dim to darkness. The curtain falls on the scene.* ANNE'S VOICE *comes to us faintly at first, and then with increasing power.*]

ANNE'S VOICE. . . . And yesterday I finished Cissy Van Marxvelt's latest book. I think she is a first-class writer. I shall definitely let my children read her. Monday the twenty-first of September, nineteen forty-two. Mr. Dussel and I had another battle yesterday. Yes, Mr. Dussel! According to him, nothing, I repeat . . . nothing, is right about me . . . my appearance, my character, my manners. While he was going on at me I thought . . . sometime I'll give you such a smack that you'll fly right up to the ceiling! Why is it that every grownup thinks he knows the way to bring up children? Particularly the grownups that never had any. I keep wishing that Peter was a girl instead of a boy. Then I would have someone to talk to. Margot's a darling, but she takes everything too seriously. To pause for a moment on the subject of Mrs. Van Daan. I must tell you that her attempts to flirt with father are getting her nowhere. Pim, thank goodness, won't play.

[*As she is saying the last lines, the curtain rises on the darkened scene.* ANNE'S *voice fades out.*]

Reader's Response: Do you think the play is going to have a happy ending? Why or why not?

_____

_____

_____

Thinking About the Skill: How does reading the **stage directions** along with the dialogue help you get a full understanding of what is happening in a play?

_____

_____

_____

The Secret Heart

Robert P. Tristam Coffin

Summary

In "The Secret Heart," the speaker recalls a simple event from childhood that has great meaning for him. The speaker recalls waking in the night to see his father standing over his bed. The father is holding a lit match in his cupped hands to help him see his sleeping child. The father's cupped hands make the shape of a heart. The speaker recalls the love and tenderness he saw on his father's face. He recognizes how strong and personal the feelings are. The boy is grateful for the gift his father gives him: a shared secret of total love.

Visual Summary

"The Secret Heart" is a poem that centers on the heart as a symbol.

Symbol	What It Stands For
Heart	Love
	Warmth
	Security
	Support

The Secret Heart
Robert P. Tristram Coffin

*This poem describes one man's memory of a single, vivid moment
from his childhood.*

Across the years he could recall
His father one way best of all.

In the stillest hour of night
The boy awakened to a light.

5 Half in dreams, he saw his sire[1]
With his great hands full of fire.

The man had struck a match to see
If his son slept peacefully.

He held his palms each side the spark
10 His love had <u>kindled</u> in the dark.

His two hands were curved apart
In the <u>semblance</u> of a heart.

He wore, it seemed to his small son,
A bare heart on his hidden one.

15 A heart that gave out such a glow
No son awake could bear to know.

It showed a look upon a face
Too tender for the day to trace.

One instant, it lit all about,
20 And then the secret heart went out.

But it shone long enough for one
To know that hands held up the sun.

Vocabulary Development: kindled (kin´ dəld) *v.* stirred up; awakened
           semblance (sem´ bləns) *n.* appearance

---

1. **sire** (sīr) *n.* father.

Reader's Response: Why do you think the speaker remembers this
moment from his childhood so vividly?

_____

_____

The Wreck of the Hesperus

Henry Wadsworth Longfellow

Summary

"The Wreck of the Hesperus" is about a ship that is destroyed by a fierce snow and sleet storm at sea. The skipper has brought his beautiful young daughter along to keep him company on the trip. An old sailor begs the skipper to sail into a port because he fears a major storm is coming. But the skipper ignores the old man's warning. Soon a cold wind is blowing and waves are crashing over the boat. The skipper wraps his daughter in his warmest coat and ties her to a mast on deck so she won't be washed overboard. The ferocious winds of the storm freeze the skipper to death, wash the crew overboard, and cause the ship to break on a reef. After the storm, a fisherman on shore finds the daughter's frozen, lifeless body, still tied to the mast.

Visual Summary

"The Wreck of the Hesperus" is a narrative poem that shows how a boat skipper's mistakes led to disaster.

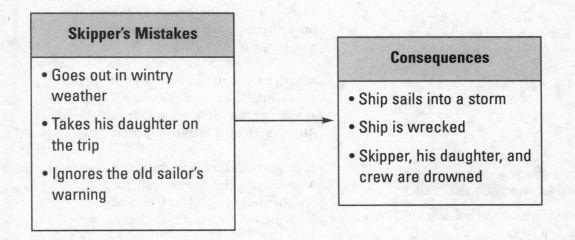

Skipper's Mistakes

- Goes out in wintry weather
- Takes his daughter on the trip
- Ignores the old sailor's warning

Consequences

- Ship sails into a storm
- Ship is wrecked
- Skipper, his daughter, and crew are drowned

Describe what happened in a ship-wreck or an adventure at sea that you know about.

_____

_____

_____

_____

_____

_____

_____

_____

What new character is introduced in the fourth stanza of the **narrative**?

_____

_____

_____

_____

What warning does the old sailor give the skipper?

_____

_____

_____

How does the skipper react?

_____

_____

_____

The Wreck of the Hesperus
Henry Wadsworth Longfellow

Narrative poems tell a story. This narrative poem is a ballad—it tells of dramatic events in a form that resembles a song. The story is based on a shipwreck that occurred off the coast of Gloucester, Massachusetts in 1839.

It was the schooner[1] Hesperus,
    That sailed the wintry sea;
And the skipper had taken his little daughter,
    To bear him company.

5 Blue were her eyes as the fairy-flax,[2]
    Her cheeks like the dawn of day,
And her bosom white as the hawthorn buds
    That ope in the month of May.

The skipper he stood beside the helm,
10   His pipe was in his mouth,
And he watched how the veering flaw[3] did blow
    The smoke now West, now South.

Then up and spake an old sailor,
    Had sailed to the Spanish Main,[4]
15 "I pray thee, put into yonder port,
    For I fear a hurricane.

"Last night the moon had a golden ring,
    And tonight no moon we see!"
The skipper he blew a whiff from his pipe,
20   And a <u>scornful</u> laugh laughed he.

Colder and colder blew the wind,
    A <u>gale</u> from the Northeast,
The snow fell hissing in the brine,
    And the billows frothed like yeast.

25 Down came the storm, and smote amain,[5]
    The vessel in its strength;

Vocabulary Development: scornful (skôrn´ fəl) *adj.* full of contempt or disdain
                   gale (gāl) *n.* strong wind

---

1. **schooner** (skoon´ ər) *n.* ship with two or more masts.
2. **fairy-flax** slender plant with delicate blue flowers.
3. **veering flaw** gust of wind that changes direction.
4. **Spanish Main** coastal region bordering the Caribbean Sea.
5. **smote** (smōt) **amain** (əmān´) struck with great, vigorous force.

She shuddered and paused, like a frighted steed,
    Then leaped her cable's length.
"Come hither! come hither! my little daughter,
30   And do not tremble so;
For I can weather the roughest gale,
    That ever wind did blow."

He wrapped her warm in his seaman's coat
    Against the stinging blast;
35 He cut a rope from a broken spar,[6]
    And bound her to the mast.

"O father! I hear the church-bells ring,
    O say, what may it be?"
"'Tis a fog-bell on a rock-bound coast!—"
40   And he steered for the open sea.

"O father! I hear the sound of guns,
    O say, what may it be?"
"Some ship in distress, that cannot live
    In such an angry sea!"

45 "O father! I see a gleaming light,
    O say, what may it be?"
But the father answered never a word,
    A frozen corpse was he.

Lashed to the helm, all stiff and stark,
50   With his face turned to the skies,
The lantern gleamed through the gleaming snow
    On his fixed and glassy eyes.

Then the maiden clasped her hands and prayed
    That savèd she might be;
55 And she thought of Christ, who stilled the wave,
    On the Lake of Galilee.[7]

And fast through the midnight dark and drear
    Through the whistling sleet and snow,
Like a sheeted ghost, the vessel swept
60   Towards the reef of Norman's Woe.

And ever the fitful gusts between
    A sound came from the land;
It was the sound of the trampling surf,
    On the rocks and the hard sea-sand.

---

6. **spar** (spär) *n.* pole supporting or extending the sail of a ship.
7. **Lake of Galilee** (gal′ ə lē′) lake in northeastern Israel.

◆ **Reading Strategy**

A dash is a type of **punctuation** that shows that a thought is not finished. When you read lines 39–40 according to punctuation, what does the dash help you guess about the skipper's unfinished thought?

_____

_____

_____

◆ **Reading Check**

What happens just before the skipper steers for the open sea?

_____

_____

_____

◆ **Literary Analysis**

What plot events does this **ballad** tell about in lines 45–56?

_____

_____

_____

_____

◆ **Reading Check**

Why does the Hesperus look "like a sheeted ghost"?

_____

_____

What is the ship doing in lines 57–60?

_____

_____

The <u>breakers</u> were right beneath her bows,
    She drifted a dreary wreck,
And a whooping billow swept the crew
    Like icicles from her deck.

She struck where the white and fleecy waves
70   Looked soft as carded[8] wool,
But the cruel rocks, they gored[9] her side
    Like the horns of an angry bull.

Her rattling shrouds,[10] all sheathed in ice,
    With the masts went by the board;
75 Like a vessel of glass, she stove[11] and sank,
    Ho! ho! the breakers roared!

At daybreak, on the bleak sea-beach,
    A fisherman stood aghast,[12]
To see the form of a maiden fair,
80   Lashed close to a drifting mast.

The salt sea was frozen on her breast,
    The salt tears in her eyes;
And he saw her hair, like the brown sea-weed,
    On the billows fall and rise.

85 Such was the wreck of the Hesperus,
    In the midnight and the snow!
Christ save us all from a death like this,
    On the reef of Norman's Woe!

Vocabulary Development: **breakers** (brāk´ ərz) *n.* waves that break
into foam

---

8. **carded** combed.
9. **gored** pierced.
10. **shrouds** ropes or wires stretched from the ship's side to the mast.
11. **stove** broke.
12. **aghast** (ə gäst´) *adj.* in horror; terrified.

Reader's Response: What would you say to the skipper about his decision not to take the old sailor's advice?

_____

_____

Thinking About the Skill: Give an example of one stanza that punctuation helps you to read effectively.

_____

_____

◆ **Reading Strategy**

Label the end of each line in the bracketed stanzas with *brief pause,* *full stop,* or *no stop,* based on punctuation. Then, read the lines aloud **according to punctuation**.

◆ **Reading Check**

Rewrite lines 73–80 in your own words. What has happened to the ship?

_____

_____

_____

_____

_____

_____

_____

_____

_____

_____

_____

_____

_____

_____

_____

_____

_____

Invocation *from* John Brown's Body
Stephen Vincent Benét

Summary

This selection from *John Brown's Body* is small part of a much longer epic poem. In this selection, the speaker calls on the "American muse," or the national spirit, to inspire him. America is so big and varied, however, that the speaker finds it hard to sum up the American spirit in words.

Visual Summary

The invocation from *John Brown's Body* describes some of the many features of the American muse.

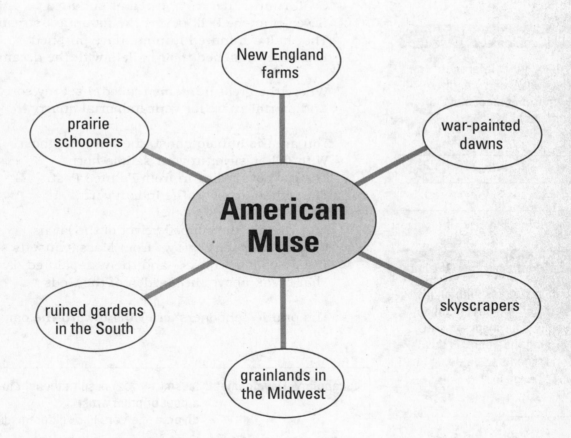

Who is the poet addressing?

_____

_____

_____

In lines 1–14, what **inference**, or educated guess, can you draw about who Benét means by "the great huntsmen"?

_____

_____

_____

_____

An **epic poem** begins with an invocation in which the poet humbly begs the muse for inspiration or help in writing the poem. Is this what Benét seems to be doing in lines 13–14? Explain.

_____

_____

_____

_____

_____

Invocation *from* John Brown's Body
Stephen Vincent Benét

John Brown was a white abolitionist who fought to abolish slavery. In 1859, he was hanged for treason and for "conspiring with slaves to rebel." His commitment to freedom, and his trial and execution, captured people's attention and moved the country toward the Civil War. This poem about him has been called "an American epic."

American <u>muse</u>, whose strong and <u>diverse</u> heart
So many men have tried to understand
But only made it smaller with their art,
Because you are as various as your land,

5 As mountainous-deep, as flowered with blue rivers,
Thirsty with deserts, buried under snows,
As native as the shape of Navajo quivers,
And native, too, as the sea-voyaged rose.

Swift runner, never captured or subdued,
10 Seven-branched elk beside the mountain stream,
That half a hundred hunters have pursued
But never matched their bullets with the dream,

Where the great huntsmen failed, I set my sorry[1]
And mortal snare for your immortal quarry.[2]

15 You are the buffalo-ghost, the broncho-ghost
With dollar-silver in your saddle-horn,
The cowboys riding in from Painted Post,
The Indian arrow in the Indian corn,

And you are the clipped velvet of the lawns
20 Where Shropshire[3] grows from Massachusetts sods,
The grey Maine rocks—and the war-painted dawns
That break above the Garden of the Gods.[4]

The prairie-schooners[5] crawling toward the oar

Vocabulary Development: muse (myo͞oz) *n.* spirit thought to inspire a poet or other artist
diverse (də vərs´) *adj.* different; dissimilar

---

1. **sorry** (sôr´ē) *adj.* inferior in quality.
2. **quarry** (kwôr´ē) *n.* something being hunted or pursued.
3. **Shropshire** (shräp´shir) county in western England.
4. **Garden of the Gods** park in the Rocky Mountains of Colorado.
5. **prairie-schooners** *n.* covered wagons used by pioneers in the 19th century to cross the American prairies.

And the cheap car, parked by the station-door.

25 Where the skyscrapers lift their foggy plumes
Of stranded smoke out of a stony mouth
You are that high stone and its arrogant fumes,
And you are ruined gardens in the South

And bleak New England farms, so winter-white
30 Even their roofs look lonely, and the deep
The middle grainland where the wind of night
Is like all blind earth sighing in her sleep.

A friend, an enemy, a sacred hag
With two tied oceans in her medicine-bag.

35 They tried to fit you with an English song
And clip your speech into the English tale.
But, even from the first, the words went wrong,
The catbird pecked away the nightingale.[6]

The homesick men begot high-cheekboned things
40 Whose wit was whittled with a different song
And Thames[7] and all the rivers of the kings
Ran into Mississippi and were drowned.

They planted England with stubborn trust.
But the cleft[8] dust was never English dust.

45 So how to see you as you really are,
So how to suck the pure, distillate,[9] stored
Essence of essence from the hidden star
And make it pierce like a riposting[10] sword.

For, as we hunt you down, you must escape
50 And we pursue a shadow of our own
That can be caught in a magician's cape
But has the flatness of a painted stone.

Vocabulary Development: essence (es´ əns) *n.* something that
exists

---

6. **catbird . . . nightingale** The catbird is native to North America; the nightingale is a
bird of Europe and Great Britain.
7. **Thames** (temz) *n.* a river in England which flows through London.
8. **cleft** (kleft) *adj.* split; divided.
9. **distillate** (dis´tə lāt) *n.* the pure essence of something.
10. **riposting** (ri pōst´iŋ) *v.* rapidly thrusting.

Invocation *from* John Brown's Body **203**

◆ **Reading Check**

In lines 15–30, what places, things,
and qualities does Benét associate
with the American muse?

_____

_____

_____

_____

◆ **Reading Strategy**

In lines 35 and 43, to whom does
the word "they" refer?

_____

Based on the footnotes and what
you know about early American
history, what can you **infer**, or
guess, about Benét's meaning in
lines 35–44?

_____

_____

_____

_____

_____

◆ **Reading Strategy**

In lines 45–52, Benét implies that
poets find it hard to write well
about America. What **inference**
can you draw about the reason?

_____

_____

_____

_____

_____

_____

◆ Reading Strategy

What do the first three things in the bracketed passage have in common?

_____

_____

From the bracketed lines, what **inference** can you draw about what Benét means by "the American thing"?

_____

_____

_____

_____

◆ Literary Analysis

In the invocation to an **epic poem**, the poet praises the muse's power to inspire him. After reading lines 59–62, what do you think most inspires Benét about the "American muse"? Circle the two characteristics of the muse that most impress him.

_____

_____

_____

_____

_____

_____

_____

_____

_____

Never the running stag, the gull at wing,
The pure elixir,[11] the American thing.

55   And yet, at moments when the mind was hot
With something fierier than joy or grief,
When each known spot was an eternal spot
And every leaf was an immortal leaf,

I think that I have seen you, not as won,
60   But clad in diverse semblances and powers,
Always the same, as light falls from the sun,
And always different, as the differing hours.

Vocabulary Development: semblances (sem´ bləns əs) *n.* outward forms or appearances

---

11. **elixir** (ē liks´ir) *n.* underlying principle.

Reader's Response: What inspires you about America?

_____

_____

_____

_____

_____

_____

Thinking About the Skill: Give at least one example of a difficult passage in this poem that drawing inferences helps you to understand.

_____

_____

_____

_____

_____

_____

Why the Waves Have Whitecaps

Zora Neale Hurston

Summary

In "Why the Waves Have Whitecaps," an African American folk tale, both the wind and the water are women. They spend a lot of time talking to each other. Mrs. Wind brags constantly to Mrs. Water about her children. Her children are breezes, gales, and other kinds of winds. Mrs. Water gets tired of listening to the bragging. One day, Mrs. Wind sends her children to Mrs. Water for a drink. Mrs. Water drowns them. When Mrs. Wind passes over the ocean calling for her lost children, white feathers come up to the top of the water. That explains why waves have whitecaps. Storms at sea are the wind and the water fighting over the children.

Visual Summary

Like many folk tales, this one seeks to explain a fact of nature.

Fact of Nature	Folk Tale's Explanation
The whitecaps of waves	• Mrs. Water gets tired of hearing Mrs. Wind brag about her children. • Mrs. Water drowns Mrs. Wind's children. • The whitecaps are feathers that appear on the waves. • The feathers appear when Mrs. Wind calls for her children.

Describe a way that wind and water are connected on an ocean or lake.

_____

_____

_____

◆ Literary Analysis

Circle words in the bracketed passage that are part of the oral tradition of **folk tales** and would probably not be found in a dictionary.

Mark the Text!

◆ Reading Strategy

What does the underlined sentence tell you about where the people who first told this story probably lived?

_____

_____

_____

_____

_____

_____

_____

_____

_____

Why the Waves Have Whitecaps
Zora Neale Hurston

Long before scientists explained causes of natural events, people developed folk tales filled with unusual and entertaining explanations.

De wind is a woman, and de water is a woman too. They useter[1] talk together a whole heap. Mrs. Wind useter go set down by de ocean and talk and patch and crochet.

They was jus' like all lady people. They loved to talk about their chillun, and brag on 'em.

Mrs. Water useter say, "Look at my chillun! Ah[2] got de biggest and de littlest in de world. All kinds of chillun. Every color in de world, and every shape!"

De wind lady bragged louder than de water woman:

"Oh, but Ah got mo' different chilluns than anybody in de world. They flies, they walks, they swims, they sings, they talks, they cries. They got all de colors from de sun. Lawd, my chillun sho is a pleasure. 'Tain't nobody got no babies like mine."

Mrs. Water got tired of hearin' 'bout Mrs. Wind's chillun so she got so she hated 'em.

One day a whole passle[3] of her chillun come to Mrs. Wind and says: "Mama, wese thirsty. Kin we go git us a cool drink of water?"

She says, "Yeah chillun. Run on over to Mrs. Water and hurry right back soon."

When them chillun went to squinch they thirst Mrs. Water grabbed 'em all and drowned 'em.

When her chillun didn't come home, de wind woman got worried. So she went on down to de water and ast for her babies.

"Good evenin' Mis' Water, you see my chillun today?"

De water woman tole her, "No-oo-oo."

Mrs. Wind knew her chillun had come down to Mrs. Water's house, so she passed over de ocean callin' her chillun, and every time she call de white feathers would come up on top of de water. And dat's how come we got white caps on waves. It's de feathers comin' up when de wind woman calls her lost babies.

When you see a storm on de water, it's de wind and de water fightin' over dem chillun.

---

1. **useter** (yōō´ stə) *v.* dialect for "used to."
2. **Ah** *pron.* dialect for "I."
3. **passle** *n.* dialect for "parcel."

Reader's Response: How do you know that the story is supposed to be funny and not serious?

_____

_____

_____

Coyote Steals the Sun and Moon

Zuni myth, retold by Richard Erdoes and Alfonso Ortiz

Summary

"Coyote Steals the Sun and the Moon" is a myth, or an ancient tale, that tells about how the sun and the moon got in the sky. It was a very dark time. Coyote and Eagle team up to go looking for a source of light. They find the Kachinas, who keep the sun and the moon in two boxes. Coyote and Eagle decide to steal the sun. Eagle flies off with the large box. Coyote runs below and begs Eagle to let him carry the box. Eagle finally agrees and gives Coyote the box. Coyote is so curious that he opens the box. He finds out that Eagle had put both the sun and the moon in one box. When Coyote opens the box, the sun and the moon escape into the sky. With the sun and the moon so far away in the sky, fall and winter come to the land.

Visual Summary

Like many myths, this one tries to answer questions about nature.

Questions About Nature	Explanations
• How did the sun and the moon get into the sky? • Why do we have the seasons of fall and winter?	• The sun and the moon escape into the sky when Coyote opens the box. • With the sun and the moon high in the sky, the earth gets colder. Fall and winter result.

Coyote Steals the Sun and Moon
Zuni Myth

In Zuni tradition, the coyote is sly and tricky, but he sometimes tricks himself, too. Imagine what would happen if the coyote got possession of the sun and moon. What might happen to the world?

Coyote is a bad hunter who never kills anything. Once he watched Eagle hunting rabbits, catching one after another—more rabbits than he could eat. Coyote thought, "I'll team up with Eagle so I can have enough meat." Coyote is always up to something.

"Friend," Coyote said to Eagle, "we should hunt together. Two can catch more than one."

"Why not?" Eagle said, and so they began to hunt in partnership. Eagle caught many rabbits, but all Coyote caught was some little bugs.

At this time the world was still dark; the sun and moon had not yet been put in the sky. "Friend," Coyote said to Eagle, "no wonder I can't catch anything; I can't see. Do you know where we can get some light?"

"You're right, friend, there should be some light," Eagle said. "I think there's a little toward the west. Let's try and find it."

And so they went looking for the sun and moon. They came to a big river, which Eagle flew over. Coyote swam, and swallowed so much water that he almost drowned. He crawled out with his fur full of mud, and Eagle asked, "Why don't you fly like me?"

"You have wings; I just have hair," Coyote said. "I can't fly without feathers."

At last they came to a pueblo,[1] where the Kachinas[2] happened to be dancing. The people invited Eagle and Coyote to sit down and have something to eat while they watched the sacred dances. <u>Seeing the power of the Kachinas, Eagle said, "I believe these are the people who have light."</u>

Coyote, who had been looking all around, pointed out two boxes, one large and one small, that the people opened whenever they wanted light. To produce a lot of light, they opened the lid of the big box, which contained the sun. For less light they opened the small box, which held the moon.

Coyote nudged Eagle. "Friend, did you see that? They have all the light we need in the big box. Let's steal it."

"You always want to steal and rob. I say we should just borrow it."

"They won't lend it to us."

---

1. **pueblo** (pweb´ lō) Native American village in the southwestern United States.
2. **Kachinas** (kə chē´ nəz) masked dancers who imitate gods or the spirits of their ancestors.

◆ **Activate Prior Knowledge**

Describe an animal in a folk tale or fairy tale that you read when you were younger. What human qualities did the animal have?

_____

_____

_____

_____

◆ **Literary Analysis**

Folk tales often explain something in nature. What do you think this tale will explain? Underline a sentence in the bracketed passage that helps you figure out the answer. Then, write the answer below.

_____

_____

_____

_____

◆ **Stop to Reflect**

Do you agree with Coyote in the underlined sentence that light gives people power? Explain.

_____

_____

_____

_____

_____

_____

"You may be right," said Eagle. "Let's wait till they finish dancing and then steal it."

After a while the Kachinas went home to sleep, and Eagle scooped up the large box and flew off. Coyote ran along trying to keep up, panting, his tongue hanging out. Soon he yelled up to Eagle, "Ho, friend, let me carry the box a little way."

"No, no," said Eagle, "you never do anything right."

He flew on, and Coyote ran after him. After a while Coyote shouted again: "Friend, you're my chief, and it's not right for you to carry the box; people will call me lazy. Let me have it."

"No, no, you always mess everything up." And Eagle flew on and Coyote ran along.

So it went for a stretch, and then Coyote started again. "Ho, friend, it isn't right for you to do this. What will people think of you and me?"

"I don't care what people think. I'm going to carry this box."

Again Eagle flew on and again Coyote ran after him. Finally Coyote begged for the fourth time: "Let me carry it. You're the chief, and I'm just Coyote. Let me carry it."

Eagle couldn't stand any more pestering. Also, Coyote had asked him four times, and if someone asks four times, you better give him what he wants. Eagle said, "Since you won't let up on me, go ahead and carry the box for a while. But promise not to open it."

"Oh, sure, oh yes, I promise." They went on as before, but now Coyote had the box. Soon Eagle was far ahead, and Coyote lagged behind a hill where Eagle couldn't see him. "I wonder what the light looks like, inside there," he said to himself. "Why shouldn't I take a peek? Probably there's something extra in the box, something good that Eagle wants to keep to himself."

And Coyote opened the lid. Now, not only was the sun inside, but the moon also. Eagle had put them both together, thinking that it would be easier to carry one box than two.

As soon as Coyote opened the lid, the moon escaped, flying high into the sky. At once all the plants shriveled up and turned brown. Just as quickly, all the leaves fell off the trees, and it was winter. Trying to catch the moon and put it back in the box, Coyote ran in pursuit as it skipped away from him. Meanwhile the sun flew out and rose into the sky.

Vocabulary Development: shriveled (shriv´ əld) v. dried up; withered
pursuit (pər sōōt´) n. following in order to overtake and capture

© Pearson Education, Inc.

Coyote Steals the Sun and Moon **209**

◆ **Reading Strategy**

What qualities does Coyote possess that are considered unworthy in the **cultural context** of the Zuni people?

_____

_____

_____

_____

_____

◆ **Literary Analysis**

Circle a Zuni custom that is included in the bracketed paragraph. Do you think this is a good custom? Why or why not?

_____

_____

_____

_____

_____

◆ **Reading Check**

On the lines below, list four events that occur after Coyote opens the box.

_____

_____

_____

_____

_____

_____

_____

According to the underlined paragraph, summer is appreciated more than winter in the Zuni **culture.** Why do you think this is so?

_____

_____

_____

_____

_____

_____

_____

_____

_____

_____

_____

_____

It drifted far away, and the peaches, squashes, and melons shriveled up with cold.

Eagle turned and flew back to see what had delayed Coyote. "You fool! Look what you've done!" he said. "You let the sun and moon escape, and now it's cold." Indeed, it began to snow, and Coyote shivered. "Now your teeth are chattering," Eagle said, "and it's your fault that cold has come into the world."

It's true. If it weren't for Coyote's curiosity and mischief making, we wouldn't have winter; we could enjoy summer all the time.

Reader's Response: What advice would you like to give to Eagle about dealing with Coyote?

_____

_____

_____

Thinking About the Skill: In what way does recognizing qualities of folk tales make them easier to understand?

_____

_____

_____

Pecos Bill: The Cyclone
Harold W. Felton

Summary

Pecos Bill's plans to enjoy a fine Fourth of July celebration are ruined when a cyclone arrives. Bill is determined not to let the cyclone ruin the fun, so he leaps onto the back of the cyclone and rides it like a bucking bronco. The cyclone tries all sorts of tricks, but it cannot throw off Pecos Bill. Gradually, the cyclone's strength drains away, so that it cannot even hold up Pecos Bill. When he falls to the ground, Death Valley is created.

Visual Summary

Every year, a cyclone breaks up Pecos Bill's Fourth of July celebration.

Pecos Bill builds "'fraid holes." People run into them when the cyclone comes.

One Fourth of July, the cyclone is very angry. Pecos Bill is the only one who does not go into a "'fraid hole."

Pecos Bill rides the cyclone until the cyclone comes apart completely.

When Pecos Bill falls from the cyclone, he creates Death Valley.

_____

_____

_____

_____

◆ Literary Analysis

In the **cultural context** of the Old West, people admired individualism and courage. Underline a sentence in the bracketed paragraph that shows Pecos Bill's courage.

◆ Reading Check

What is a posthole?

_____

_____

_____

Notice the underlined sentence. Can a posthole really be blown away by a cyclone? Why or why not?

_____

_____

_____

Pecos Bill: The Cyclone
Harold W. Felton

If you came face to face with a cyclone, would you run away or hide—or would you just climb on board for a wild ride like Pecos Bill does?

One of Bill's greatest feats, if not the greatest feat of all time, occurred unexpectedly one Fourth of July. He had invented the Fourth of July some years before. It was a great day for the cowpunchers.[1] They had taken to it right off like the real Americans they were. But the celebration had always ended on a dismal note. Somehow it seemed to be spoiled by a cyclone.

Bill had never minded the cyclone much. The truth is he rather liked it. But the other celebrants ran into caves for safety. He invented cyclone cellars for them. He even named the cellars. He called them "'fraid holes." Pecos wouldn't even say the word "afraid." The cyclone was something like he was. It was big and strong too. He always stood by musing[2] pleasantly as he watched it.

The cyclone caused Bill some trouble, though. Usually it would destroy a few hundred miles of fence by blowing the postholes away. But it wasn't much trouble for him to fix it. All he had to do was to go and get the postholes and then take them back and put the fence posts in them. The holes were rarely ever blown more than twenty or thirty miles.

In one respect Bill even welcomed the cyclone, for it blew so hard it blew the earth away from his wells. The first time this happened, he thought the wells would be a total loss. There they were, sticking up several hundred feet out of the ground. As wells they were useless. But he found he could cut them up into lengths and sell them for postholes to farmers in Iowa and Nebraska. It was very profitable, especially after he invented a special posthole saw to cut them with. He didn't use that type of posthole himself. He got the prairie dogs to dig his for him. He simply caught a few gross[3] of prairie dogs and set them down at proper intervals. The prairie dog would dig a hole. Then Bill would put a post in it. The prairie dog would get disgusted and go down the row ahead of the others and dig another hole. Bill fenced all of Texas and parts of New Mexico and Arizona in this manner. He took a few contracts and fenced most of the Southern Pacific right of way too. That's the reason it is so crooked. He had trouble getting the prairie dogs to run a straight fence.

As for his wells, the badgers dug them. The system was the same as with the prairie dogs. The labor was cheap so it

---

1. **cowpunchers** (kou´ pun chərz) *n.* cowboys.
2. **musing** (myo͞o´ zin) *adj.* thinking deeply.
3. **gross** (grōs) *n.* twelve dozen.

didn't make much difference if the cyclone did spoil some of the wells. The badgers were digging all of the time anyway. They didn't seem to care whether they dug wells or just badger holes.

One year he tried shipping the prairie dog holes up north, too, for postholes. It was not successful. They didn't keep in storage and they couldn't stand the handling in shipping. After they were installed they seemed to wear out quickly. Bill always thought the difference in climate had something to do with it.

It should be said that in those days there was only one cyclone. It was the first and original cyclone, bigger and more terrible by far than the small cyclones of today. It usually stayed by itself up north around Kansas and Oklahoma and didn't bother anyone much. But it was attracted by the noise of the Fourth of July celebration and without fail managed to put in an appearance before the close of the day.

On this particular Fourth of July, the celebration had gone off fine. The speeches were loud and long. The contests and games were hard fought. The high point of the day was Bill's exhibition with Widow Maker, which came right after he showed off Scat and Rat. People seemed never to tire of seeing them in action. The mountain lion was almost useless as a work animal after his accident, and the snake had grown old and somewhat infirm, and was troubled with rheumatism in his rattles. But they too enjoyed the Fourth of July and liked to make a public appearance. They relived the old days.

Widow Maker had put on a good show, bucking as no ordinary horse could ever buck. Then Bill undertook to show the gaits[4] he had taught the palomino.[5] Other mustangs[6] at that time had only two gaits. Walking and running. Only Widow Maker could pace. But now Bill had developed and taught him other gaits. Twenty-seven in all. Twenty-three forward and three reverse. He was very proud of the achievement. He showed off the slow gaits and the crowd was eager for more.

He showed the walk, trot, canter, lope, jog, slow rack, fast rack, single foot, pace, stepping pace, fox trot, running walk and the others now known. Both men and horses confuse the various gaits nowadays. Some of the gaits are now thought to be the same, such as the rack and the single foot. But with Widow Maker and Pecos Bill, each one was different. Each was precise and to be distinguished from the others. No one had ever imagined such a thing.

Then the cyclone came! All of the people except Bill ran into the 'fraid holes. Bill was annoyed. He stopped the performance. The remaining gaits were not shown. From that day to this horses have used no more than the gaits Widow

---

4. **gaits** (gāts) *n.* foot movements of a horse.
5. **palomino** (pal′ ə mē′ nō) *n.* a light-tan or golden-brown horse with a cream-colored mane and tail.
6. **mustangs** (mus′ taŋz) *n.* wild horses.

◆ Stop to Reflect

Does the author think people will believe that Bill really shipped prairie dog holes up north? Why does he tell this "fact"?

_____

_____

_____

_____

◆ Reading Strategy

What do you **predict** the cyclone will do? What detail leads you to this prediction?

_____

_____

_____

_____

◆ Literary Analysis

In the **cultural context** of the Old West, people admired experts at horseback riding. Underline sentences in the bracketed passage that show that Pecos Bill was an expert horseman.

Story Clue	My Prediction

Proved   ☐ True
          ☐ False

◆ **Reading Check**

The author gives the cyclone human qualities and feelings. Underline some of these human emotions mentioned in the brack-eted passage.

Maker exhibited that day. It is unfortunate that the really fast gaits were not shown. If they were, horses might be much faster today than they are.

Bill glanced up at the cyclone and the quiet smile on his face faded into a frown. He saw the cyclone was angry. Very, very angry indeed.

The cyclone had always been the center of attention. Everywhere it went people would look up in wonder, fear and amazement. It had been the undisputed master of the country. It had observed Bill's rapid climb to fame and had seen the Fourth of July celebration grow. It had been keeping an eye on things all right.

In the beginning, the Fourth of July crowd had aroused its curiosity. It liked nothing more than to show its superiority and power by breaking the crowd up sometime during the day. But every year the crowd was larger. This preyed on the cyclone's mind. This year it did not come to watch. It deliberately came to spoil the celebration. Jealous of Bill and of his success, it resolved to do away with the whole institution of the Fourth of July once and for all. So much havoc and destruction would be wrought that there would never be another Independence Day Celebration. On that day, in future years, it would circle around the horizon leering[7] and gloating. At least, so it thought.

The cyclone was resolved, also, to do away with this bold fellow who did not hold it in awe and run for the 'fraid hole at its approach. For untold years it had been the most powerful thing in the land. And now, here was a mere man who threatened its position. More! Who had <u>usurped</u> its position!

When Bill looked at the horizon and saw the cyclone coming, he recognized the anger and rage. While a cyclone does not often smile, Bill had felt from the beginning that it was just a grouchy fellow who never had a pleasant word for anyone. But now, instead of merely an unpleasant character, Bill saw all the viciousness of which an angry cyclone is capable. He had no way of knowing that the cyclone saw its kingship tottering and was determined to stop this man who threatened its supremacy.

But Bill understood the violence of the onslaught even as the monster came into view. He knew he must meet it. The center of the cyclone was larger than ever before. The fact is, the cyclone had been training for this fight all winter and spring. It was in best form and at top weight. It headed straight for Bill intent on his destruction. In an instant it was upon him. Bill had sat quietly and silently on the great

---

Vocabulary Development: usurped (yо̅о̅ surpt´) *v.* took power or authority away from

---

7. **leering** (lir´ iŋ) *adj.* looking with malicious triumph.

pacing mustang. But his mind was working rapidly. In the split second between his first sight of the monster and the time for action he had made his plans. Pecos Bill was ready! Ready and waiting!

Green clouds were dripping from the cyclone's jaws. Lightning flashed from its eyes as it swept down upon him. Its plan was to envelop Bill in one mighty grasp. Just as it was upon him, Bill turned Widow Maker to its left. This was a clever move for the cyclone was right-handed, and while it had been training hard to get its left in shape, that was not its best side. Bill gave rein to his mount. <u>Widow Maker wheeled and turned on a dime</u> which Pecos had, with great foresight[8] and accuracy, thrown to the ground to mark the exact spot for this maneuver. It was the first time that anyone had thought of turning on a dime. Then he urged the great horse forward. The cyclone, filled with surprise, lost its balance and rushed forward at an increased speed. It went so fast that it met itself coming back. This confused the cyclone, but it did not confuse Pecos Bill. He had expected that to happen. Widow Maker went into his twenty-first gait and edged up close to the whirlwind. Soon they were running neck and neck.

At the proper instant Bill grabbed the cyclone's ears, kicked himself free of the stirrups and pulled himself lightly on its back. Bill never used spurs on Widow Maker. Sometimes he wore them for show and because he liked the jingling sound they made. They made a nice accompaniment for his cowboy songs. But he had not been singing, so he had no spurs. He did not have his rattlesnake for a quirt.[9] Of course there was no bridle. It was man against monster! There he was! Pecos Bill astride a raging cyclone, slick heeled and without a saddle!

The cyclone was taken by surprise at this sudden turn of events. But it was undaunted. It was sure of itself. Months of training had given it a conviction that it was <u>invincible</u>. With a mighty heave, it twisted to its full height. Then it fell back suddenly, twisting and turning violently, so that before it came back to earth, it had turned around a thousand times. Surely no rider could ever withstand such an attack. No rider ever had. Little wonder. No one had ever ridden a cyclone before. But Pecos Bill did! He fanned the tornado's ears with his hat and dug his heels into the demon's flanks and yelled, "Yipee-ee!"

The people who had run for shelter began to come out. The audience further enraged the cyclone. It was bad enough

---

Vocabulary Development: invincible (in vin´ sə bəl) *adj.* unbeatable

---

8. **foresight** (fôr´ sīt) *n.* the act of seeing beforehand.
9. **quirt** (kwurt) *n.* short-handled riding whip with a braided rawhide lash.

◆ **Literary Analysis**

Mark the Text

In the Old West, wrestling and horseback riding were important activities. As you read the next few paragraphs, underline parts that describe a wrestling match between Pecos Bill and the cyclone. Circle parts that describe horseback riding.

◆ **Reading Check**

What do you think the underlined expression "turned on a dime" means? Check your answer by looking in a dictionary entry for the word *dime*.

_____

_____

_____

_____

_____

◆ **Reading Check**

The cyclone and Pecos Bill are both good fighters. List two qualities that make each of them a tough opponent.

Cyclone

1. _____

2. _____

Pecos Bill

1. _____

2. _____

Predict what the cyclone will do after being embarrassed by Pecos Bill. Then, read ahead to check your prediction.

_____

_____

_____

_____

_____

◆ Literary Analysis

What qualities does Bill show in the bracketed paragraph that make him seem like a hero in the **cultural context** of the Old West? To help make your list, circle some of his actions that demonstrate these qualities.

_____

_____

_____

_____

_____

_____

◆ Reading Check

According to the story, how were Death Valley and the Grand Canyon formed?

_____

_____

_____

to be disgraced by having a man astride it. It was unbearable not to have thrown him. To have all the people see the failure was too much! It got down flat on the ground and rolled over and over. Bill retained his seat throughout this ruse.[10] Evidence of this desperate but <u>futile</u> stratagem[11] remains today. The great Staked Plains, or as the Mexicans call it, *Llano Estacado,* is the result. Its small, rugged mountains were covered with trees at the time. The rolling of the cyclone destroyed the mountains, the trees, and almost everything else in the area. The destruction was so complete, that part of the country is flat and treeless to this day. When the settlers came, there were no landmarks to guide them across the vast unmarked space, so they drove stakes in the ground to mark the trails. That is the reason it is called "Staked Plains." Here is an example of the proof of the events of history by careful and painstaking research. It is also an example of how seemingly <u>inexplicable</u> geographical facts can be explained.

It was far more dangerous for the rider when the cyclone shot straight up to the sky. Once there, the twister tried the same thing it had tried on the ground. It rolled on the sky. It was no use. Bill could not be unseated. He kept his place, and he didn't have a sky hook with him either.

As for Bill, he was having the time of his life, shouting at the top of his voice, kicking his opponent in the ribs and jabbing his thumb in its flanks. It responded and went on a wild bucking rampage over the entire West. It used all the bucking tricks known to the wildest broncos as well as those known only to cyclones. The wind howled furiously and beat against the fearless rider. The rain poured. The lightning flashed around his ears. The fight went on and on. Bill enjoyed himself immensely. In spite of the elements he easily kept his place. . . .

The raging cyclone saw this out of the corner of its eye. It knew then who the victor was. It was twisting far above the Rocky Mountains when the awful truth came to it. In a horrible heave it disintegrated! Small pieces of cyclone flew in all directions. Bill still kept his seat on the main central portion until that rained out from under him. Then he jumped to a nearby streak of lightning and slid down it toward earth. But it was raining so hard that the rain put out the lightning. When it fizzled out from under him, Bill dropped the rest of the way. He lit in what is now called Death Valley. He hit quite hard, as is apparent from the fact that he so compressed the place that it is still two hundred and seventy-six feet below sea level. The Grand Canyon was washed out by the rain, though it must be

---

Vocabulary Development: futile (fyo͞ot′ əl) *adj.* useless; hopeless
inexplicable (in eks′ pli kə bəl) *adj.* unexplainable

---

10. **ruse** (ro͞oz) *n.* trick.
11. **stratagem** (strat′ ə jəm) *n.* plan for defeating an opponent.

understood that this happened after Paul Bunyan had given it a good start by carelessly dragging his ax behind him when he went west a short time before.

The cyclones and the hurricanes and the tornadoes nowadays are the small pieces that broke off of the big cyclone Pecos Bill rode. In fact, the rainstorms of the present day came into being in the same way. There are always skeptics, but even they will recognize the logic of the proof of this event. They will recall that even now it almost always rains on the Fourth of July. That is because the rainstorms of today still retain some of the characteristics of the giant cyclone that met its comeuppance at the hands of Pecos Bill.

Bill lay where he landed and looked up at the sky, but he could see no sign of the cyclone. Then he laughed softly as he felt the warm sand of Death Valley on his back. . . .

It was a rough ride though, and Bill had resisted unusual tensions and pressures. When he got on the cyclone he had a twenty-dollar gold piece and a bowie knife[12] in his pocket. The tremendous force of the cyclone was such that when he finished the ride he found that his pocket contained a plugged nickel[13] and a little pearl-handled penknife. His two giant six-shooters were compressed and transformed into a small water pistol and a popgun.

It is a strange circumstance that lesser men have monuments raised in their honor. Death Valley is Bill's monument. Sort of a monument in reverse. Sunk in his honor, you might say. Perhaps that is as it should be. After all, Bill was different. He made his own monument. He made it with his hips, as is evident from the great depth of the valley. That is the hard way.

Vocabulary Development: skeptics (skep′ tiks) *n.* people who frequently doubt and question matters generally accepted

---

12. **bowie** (bō′ ē) **knife** a strong, single-edged hunting knife named after James Bowie (1799–1836), a soldier who died fighting at the Alamo.
13. **plugged nickel** fake nickel.

Reader's Response: Did this story make you laugh? Why or why not?

_____

_____

Thinking About the Skill: How does **making predictions** help you stay involved in a story you are reading?

_____

_____

Reread the underlined sentences. What are some of the characteristics of the cyclone that rainstorms today still seem to have?

_____

_____

_____

_____

_____

_____

◆ Literary Analysis

What is Pecos Bill's monument? Why is it important in the **culture** of the Old West for a person to make his own monument?

_____

_____

_____

_____

_____

_____

_____

_____

_____

_____

Part 2

Selection Summaries With Alternative Reading Strategies

Part 2 contains summaries of all selections in *Prentice Hall Literature: Timeless Voices, Timeless Themes*. An alternative reading strategy follows each summary.

- Use the selection summaries in Part 2 to preview what you will read in *Prentice Hall Literature: Timeless Voices, Timeless Themes*.

- Read the selection in *Prentice Hall Literature: Timeless Voices, Timeless Themes*.

- Use the alternative reading strategies in Part 2 to guide your reading or to check your understanding of the selection.

"The Drummer Boy of Shiloh" by Ray Bradbury

Summary During the Civil War, an army sleeps. The next day, a few thousand young boys will fight the battle of Shiloh. Except for Joby, age fourteen, all soldiers have guns. Without even a shield to protect himself, Joby will carry only his drum. He almost decides not to go to battle, but a talk with the general changes his mind. Stopping beside Joby, the general tells him the soldiers are young and untrained. He explains that the drummer helps soldiers pull together as one army. The beat gives soldiers courage. If the drum beats slowly, the soldiers move slowly. A steady, fast beat moves them faster. Now knowing his job is important, Joby waits with his drum for morning.

Paraphrase Some of the sentences in this story are hard to understand because they seem to have so many ideas. One way to make them clear is to paraphrase, or restate, the main idea in the sentence.

DIRECTIONS: Choose three sentences from the story to paraphrase. Use this example as a guide.

Example:

A mile yet farther on, another army was strewn helter-skelter, turning slow, basting themselves with the thought of what they would do when the time came: a leap, a yell, a blind plunge their strategy, raw youth their protection and benediction.

Paraphrase: The men of both armies were worried about the coming battle and how they would behave.

Sentence 1 Original: _____
_____
_____

Sentence 1 Paraphrase: _____
_____
_____

Sentence 2 Original: _____
_____
_____

Sentence 2 Paraphrase: _____
_____
_____

Sentence 3 Original: _____
_____
_____

Sentence 3 Paraphrase: _____
_____
_____

"Charles" by Shirley Jackson

Summary After Laurie's first day of kindergarten, he is rude to his parents. He spills milk and uses bad language. Then he tells his parents the teacher spanked a classmate named Charles for being fresh. Each day, Laurie has a story about Charles. Charles hits, kicks, and uses bad language. He does not obey. When Charles must stay after school, Laurie stays with him and comes home late. After a few weeks, Laurie reports that Charles is behaving well and helping the teacher. When Laurie's mother goes to a parent-teacher meeting, she meets his teacher. The teacher says Laurie made trouble at first, but now he is a helper. Laurie's mother learns there is no Charles in the class.

Break Down Long Sentences To understand a long sentence, it is helpful to find the key idea and to note the details the writer uses to support that idea.

DIRECTIONS: Working with a partner, list the key ideas in long sentences in this story. Then find and list the supporting details for each key idea. The first sentence has been modeled for you. Do the next two sentences on this page. Then use a separate sheet of paper to continue the strategy with other long sentences you find in the story.

> The day my son Laurie started kindergarten he renounced corduroy overalls with bibs and began wearing blue jeans with a belt; I watched him go off the first morning with the older girl next door, seeing clearly that an era of my life was ended, my sweet-voiced nursery-school tot replaced by a long-trousered, swaggering character who forgot to stop at the corner and wave goodbye to me.

1. **Key Idea:** A boy acts grown-up on his first day of kindergarten.
   Supporting Details: my son Laurie started kindergarten; he began wearing blue jeans with a belt; ____
   sweet-voiced nursery-school tot replaced by a long-trousered, swaggering character; [he] forgot
   to … wave goodbye to me. ____

2. He came home the same way, the front door slamming open, his cap on the floor, and the voice suddenly became raucous shouting, "Isn't anybody here?"
   Key Idea: _____
   Supporting Details: _____
   _____

3. At lunch he spoke insolently to his father, spilled his baby sister's milk, and remarked that his teacher said we were not to take the name of the Lord in vain.
   Key Idea: _____
   Supporting Details: _____
   _____

from *I Know Why the Caged Bird Sings* by Maya Angelou

Summary Marguerite's favorite place is her grandmother's store in a black neighborhood of Stamps, Arkansas. Marguerite lives with her grandmother behind the store. After visiting her mother in St. Louis, she is depressed and withdrawn. Although she reads and writes well, she talks little. Marguerite is overjoyed when the well-bred Mrs. Flowers invites her home. Marguerite admires Mrs. Flowers for her fine manners, speech, and dress. Mrs. Flowers encourages Marguerite to talk as well as write. When Mrs. Flowers reads aloud, the lines take on magic and new meaning for Marguerite. Mrs. Flowers lends Marguerite books and tells her to read them aloud. She invites Marguerite back to recite poetry. Being liked by Mrs. Flowers gives Marguerite joy and new confidence.

Reread or Read Ahead It is easy to miss important details if you just read something straight through. Often, it is a good idea to reread or read ahead to keep details straight and to answer any questions you might have.

DIRECTIONS: Fill in the following chart as you read the excerpt from *I Know Why the Caged Bird Sings*. An example is provided.

Notes	Questions	Reread/Read Ahead Answers/Details
1. Narrator lives with grandmother in store	What kind of store?	General Merchandise: food staples, colored thread, corn, coal oil, light bulbs, shoestrings, hair dressing, balloons, flower seeds
2.		
3.		
4.		

"The Road Not Taken" by Robert Frost
"All But Blind" by Walter de la Mare
"The Choice" by Dorothy Parker

Summary As people come of age, they face choices. Yet, like the speakers in these three poems, people facing choices cannot know the future. In "The Road Not Taken," the speaker reaches a fork in the road. He chooses a road that fewer people have traveled, and the choice affects his life. In "All But Blind," the speaker describes nearly blind animals. He realizes someone who sees and knows more must think him blind. In "The Choice," the speaker is courted by two men. Rather than choose the rich man, she chooses the poor man whom she loves. She recognizes that hers was an emotional decision, rather than a sensible and practical decision.

Paraphrase Some of the phrases in these poems might be confusing. One way to understand unfamiliar poetic language is to restate it in everyday language. Work with two or three of your classmates, and discuss what the following lines from the poems mean. An example from each poem has been given. Choose three more examples, and explain what each one means.

Unfamiliar Language	Everyday Language
1. And both that morning equally lay / In leaves no step had trodden black. (from "The Road Not Taken")	1. Both roads were covered in leaves.
2. Never a thought for another had I. (from "The Choice")	2. I never thought about anyone else.
3. All but blind / In his chambered hole / Gropes for worms / The four-clawed Mole (from "All But Blind")	3. The mole looks for food in the darkness of his underground home.
4.	4.
5.	5.
6.	6.

Name _____ Date _____

from *E-Mail from Bill Gates* by John Seabrook

Summary The writer of this nonfiction piece includes actual E-mail messages to help convey to the reader how E-mail functions as a form of communication. First of all, E-mail messages have their own system of etiquette, with no time wasted on "Dear" and "Yours." More important, E-mail helps to break down barriers. It allows users to reach quickly other people who may be practically unreachable through other forms of communication, such as the telephone. This point is demonstrated by Bill Gates's quick responses to E-mail messages sent by the writer. Reading those thoughtfully written responses provides a sense of Bill Gates as a real person. A unique relationship forms between the writer and Bill Gates via E-mail. The relationship is different, perhaps less spontaneous, from what it would be if the conversation were taking place in person.

Context Clues While you are reading, you may come across a word or phrase whose meaning you don't know. The context, or the words before and after the unfamiliar word, can provide clues to help you understand the meaning. Context clues may be in the same sentence in which the unfamiliar word appears or in sentences before or after the word.

DIRECTIONS: Read the sentences below from the selection. Use context clues to figure out the meaning of the words in bold type. Underline the context clues. Write the meaning of the bold-face words on the lines provided. The first one is done for you.

1. The best way to communicate with another person on the information highway is to ex-change **electronic mail:** <u>to write a message on a computer and send it through the tele-phone lines into someone else's computer.</u>

    electronic mail: messages sent by computer from one person to another

2. In the future, people will send each other sound and pictures, as well as text, and do it in real time, and **improved technology** will make it possible to have rich, human electronic messages, but at present E-mail is the closest thing we have to that.

    improved technology: _____

3. I am the only person who reads my E-mail so no one has to worry about embarrassing themselves or going around people when they send a message. Our E-mail is completely **secure.**

    secure: _____

4. Nor were there any fifth-grade-composition book standards like "It may have come to your attention that" and "Looking forward to hearing from you." **Social niceties** are not what Bill Gates is about.

    social niceties: _____

5. I worried that he might think I was being **"random"** (a big problem at Microsoft) because I jumped from topic to topic.

    random: _____

    _____

    _____

"Grandma Ling" by Amy Ling
"Old Man" by Ricardo Sánchez
"The Old Grandfather and His Little Grandson" by Leo Tolstoy

Summary Aging is viewed differently in each of these pieces. The speaker in the poem "Grandma Ling" looks upon her ancient grandmother as if seeing into both her own future and her past. The grandmother is an older mirror image of the speaker. In "Old Man," the speaker is talking about the grandfather. He describes the age showing on the old man's face as rich with memories rather than marred by lines. In the way the speaker talks about the grandfather's memories of his people, the reader learns a respect for history and for the wisdom that comes with age. In "The Old Grandfather and His Little Grandson," the aging grandparent is becoming a burden to his children and is treated cruelly. When the grandson reminds his parents that they too will be old someday, the parents once again treat the old man with dignity.

Relate to What You Know When you are reading, it is easier to understand what the characters are going through if you relate their experiences to your own. Your own life experiences and knowledge can help you get inside the characters' heads and can help you get more out of what you read.

Work with a partner. Take turns reading lines from each of the works aloud. Then choose your favorite work and select one of the situations described below. Describe to your partner an experience of your own that helped you understand the situation. You may use the lines provided to jot down notes about your experience.

"Grandma Ling" by Amy Ling

- Digging a hole to China as a child
- Traveling a great distance to meet a relative
- Communicating with a relative who doesn't speak English

"Old Man" by Ricardo Sánchez

- Feeling proud of an older relative
- Learning about family history
- Imagining life 100 years ago

"The Old Grandfather and His Little Grandson" by Leo Tolstoy

- Caring for an elderly family member
- Making a gift for a special friend or family member
- Showing kindness to those who need help

_____
_____
_____
_____

"Ring Out, Wild Bells" by Alfred, Lord Tennyson
"Poets to Come" by Walt Whitman
"Winter Moon" by Langston Hughes

Summary In "Ring Out, Wild Bells," the speaker addresses the bells on New Year's Eve. He urges them to ring out the old year to make room for a new and better year. Often, growth and talent do not appear until after coming of age. In these three poems, speakers write of the promise that is present before coming of age. In "Poets to Come," the speaker addresses great poets of the future who will show their talent when the time comes. In "Winter Moon," the speaker sees the new, thin moon which will soon be a full moon.

Read Poetry According to Punctuation Poetry makes more sense if you read it according to punctuation. You should stop at a period, colon, and semicolon; pause at a comma; and change your tone and stop at an exclamation point or question mark.

Listen to the audiocassette recordings of the poems as you follow along in your textbook. Listen carefully for the places where the reader pauses, stops, and/or changes tone. Then, with a partner, take turns reading the poems aloud. Practice pausing briefly at commas, dots, and dashes and longer at end marks. Don't stop at the end of lines if there is no punctuation. You may use the following chart to note the various places in the poems where you should pause.

Poems	Pausing Points
"Ring Out, Wild Bells"	
"Poets to Come"	
"Winter Moon"	

"Cub Pilot on the Mississippi" by Mark Twain

Summary With wit and candor, the author describes his experiences as a riverboat cub pilot serving under the tyrannical "fault-hunting" pilot, Brown. Twain, the well-mannered, well-spoken cub, suffers the indignities of Brown's treatment; no matter what the boy does, he earns an insult. But he cannot stand by while the malicious pilot mistreats his younger brother Henry. At this point, the cub pilot defends his brother, protecting him by hitting Brown and then hitting him some more. Although attacking a ship's pilot on duty is the "crime of crimes," the captain of the boat, who knows Brown's evil ways, sympathizes with the boy and excuses his behavior.

Ask Questions For a better understanding of what you read, ask questions about what you are reading. Question the character's motives and judgments. Keeping such questions in mind as you read, and purposely seeking out the answers to those questions, will increase your comprehension of a selection.

With a partner, take turns asking questions about the characters in "Cub Pilot on the Mississippi." Write each question and the answer you discover in the chart below. If you need more space for questions, use an additional sheet of paper. A sample question and answer have been done for you.

Question	Answer
1. Why does Twain tell us that he had met all kinds of people when he was an apprentice?	1. He is going to tell us about one of the meanest people he had ever met.
2.	
3.	
4.	
5.	
6.	

Name _____   Date _____

"The Secret" by Arthur C. Clarke

Summary In this science-fiction tale, Henry Cooper is a science reporter visiting the moon at the request of the United Nations Space Administration. When the moon's Medical Research Department proves uncooperative, a suspicious Cooper contacts Chandra Coomaraswamy, Inspector General of the moon's Police Department, who promises to investigate. Two weeks later, Chandra takes Cooper to a research laboratory that studies animals from Earth. A lab scientist, Dr. Hastings, shares a recent discovery: hamsters on the moon can survive ten years, even though they normally live only about two years on Earth. The moon's lack of gravity prolongs life, and humans there might live 200 years or more. Hastings worries about the reactions of people on Earth once they learn this. Cooper must decide how to break the news to them.

Ask Questions When you read a story, you can usually understand it better if you ask questions while you read. Your questions should focus on important characters and events in the story. They should usually ask *who, what, when, where, why,* and *how*. Once you ask a question, keep reading to see if you can figure out the answer.

Listen to the audiocassette recording of "The Secret". Stop the recording when you have a question about *who, what, when, where, why,* or *how*. Jot down the questions on this chart. Also write the answers when you figure them out. An example is done for you.

Question Word	Questions	Answers
Who	Who is Henry Cooper?	He is a journalist (science reporter).
What		
When		
Where		
Why		
How		

Part 2 **229**

"Harriet Tubman: Guide to Freedom" by Ann Petry

Summary Harriet Tubman, a former slave, was a brave and determined woman who repeatedly led runaway slaves to freedom in Canada. This is the story of one such trip, a dangerous month-long escape from Maryland to Canada in 1851. Harriet and the runaway slaves traveled by night and slept by day so that they would not be seen. The journey, entirely on foot, was cold and strenuous. The runaway slaves were dreadfully hungry and tired, and Tubman tried to keep up their morale. She urged them on, telling them of the joys of freedom and of the good people along the way who were sympathetic toward slaves and would provide food and shelter. When Tubman's party finally reached St. Catharines in what is now Ontario, Canada, they could begin their new lives in freedom.

Set a Purpose for Reading You will usually get more out of your reading if you set a purpose for reading beforehand. Then, as you read, keep that purpose in mind. To help you set a purpose for your reading, ask yourself the following questions.

- What do I already know about the topic?

- What do I want to know about the topic?

Fill out the first two columns in this chart before you read "Harriet Tubman: Guide to Freedom." Then fill out the third column as you read, or just after you finish reading.

Topic

Harriet Tubman

What I Know	What I Want to Know	What I Learned

"Columbus" by Joaquin Miller
"Western Wagons" by Stephen Vincent Benét
"The Other Pioneers" by Roberto Félix Salazar

Summary These poems celebrate the spirit of exploration. "Columbus" presents a conversation between a crew member and Christopher Columbus during his famous voyage. As the mate mentions each difficulty of the journey, Columbus bravely responds, "Sail on!" and eventually proves triumphant. In "Western Wagons," the speaker praises the rugged pioneers who left their Midwestern homes to ride west across America in search of gold and a better life. In "The Other Pioneers," the speaker pays tribute to the brave, hard-working Spanish pioneers who settled the territory of Texas long before other Europeans arrived.

Relate to What You Know Lots of subjects you read about are things you already know something about. You will understand your reading better if you **relate it to what you already know**. A good way to consider what you already know on a subject is to talk about it with a classmate. It will also be helpful to find out what your classmate already knows on the subject.

With a classmate, discuss what you already know about the subjects of these three poems: Christopher Columbus, the westward expansion of America's pioneers, and early Spanish settlers in what is now the United States. Jot down what you know on the chart below.

What We Know About Columbus	
What We Know About U.S. Westward Expansion	
What We Know About Early Spanish Settlers in What Is Now the U.S.	

"Up the Slide" by Jack London

Summary Seventeen-year-old Clay Dilham and his partner, Swanson, are headed to the city of Dawson in Canada's Yukon territory. Clay leaves their camp site by dog sled to get a load of firewood, confident he'll return in half an hour. Swanson doubts that good firewood is so near. Traveling on the frozen river, Clay spots a tree on a nearby mountain cliff. But climbing the icy cliff proves perilous. Clay slips several times along the way. After felling the tree, he struggles to maneuver down the cliff, but slips many more times. Freezing, Clay struggles for hours before winding up in a gully, where he discovers a hidden grove of pine trees. Clay finally returns to Swanson. A week later, he and Swanson sell fifty cords of the pine wood in Dawson.

Predict Active readers think about what they read and understand it better. One way to be an active reader is to **predict**, or make reasonable guesses, about what will happen in a story.

Read the first ten paragraphs of "Up the Slide." Then fill in this question sheet to help you make predictions about the rest of the story.

1. What is the main character like? _____

2. What usually happens to people like him? _____
   _____

3. What do other characters think will happen to him? _____
   _____

4. What is the setting like? _____

5. What usually happens in settings of this kind? _____
   _____

6. How would you describe the story events so far? _____

7. What themes, or general messages about life, do you think the author is trying to convey?
   _____

8. What future events would help convey those themes? _____
   _____

9. Do any comments by the narrator hint at what will happen? If so, what do they say?
   _____
   _____

10. Reread the information about Jack London in your textbook. Does anything about his life or other works give clues about what will happen in this story? If so, what are the clues?
    _____
    _____

"Thank You, M'am" by Langston Hughes

Summary In this moving story, a caring woman teaches a teenage boy a lesson he is never likely to forget. About eleven o'clock one night on the street, a boy tries to snatch the purse of a large woman. When he trips, the woman grabs him and scolds him. Annoyed by his dirty face, she drags him to her home to clean up. The boy says he wanted money for a pair of blue suede shoes. When he says there's no one at his home, the woman makes dinner for the two of them. Not wishing to betray the woman's trust, the boy doesn't run away when the opportunity arises. After eating, the woman gives him ten dollars for shoes and warns him never to steal again. The boy, nearly speechless, says, "Thank you," and leaves.

Respond to Characters' Actions You'll get more out of any story you read if you respond to the characters' actions while you read. **Responding to the characters' actions** means getting involved in the story, deciding what you think of the things characters do and say. Here are some questions you might ask yourself about a particular character's action.

- Do I understand the action? If so, what might be the motives behind it?
- Do I approve of the action? Why or why not?
- How would I probably behave if I were in the same situation as the character?

Respond to each Character's Action from "Thank You, M'am" listed below, by answering the questions that follow.

Character's Action: Mrs. Jones prevents Roger from stealing her purse.

1. Do I approve of Mrs. Jones's action? Why or why not?

_____

2. How would I behave if I were in the same situation as Mrs. Jones?

_____

Character's Action: Mrs. Jones takes Roger home.

1. Do I approve of Mrs. Jones's action? Why or why not?

_____

2. How would I behave if I were in the same situation as Mrs. Jones?

_____

Character's Action: Mrs. Jones gives Roger ten dollars.

1. Do I approve of Mrs. Jones's action? Why or why not?

_____

2. How would I behave if I were in the same situation as Mrs. Jones?

_____

Name _____ Date _____

"Flowers for Algernon" by Daniel Keyes

Summary This story is told through a series of progress reports written by Charlie Gordon, a retarded factory worker. After undergoing psychological tests, Charlie is chosen for experimental brain surgery that doctors hope will increase his intelligence. His progress is monitored and compared with that of Algernon, a mouse. Over several months, Charlie's intelligence soars. Soon he can read classical literature and speak foreign languages. Charlie's co-workers, who once enjoyed making fun of him, now feel uncomfortable, and Charlie must quit his job. At a restaurant, Charlie gets angry when customers make fun of a retarded dishwasher. Sadly, Algernon's brain eventually regresses, as does Charlie's. Charlie mourns the mouse's death, knowing he is likely doomed as well. He leaves home, but with the determination to get smart again.

Summarize When you **summarize**, you state in your own words the main ideas and details of a piece of writing. For example, you could summarize progress report 1 from "Flowers for Algernon" by saying "Charlie begins keeping a journal." Pausing to summarize portions of a story while you read will help you clarify events and remember them better.

On the following chart, summarize the listed progress reports and portions of progress reports from "Flowers for Algernon." The first one has been done for you as an example.

Progress Report	Summary
Progress Report 2	**Charlie is given a Rorschach test, but doesn't see any pictures in the inkblots. He thinks he has failed the test.**
Progress Report 4	
Progress Report 6	
Progress Report 8: March 28, March 29	
Progress Report 11: April 22	
Progress Report 12: April 30	
Progress Report 13: May 23, May 24, May 25, May 29	
Progress Report 13: June 5, June 10	
Progress Report 13: June 22, June 23, June 30	
Progress Report 13: July 27, July 28	

Name _____ Date _____

"Brown *vs.* Board of Education" by Walter Dean Myers

Summary In the 1950's a number of states required or allowed separate public schools for African American and white students. Those who supported this practice claimed that education would be "separate but equal." Those who objected said that education could not be truly equal if the races were separated. Brown *vs.* Board of Education of Topeka was a case in which the Supreme Court of the United States ruled racial segregation in public schools to be unconstitutional. In 1951, Oliver Brown, an African American railroad worker, and thirteen other families sued the Topeka, Kansas, board of education for not allowing their children to attend an all-white school near their homes. Thurgood Marshall, who later became the first African American justice of the Supreme Court, presented the legal argument for Brown. The court ruled unanimously that segregated schools deprive minorities of equal educational opportunities.

Make Inferences: A writer doesn't always state every idea he or she wants readers to know. Often, readers must "read between the lines," or make inferences, in order to discover important ideas. An **inference** is a reasonable conclusion that you draw from the details or clues an author provides. Read the following sentence from "Brown *vs.* Board of Education" about Thurgood Marshall's father:

When it was time for the Marshall boys to go to college, he was more than willing to make the sacrifices necessary to send them.

From the details presented in the sentence, you can infer, or figure out, that Thurgood Marshall's father believed that getting a good education was most important. Why can you infer that? You can do so because anyone who is willing to make sacrifices to send someone to college obviously values education.

Read each detail from "Brown *vs.* Board of Education" and the inference based on that detail. Then write the reason you can make such an inference from the given detail. The first item has been done for you.

1. Detail: "He [Thurgood Marshall] was graduated, first in his class, from Howard University Law School."

Inference: Thurgood Marshall was a very intelligent person who studied hard.

Why: To graduate first in the class, a student must be intelligent and hard working.

2. Detail: When psychologist Dr. Kenneth B. Clark presented white dolls and black dolls to black children, the children rejected the black dolls.

Inference: The black children felt inferior to white children.

Why: _____

3. Detail: After the Supreme Court decision in Brown *vs.* Board of Education, "the major struggle would be in the hearts and minds of people."

Inference: Although the law now made segregation illegal, the law would mean little unless the American people believed that segregation was wrong.

Why: _____

"A Retrieved Reformation" by O. Henry

Summary Safecracker Jimmy Valentine walks out of prison with a smile and no intention of changing his ways. He is soon back at his criminal craft, using special tools to open vaults others can't penetrate. One day, Jimmy travels to a small town, falls in love at first sight with the banker's daughter, and decides to reform. He assumes a new identity, becomes a successful shoe salesman, and is set to marry the banker's daughter when fate intervenes. The very day he plans to give his tools to an old pal, the niece of Jimmy's fiancée gets locked in the bank's vault. At the same time, a detective arrives in town to arrest Jimmy. Using his tools, Jimmy calls upon his safe-cracking skills, opens the vault, and saves the child. Seeing this heroic action, the detective changes his mind and doesn't arrest Jimmy.

Ask Questions: When you read a story, you can usually understand it better if you ask questions while you read. Your questions should focus on the story's important characters and events by asking *who, what, when, where, why,* and *how.* Once you ask a question, keep reading to see if you can figure out the answer.

Listen to the audiocassette recording of "A Retrieved Reformation." Stop the recording when you have a question about *who, what, when, where, why,* or *how.* Write down the questions on the chart below. Also write the answers when you figure them out. An example has been done for you.

Question Word	Questions	Answers
Who	Who is Jimmy Valentine?	He is a convicted safe-cracker just released from prison.
What		
When		
Where		
Why		
How		

Name _____ Date _____

"Emancipation" by Russell Freedman
"O Captain! My Captain!" by Walt Whitman

Summary These two selections demonstrate how history remembers President Abraham Lincoln in life and in death. In "Emancipation," historian Russell Freedman explains the struggles Lincoln faced in deciding to abolish slavery during the Civil War. Knowing he needed to take a dramatic stand on the issue of slavery, he crafted the Emancipation Proclamation. On New Year's Day in 1863, Lincoln signed the document that proclaimed freedom for all slaves, knowing he would be remembered for this act that changed the course of American history. Poet Walt Whitman captures the nation's mood upon Lincoln's death in "O Captain! My Captain!" In this tribute to Lincoln, the speaker of the poem laments the tragic and untimely death of a great president who led the nation through the Civil War.

Determine Cause and Effect: When you read about historical events, look for cause-and-effect relationships. Doing so will help you to understand better what you are reading. Remember the following definitions.

- A **cause** is an event, an action, or a situation that produces a result.

- An **effect** is the result produced by the event, action, or situation.

As you read the selection "Emancipation" or listen to the audiocassette recording of it, fill in the missing causes and effects in the chart below.

CAUSES		EFFECTS
Slavery practiced in most border states loyal to Union.	→	Some in border states sympathize with Confederacy.
	→	Many Republicans think Lincoln should end slavery.
Lincoln fears driving border states from the Union.	→	
Confederacy enjoys most of the early victories in the Civil War.	→	
	→	Lincoln waits for a Union victory before issuing the Emancipation Proclamation.
	→	Lincoln's proclamation ends slavery in the Confederacy but not the border states.
Many freed African-American slaves join the Union army.	→	

"Gentleman of Río en Medio" by Juan A. A. Sedillo
"Saving the Wetlands" by Barbara A. Lewis

Summary Land is central to these stories. In "The Gentleman of Río en Medio," Don Anselmo sells his property to Americans who become upset when the village children continue playing noisily in their orchard. Don Anselmo explains that the Americans bought the land, not the trees. He planted each tree for each child. It is that individual's decision to sell or not. "Saving the Wetlands" tells of a twelve-year-old boy named Andy who treasures the many plants and animals that live in the local wetlands. When he learns that a developer wants to build housing units there, Andy decides to protect the land and the wildlife. He researches information about wetlands and endangered species. He encourages neighbors to sign petitions, educating them about the important role the wetlands have. Andy then leads the fight against the developer. The boy proves his point, the developer's application is denied, and the endangered species and wetlands are protected.

Make Inferences: An **inference** is a reasonable conclusion that you draw from the details or clues an author provides. An active reader is always making inferences as he or she reads. Read this remark made by Don Anselmo:

"I am the oldest man in the village. Almost everyone there is my relative and all the children of Río en Medio are my sobrinos and nietos, my descendants. Every time a child has been born in Río en Medio since I took possession of that house from my mother, I have planted a tree for the child."

From these details you might infer, or figure out, that

- Don Anselmo is an important elder in his community.
- Don Anselmo has a deep respect for tradition and family.

For each detail below, make an inference about the characters, settings, events, or ideas of "Gentleman of Río en Medio." Write your inferences on the lines provided.

1. Detail: It takes months of negotiation to come to an understanding with Don Anselmo.

   Inference: _____

2. Detail: Don Anselmo's house is described as "small and wretched, but quaint."

   Inference: _____

3. Detail: Don Anselmo refuses the additional money, saying, "I have agreed to sell my house and land for twelve hundred dollars and that is the price."

   Inference: _____

4. Detail: When the purchasers complain that the children of the village are overrunning their property, Don Anselmo says, "I sold them my property because I knew they were good people, but I did not sell them the trees in the orchard."

   Inference: _____

5. Detail: The narrator, as agent for the purchasers, must buy each tree individually from Don Anselmo.

   Inference: _____

"Raymond's Run" by Toni Cade Bambara

Summary Street-smart Squeaky is the fastest kid in the neighborhood, with the possible exception of Gretchen. When she's not in school or training to race, Squeaky cares for Raymond, her "not quite right" older brother, and is very protective of him. But running is the most important thing in her life and what she does best. In a close race on May Day, Squeaky beats Gretchen. The girls smile at each other in a way that indicates a newly expressed respect for each other. This delights Squeaky, who has experienced very few instances of being treated like a person by other girls. And although winning this race is important to Squeaky, she actually takes more pleasure in noticing how well Raymond has run his own race off to the side. Squeaky sees a new, meaningful direction for herself—as Raymond's track coach. She also sees the possibility that Gretchen might want to help her.

Predict: One way to appreciate what you read is to **predict**, or make reasonable guesses, about what will happen in a story. You can make logical predictions by basing them on details from the story.

   Read the first four pages of "Raymond's Run." Then answer the following questions to help you make predictions about the rest of the story.

1. What is Squeaky's biggest talent?

   _____

2. Who else in Squeaky's family shares her talent?

   _____

3. What is Squeaky about to do?

   _____

4. Who is her greatest rival?

   _____

5. What is Squeaky's biggest family responsibility?

   _____

6. What is Raymond like?

   _____

7. Where is Raymond when the race is about to begin?

   _____

8. What does the title suggest about Raymond's future actions?

   _____

9. Based on all these details, what do you think is going to happen?

   _____

"Paul Revere's Ride" by Henry Wadsworth Longfellow

Summary In "Paul Revere's Ride," Longfellow looks back in history and writes of the solitary man who gallops courageously through the night to warn Boston villagers that the British soldiers are coming. Revere and a friend set up a signal system: His friend will watch for British ships from the bell tower of the Old North Church. If a ship is spotted, his friend will hang a lantern in the tower. Across the shore, Revere watches and waits. When the light appears in the tower, he leaps on his horse and rides through the countryside warning the patriots that they need to come and fight. Revere's early warning helps the colonists defeat the British in America's first battle for independence.

Interpret the Meaning: When you read a poem, you need to think about the ideas and feelings the poet is trying to convey. The poet usually does not state all those ideas and feelings directly. Instead, he or she often uses images to convey ideas and feelings. Here are some steps that can help you interpret the poet's meaning.

- Identify the images in the poem. Remember, an image is something that appeals to one or more of the five senses (sight, hearing, taste, smell, and touch).
- Try to picture the poem's images in your mind.
- Think about why the poet chose those images.
- Think about how those images relate to your own experience.
- Decide on the ideas and feelings the images are trying to convey.

As you read or listen to the audiocassette recording of the poem, use the lines below to jot down four images from the poem. Then follow the steps listed above to help you interpret the meaning of each image.

Title of Poem: _____

1. _____

   _____

2. _____

   _____

3. _____

   _____

4. _____

   _____

"Always to Remember: The Vision of Maya Ying Lin"
by Brent Ashabranner

Summary Yale University architecture student Maya Ying Lin won a national competition to design the Viet Nam Veterans Memorial in Washington, D.C. The winning design would be one that would soothe pain, display the names of all soldiers killed or missing in action in Viet Nam, and enhance the landscape. For Maya Lin, the competition began as a class assignment. Prior to creating her design, Maya Lin visited and studied the site of the proposed memorial—the area between the Lincoln Memorial and the Washington Monument. While there, she envisioned the kind of memorial that would be best. Maya Lin then entered the contest and hoped for the best. She soon received word that she had won. Her design was selected over entries by famous sculptors and artists. Today, Maya's vision of the Viet Nam Veterans Memorial is a reality.

Identify Important Ideas: Biographical works often contain many ideas and details. Some of them are very important; others are less important. To get the most from nonfiction reading, you need to identify the important ideas. Think about the subject of the selection and the details that matter most about the subject. For example, if the subject is a person, focus on the achievements or events that mattered most in his or her life.

Read the selection, or listen to the audiocassette recording of it. Then, to identify the important ideas of the selection, answer the following questions on the lines provided.

1. Who is the subject of the selection?

   _____

2. What was this person's main achievement in the selection?

   _____

   _____

3. When did this achievement take place?

   _____

4. Where did this achievement take place?

   _____

5. Why did this achievement take place?

   _____

   _____

6. How did this achievement or event affect others?

   _____

   _____

from "The People, Yes" by Carl Sandburg

Summary: This selection is excerpted from a 200-page free verse poem published in 1936 that affirmed Sandburg's faith in the common American people. This excerpt catalogs some of the exploits of characters such as Pecos Bill, Paul Bunyan, and John Henry in American tall tales.

Respond: When you **respond** to a poem, you react to it personally. Your response can include many aspects of a poem. For example, you might enjoy some of the images of the poem, like or dislike the poem as a whole, or agree or disagree with its message. It is important to remember that you respond by bringing your own experiences and memories to the poem you read. Your response might be formed by the following factors:

- Your understanding of different details in the poem
- Your opinions about the ideas expressed in the poem
- Your reactions to sounds and images in the poem
- Your ability to identify with people or situations described in the poem.

Your response to an entire poem can depend upon your responses to passages of that poem. Respond to each of the following passages from "The People, Yes," by answering each question. Write your answers on the lines provided.

1. Of pancakes so thin they had only one side

   Do I enjoy this kind of humorous exaggeration? Why or why not?

   _____

   _____

2. Of a mountain railroad curve where the engineer in his cab can touch the caboose and spit in the conductor's eye

   Do I believe that these words successfully present an image of a curvy mountain railroad? Why or why not?

   _____

   _____

3. They have yarns / Of a skyscraper so tall they had to put hinges / On the two top stories so to let the moon go by.

   What do these lines say about what "the people" think they can accomplish? Do I agree with this idea? Why or why not?

   _____

   _____

4. Of Paul Bunyan's big blue ox, Babe, measuring between the eyes forty-two ax-handles and a plug of Star tobacco exactly

   Can I enjoy this passage fully even if I don't know the story of Paul Bunyan? Why or why not?

   _____

   _____

Name _____ Date _____

from *Travels with Charley* by John Steinbeck

Summary Author John Steinbeck decides to leave his New York home and drive across the United States. As an American writer, he feels an obligation to observe the country and its people firsthand. He buys a special pick-up truck mounted with a small house. Steinbeck travels anonymously in order to interact with people as they really are, without their being affected by his celebrity. His only companion is his French poodle, Charley. In North Dakota, Steinbeck is frightened by the wind in a desolate area. He dislikes the Bad Lands, where he meets a stranger but has little to say to him. In the late afternoon, however, the hills lose their dreadful look and take on a beautiful glow. On a gorgeous night, as he prepares to sleep, Steinbeck reevaluates the Bad Lands as Good Lands.

Clarify Details: To **clarify** is to make something clear in your own mind. When you read a passage and don't completely understand it, it's important to take time to clarify the details. To do so, use the following steps:

- Stop and think about what the detail means.

- Reread the passage to see if a second reading makes the detail clearer.

- Read ahead to see if later information helps you understand the detail.

- Go outside the text, consulting a reference book or another person to help clarify the detail.

Follow the steps above as you read the first four paragraphs of the selection or listen to them on audiocassette tape. Then clarify details by answering these questions.

1. Why does Steinbeck compare New York, Paris, and London? What do they have in common?

   _____

   _____

2. What does Steinbeck mean by "peripatetic eyes and ears"?

   _____

   _____

3. How can he travel across America without signing hotel registers?

   _____

   _____

4. What is the butane that operates the refrigerator and lights?

   _____

   _____

5. How can you find out how to pronounce Rocinante?

   _____

   _____

"Choice: A Tribute to Dr. Martin Luther King, Jr." by Alice Walker
"The New Colossus" by Emma Lazarus
"Ellis Island" by Joseph Bruchac
"Achieving the American Dream" by Mario Cuomo

Summary These selections focus on American heritage and immigration. Alice Walker pays homage to Dr. Martin Luther King, Jr., who inspired her to allow no one to deprive her of her rights, as her ancestors had been deprived. "The New Colossus" depicts the Statue of Liberty as an inspirational light that welcomes desperate immigrants to America's shores. In "Ellis Island," the author, a product of two cultures—one Native American, one European—describes how his visit to the Statue of Liberty triggers two contrasting reactions: a fond memory of his grandparents' immigration from Europe to America, yet a bitter memory of Native Americans being invaded by outsiders. In "Achieving the American Dream," Mario Cuomo recalls how his Italian parents came to America with nothing but the desire to succeed, and how they finally achieved their goal through hard work.

Summarize: When you **summarize**, or make a summary, you state in your own words the main ideas and key details that a passage or selection contains. To do so, ask yourself these questions:

- What main point or points does this passage or selection make?
- What key details help make the main point or points?

   Read the poem "Ellis Island," or listen to the audiocassette tape of it. Then answer the questions on the lines provided.

1. What main points does the poem make?

   _____

   _____

   _____

2. What key details help make these main points?

   _____

   _____

   _____

3. Incorporate your answers to 1 and 2 into a one- or two-sentence summary of the poem.

   _____

   _____

   _____

"A Ribbon for Baldy" by Jesse Stuart
"The White Umbrella" by Gish Jen

Summary These stories relate touching experiences of children struggling to overcome embarrassment. In "A Ribbon for Baldy," a schoolboy whom classmates mock because of his poor, rural upbringing hopes to win their respect by creating an outstanding science project. With great effort, he plants and grows a twenty-three-mile row of corn that wraps around a hilltop called Little Baldy. The newspaper reports the boy's achievement, and after visiting his project, classmates stop making fun of him. In "The White Umbrella," two young Chinese sisters are concerned because their mother has taken a job, making her late for family duties. One sister happily accepts their piano teacher's beautiful umbrella as a gift. She tries to hide it when the mother picks the girls up, but after it contributes to a car accident, she throws her umbrella away.

Predict: One way to understand a story better is to **predict**, or make reasonable guesses about, what will happen before it happens.

Read the first ten paragraphs of "A Ribbon for Baldy" or listen to them on the audiocassette recording. Then, answer the following questions to help you make predictions about the rest of the story.

1. What are the narrator's character traits and motives?

   _____

   _____

2. What are some of the hardships of his life?

   _____

   _____

3. What are some of the important features of the setting?

   _____

   _____

4. What message or moral do you think the author may try to convey?

   _____

   _____

5. What activities or events would help convey that message or moral?

   _____

   _____

6. Do any comments by the narrator hint at what will happen? If so, what are the comments and what do they hint at?

   _____

   _____

7. Does the title hint at what will happen? If so, what hint does it give?

   _____

   _____

"Those Winter Sundays" by Robert Hayden
"Taught Me Purple" by Evelyn Tooley Hunt
"The City Is So Big" by Richard García

Summary These three poems focus on people and places seen from a special perspective. In "Those Winter Sundays," the speaker recalls how her father always arose early on cold mornings to make a fire to warm the house, although no one ever thanked him for this lonely task. In "Taught Me Purple," the speaker recalls how her mother toiled in poverty while trying to give her child a better life. The speaker sadly remembers that her mother "knew so much of duty, she could not teach me pride." In "The City Is So Big," the speaker observes images of the city that are awesome to him, such as bridges quaking with fear, machines eating houses, and people disappearing through closing elevator doors.

Respond: When you **respond** to a poem, you react to it personally. You do so by bringing your own experiences and memories to the poem you read. For example, you might like or dislike the poem, agree or disagree with its message. Your response might take the following into account:

- your understanding of different details in the poem
- your opinions about the ideas expressed in the poem
- your reactions to sounds and images in the poem
- your ability to identify with people or situations described in the poem

Choose one of the three poems in this grouping and indicate your response to it by answering the following questions. Write your answers on the lines provided.

Poem Title:_____

1. Which of the poem's details do I understand clearly?

_____

_____

_____

2. What are my opinions of the poem's main ideas?

_____

_____

_____

3. What reactions do I have to some of the poem's images and sounds?

_____

_____

_____

4. With which people or experiences in the poem, if any, do I identify?

_____

_____

_____

"Lights in the Night" by Annie Dillard

Summary Annie Dillard writes about a childhood experience she had while growing up in America in the 1950's. The experience teaches Annie about imagination and reason. Each night in Annie's bedroom, something luminous and scary appears, casting a pale glow as it travels across the darkened room. Just before it reaches Annie, it roars and sinks away. Only Annie sees it. Her younger sister sleeps innocently through the entire event each night. After many fearful nights, Annie finally figures out what this scary thing is. It's the light reflection from a passing car. The roaring noise she hears is the car's engine changing gears as it pulls away from a stop sign. Annie walks through her thought process, solving the mystery and learning about what her imagination does with the world of things that exist outside of her room.

Recognize the Author's Purpose An author's **purpose** is his or her reason for writing a work. For example, the purpose of an author who writes directions for preparing a roast beef dinner would be to teach or explain. Other common purposes for writing include the following ones: to describe, to tell a story, to persuade, and to entertain and amuse.

You can determine an author's purpose by paying attention to the details of what you are reading. Often, the details—such as specific instructions or humorous dialogue—are clues to an author's purpose. For example, if an author's purpose were to amuse, he or she might include comical incidents or humorous conversations.

One of the purposes of "Lights in the Night" is to explain that some things that seem strange and even frightening have logical explanations. After reading or listening to the audiocassette recording of "Lights in the Night," write, on the lines below, the details from the story that support the purpose. One detail has been written for you.

Purpose of "Lights in the Night": To Explain

Details Supporting the Purpose
The author was only five years old when she thought something scary came into her room.

_____

_____

_____

_____

_____

_____

_____

_____

_____

_____

"What Stumped the Blue Jays" by Mark Twain
"Why Leaves Turn Color in the Fall" by Diane Ackerman

Summary Both of these selections deal with the natural world. In "What Stumped the Blue-Jays," Jim Baker is a miner living in the days of the American frontier. He speaks to animals and interprets their language. Baker tells about a blue jay trying to fill with acorns an empty knothole in the roof of a house. The jay drops tons of acorns through the knothole but never hears them fall. Another bird wanders into the house, discovering that the hole opens into the entire house. All the jays laugh at this discovery, proving that jays have a sense of humor. "Why Leaves Turn Color in the Fall" describes the natural processes that change the color of leaves each autumn. The author explains how sunlight, temperature, nutrients, chlorophyll, and photosynthesis all play a part in determining what happens in the fall when the foliage is made up of bright reds, oranges, and yellows.

Recognize the Author's Purpose An **author's purpose** is his or her reason for writing a work. Six common purposes for writing are

- to describe
- to teach or explain
- to tell a story or recount events
- to persuade
- to entertain or amuse

You can determine an author's purpose by the details he or she includes in a written work. For example, if an author's purpose were to describe a wilderness area, he or she would include detailed information about the kinds of plants, animals, and terrain found in the area.

After reading or listening to the audiocassette recording of "What Stumped the Blue Jays" and "Why Leaves Turn Color in the Fall," decide which of the five purposes listed above was the author's main purpose in writing. Then fill in the chart below.

Selection Title	Main Purpose	Details That Support This Purpose

Name _____ Date _____

"Los New Yorks" by Victor Hernández Cruz
"Southbound on the Freeway" by May Swenson
"The Story-Teller" by Mark Van Doren

Summary These three poems illustrate how common objects can take on unusual characteristics if looked at from a different perspective. "Los New Yorks" shows how strange the city of New York might look through the eyes of someone of another culture. The city creates such an unsettling feeling that the speaker compares components of the city to things that are familiar, such as viewing " ...the tall skyscrapers / as merely huge palm trees with lights." These three poems illustrate how common objects can take on unusual characteristics if looked at from a different perspective. "Southbound on the Freeway" describes everyday traffic, streets, and cars from the viewpoint of an alien being from outer space. The cars become living creatures rather than objects. Headlights become eyes and streets become measuring tapes. In "The Story-Teller," the art of good storytelling tricks the imagination into thinking something is other than what it is. An inanimate object like wallpaper comes alive or maps suddenly develop mouths.

Understand the Author's Bias The **author's bias** is the slant or prospective he or she brings to a particular topic. For example, a poet who loves city life would write a very different poem about New York City than a poet who dislikes cities and prefers country life. When you read a poem or another work, try to determine the author's bias by considering the following three things:

- the details that the author presents about the topic
- the details that you may already know about the topic
- any information you may know about the author's background and interests.

   Read the three poems in this grouping, or listen to them on the audiocassette recording. Then, in the third column on the chart below, jot down what you consider to be the authors' biases about the topics listed in the second column.

Author	Topic	Bias
May Swenson	Automobile Travel	_____ _____ _____
Mark Van Doren	Storytelling	_____ _____ _____
Victor Hernández Cruz	New York City's Puerto Rican neighborhoods	_____ _____ _____

"The Adventure of the Speckled Band" by Sir Arthur Conan Doyle

Summary English detective Sherlock Holmes solves a mystery that proves deadly. Dr. Watson, friend and associate of the popular detective, tells the story. Miss Stoner, fearing for her life and upset over her twin's mysterious death, seeks help from Holmes. She relays the facts of her sister's death and her final words about a "speckled band." By surveying the dead sister's room, now used by Miss Stoner, and by examining her stepfather's chamber, too, Holmes pieces together a sinister murder plot. To prove it, he and Watson must stay alert in Miss Stoner's room overnight. The detective's keen skills of observation, coupled with his research on Miss Stoner's family history, help him to determine that "speckled band" refers to a deadly snake. In proving this, he prevents Miss Stoner's murder, but causes the death of the murderer.

Identify the Evidence When you read a mystery, you will usually enjoy it more if you follow the **evidence**, or clues, and try to solve the crime along with the detective. To do so, you need to use your powers of observation and logical reasoning to try to answer the following questions:

- **What** is the crime?
- **When** did it take place?
- **Where** did it take place?
- **Who** might the culprit be?
- **How** might the crime have been committed?
- **Why** might the crime have been committed?

Listen to the first half of the story on the audiocassette recording, pausing at the point where Holmes and Watson catch the train from Waterloo Station. When you pause, use the evidence up to that point to try to answer the six questions in the Evidence Chart below. Be sure to write your answers on the Chart. Include more than one guess whenever you think the evidence points to more than one possibility.

Evidence Chart					
What?					
When?					
Where?					
Who?					
How?					
Why?					

Name_____ Date_____

"A Glow in the Dark" by Gary Paulsen

"Mushrooms" by Sylvia Plath

"Southern Mansion" by Arna Bontemps

"The Bat" by Theodore Roethke

Summary These selections focus on their subjects in an unusual manner. In "A Glow in the Dark," the night-time glow of a strange light in the Alaskan wilderness frightens Gary Paulsen's sled dogs into an abrupt stop. Paulsen and the dogs creep forward and discover that the light emanates from a tree stump containing phosphorous. "Mushrooms" is about an edible fungus that takes on the qualities of an army. Because mushrooms grow with little or no notice until they are in abundance, they are able to quietly take over the world. The mansion described in "Southern Mansion" stands as a symbol for a way of life that has vanished. Silently decaying, the mansion is a reminder of slavery and the Civil War period in American history. "The Bat" presents one of nature's nocturnal creatures in a way that causes unease. By pointing out the bat's "human" characteristics, the poet changes perceptions of the creature.

Make Inferences An **inference** is a reasonable conclusion that you draw from the details an author provides. For example, consider this passage from the selection by Gary Paulsen:

> We had been running all morning and were tired; some of the dogs were young and could not sustain a long run. So we stopped in the middle of the afternoon when they seemed to want to rest.

From these details you might infer, or figure out, that

- the narrator is traveling with dogs, probably via dogsled.
- the narrator is considerate of the dogs' needs and feelings.

For each detail below from "A Glow in the Dark," make at least one inference and write it on the line provided.

1. Detail: It hadn't snowed yet so we had been running with a three-wheel cart, which meant we had to run on logging roads and open areas.

   Inference: _____

2. Detail: Without a lamp I could not tell when the rig was going to hit a rut or a puddle. ... Without the moon or even starlight I had no idea where the puddles were until they splashed me.

   Inference: _____

3. Detail: It was a form. Not human. A large, standing form glowing in the dark.

   Inference: _____

Name _____ Date _____

"The Tell-Tale Heart" by Edgar Allan Poe

Summary The murderer himself tells this gruesome story of how he kills an old man whose chilling glance disturbs him. First, the murderer practices carefully opening the door to the old man's room every night for a week. On the eighth night, he enters the room and hears the beating of the old man's heart. The killer leaps upon his victim and kills him. The murderer then dismembers the corpse and hides the pieces under the floor boards of the room. When police arrive because of a neighbor's complaint of a shriek in the night, the murderer confidently lets them in to search the premises. The officers remain on the scene where the murderer begins to hear the dead man's heartbeat. The sound increases and upsets the murderer so much that he confesses his crime.

Predict: One way to get the most from a story is to **predict**, or make reasonable guesses, about what will happen next and what will happen in the end.

Read the first nine paragraphs of "The Tell-Tale Heart." Then answer the questions to help you make predictions about the rest of the story.

1. How would you describe the main character?

_____

_____

2. What do you think he will do to the old man?

_____

_____

3. How would you describe the setting?

_____

_____

4. What might happen in a setting of this kind?

_____

_____

5. How would you describe the story events so far?

_____

_____

6. Do any comments by the narrator hint at what will happen? If so, what are the comments?

_____

_____

Name _____ Date _____

"Hamadi" by Naomi Shihab Nye
"The Day I Got Lost" by Isaac Bashevis Singer

Summary Accepting who you are is the message of both of these short stories. "Hamadi" tells a more complex tale of acceptance by using a teenage girl's friendship with an odd, old-world philosopher named Hamadi as a bridge between different cultures. Hamadi helps Susan to find balance in a place in which she doesn't always feel comfortable. Now in Texas, far away from Jerusalem and her grandmother, Susan is finding ways to accept her cultural differences while learning new customs. In his funny tale about an absent-minded professor, Isaac Bashevis Singer creates a character that speaks openly about his shortcomings. He is so absent-minded that he can't remember where he lives. Rather than depicting the professor as an embarrassment, the writer makes the professor more human and lovable because he is so accepting of himself.

Identify with the Characters: Identifying with characters can help you appreciate their stories and the themes or ideas about life that those stories convey. When you **identify** with a character, you imagine yourself in the character's situation and try to understand the character's actions and reactions. The more you have in common with a character, the more you can identify with him or her. To identify with a character, keep in mind the following points.

- Look for any similarities between the character's situation and your own.

- Consider how problems that the character faces might be similar to those that you have faced.

- Consider the character's values and interests and whether you share any of them.

- Focus on the character's emotional reactions, and recall times when you have experienced similar emotions.

Choose a character from either story, and try to identify with him or her by answering these questions on the lines provided.

1. How is the character's situation in life similar to your own?

   _____

   _____

2. In what ways, if any, are the character's problems similar to those that you have faced?

   _____

   _____

3. When have you felt joy, sorrow, and other emotions similar to those that the character experiences?

   _____

   _____

4. Which, if any, of the character's values and interests do you share?

   _____

   _____

"The Finish of Patsy Barnes" by Paul Laurence Dunbar
"Tears of Autumn" by Yoshiko Uchida

Summary Having belief in yourself and your purpose is the lesson learned from the African American boy Patsy—in "The Finish of Patsy Barnes"—and from the Japanese girl Hana—in "Tears of Autumn." Both travel great distances to find where they belong. For Patsy, the road is to maturity. Once an angry, fatherless child surrounded by strangers, he becomes a caring adolescent, placing his mother's needs first. The cause of the transformation is a horse—the very horse that killed his dad—and Patsy's determination to win. Hana's distance is measured in miles. She leaves her beloved Japan to marry a stranger in America. Hana chooses this path because she wants more than the woman's traditional role in Japanese society. Fear and doubt cloud her journey, and disappointment greets her arrival. Then Hana remembers how far she has come and why. She puts herself in the frame of mind to look forward, not back.

Ask Questions: While you read a story, you will usually understand it better if you **ask your-self questions** about it. Your questions should deal with important characters and events in the story. They should usually ask *who, what, when, where, why,* and *how.* Once you ask a question, keep reading to see if you can figure out the answer. If you can't, see if you can learn the answers by talking with your teacher or with other students, or by looking in a reference book such as a dictionary or an encyclopedia.

Listen to the audiocassette recording of either "The Finish of Patsy Barnes" or "Tears of Au-tumn." Stop the tape whenever you have a question about *who, what, when, where, why,* and *how.* Write your questions on the chart below. Also write the answers if you can find them. An example has been done for you.

Question Words	Questions	Answers
Who	Who is Patsy Barnes?	He is a Kentucky-born African American boy who loves horses.
What		
When		
Where		
Why		
How		

Name _____ Date _____

"The Medicine Bag" by Virginia Driving Hawk Sneve
"The Story-Teller" by Saki (H. H. Munro)

Summary These two selections, in very different ways, express how stories can offer valuable lessons. "The Medicine Bag" illustrates how stories passed down through generations can teach acceptance and understanding. Native American Grandpa Joe Iron Shell tells his great-grandson Martin the story of a Sioux warrior's vision quest and how the "Iron Shell" name came to be. As Martin listens to the story, he learns that even in modern society, away from the Indian reservation, there is a place in his life for cultural pride, celebration of heritage, and preservation of ritual. In "The Story-Teller," a stranger on a train weaves a colorful story that captivates three children and teaches their smug aunt a lesson. In this story, bad outsmarts good in the end, turning the aunt's sermons on proper behavior topsy-turvy.

Make Inferences: An **inference** is a reasonable conclusion that you draw from the evidence an author provides. What inferences would you make from this remark from "The Story-Teller"?

The smaller girl created a diversion by beginning to recite "On the Road to Mandalay." She only knew the first line, but she put her limited knowledge to the fullest possible use. She repeated the line over and over again in a dreamy but resolute and very audible voice: it seemed to the bachelor as though someone had had a bet with her that she could not repeat the line aloud two thousand times without stopping. Whoever it was who had made the wager was likely to lose his bet.

From these details you might infer, or figure out, that the girl's repetitious recital is really annoying, and the bachelor has a sense of humor.

For each detail below, make an inference about the characters or theme of "The Medicine Bag." Write your inferences on the lines provided.

1. Detail: The narrator brags about his Sioux grandfather but won't show the grandfather's picture.

   Inference: _____

2. Detail: Grandpa, believing he is near death, has come to give the narrator the medicine bag.

   Inference: _____

3. Detail: The narrator almost tells Grandpa that he does not want the medicine bag.

   Inference: _____

4. Detail: Grandpa wears full Sioux costume when he meets the narrator's friends, and he tells the narrator that the narrator need not wear the medicine bag in the city.

   Inference: _____

5. Detail: Two weeks after Grandpa goes to the hospital, the narrator stands alone on the prairie of the reservation and puts the sacred sage in his medicine bag.

   Inference: _____

"Animal Craftsmen" by Bruce Brooks

Summary The writer of this selection uses personal experience to remind readers about the keen craftsmanship abilities of animals. The author first comes across an example of these talents when, at about age five, he admires what turns out to be a wasp's nest in a barn. The nest is so intricately built that the author assumes it's made by humans and that, like some birdhouses, it is taken inside for the winter. Learning that the wasps themselves built the nest makes it even more awesome. As a result of this experience, the author contemplates about the many creatures that have the ability to craft delicate designs that withstand a variety of conditions. The reader learns to think about these living conditions not from a human viewpoint, but from an animal's point of reference. In doing so, the nests, webs, or tunnels the animals create become more wondrous.

Identify the Author's Main Points An author's **main points** are the most important ideas in a selection. Often, you can find one or more main points in practically every paragraph of a written work. To identify the author's main points, ask yourself, "What does the author want me to discover or think?" For example, read what author Bruce Brooks writes about his thoughts upon discovering, at about age five, an intricately fashioned wasp's nest:

> I assumed the designer was a human being: someone from the farm, someone wise and skilled in a craft that had so far escaped my curiosity.

If you ask yourself what the author wants you to conclude or think, you will probably decide that he wants you to realize that animals can make structures so incredibly complex and durable that they appear to be made by people.

Read "Animal Craftsmen," pausing after each paragraph to determine the one or more main points of that paragraph. Write those main points on the lines below.

"Animal Craftsmen" Main Points

_____

_____

_____

_____

_____

_____

_____

_____

_____

_____

_____

_____

_____

_____

Name _____ Date _____

from *One Writer's Beginnings* by Eudora Welty
"**Baseball**" by Lionel García

Summary These two autobiographies show how children use imagination to create their own world. In *One Writer's Beginnings,* writer Eudora Welty explains that a child's learning is made up of moments. She recalls one such moment when, as a child, she connected the rising moon with the setting sun and grew up believing the moon rises opposite the sun. When years later, in a story she wrote, she placed the moon in the wrong part of the sky, someone finally corrected her. In "Baseball," the writer recalls a version of baseball he and his childhood friends played. The children's baseball rules included some actual basics, such as having a pitcher and a batter. However, instead of running the bases, the batter ran to avoid being hit by a thrown ball. Often, the batter ran all the way into town. The writer's uncle marveled at the children's ignorance of baseball rules.

Understand the Author's Purpose An **author's purpose** is his or her reason for writing a work. Five common purposes for which authors write are to describe, to teach or explain, to recount events, to persuade, and to entertain. Often, different portions of a selection have different purposes, or writing has more than one purpose. For example, a writer may hope to entertain while teaching or explaining.

On the chart below, list examples from the two selections that you think have the purposes indicated in the left column. Try to include at least one example of each purpose.

Purposes	Examples
to describe	
to teach or explain	
to recount events	
to persuade	
to entertain	

"Hokusai: The Old Man Mad About Drawing" by Stephen Longstreet
"Not to Go With the Others" by John Hersey

Summary A desire to live a full life motivates the subjects of these biographies. In "Hokusai: The Old Man Mad About Drawing," the Japanese artist Katsushika Hokusai recharges himself by experimenting with new ways of drawing. He adopts a new name with each change of direction. Intending to live to be 110, he sets goals for the ages in his lifetime. In "Not to Go With the Others," Frantizek Zaremski is marked for certain death in a Nazi camp for Polish political prisoners. Zaremski finds a way to escape each attack on his life. When he is grazed by Nazi gunfire, he feigns death. When the Nazis set fire to the building he is in, he submerges himself in the building's water tank. When others are shot trying to escape, Zaremski hides inside a box in a storeroom. Then, when he hears voices speaking Polish, he knows it is safe to come out.

Identify the Author's Main Points An author's **main points** are the most important ideas in a selection. To identify the author's main points, ask yourself, "What does the author want me to discover or think?" For example, consider this paragraph about Hokusai:

He didn't reach a hundred and ten, but he nearly reached ninety. On the day of his death, in 1849, he was cheerfully at work on a new drawing.

If you ask yourself what the author wants you to conclude or think, you may decide that he makes this main point in the paragraph: Hokusai's achievements in art continued in old age.

As you listen to the audiocassette recording of "Not to Go With the Others," jot down the points you think the author is trying to make. When you are done, mentally review the points you list to come up with what you think are the two or three main points for the entire selection.

Points Author Makes:

_____

_____

_____

_____

_____

Main Points of Selection:

_____

_____

_____

_____

"Debbie" by James Herriot
"Forest Fire" by Anaïs Nin

Summary "Debbie" is a heartwarming essay about a dying cat. Debbie the cat visits Mrs. Ainsworth's home for short periods of time. On Christmas Day, a weak Debbie carries her kitten into Mrs. Ainsworth's home and then dies. Mrs. Ainsworth lovingly raises the kitten, which grows into a fine cat with a playful personality. "Forest Fire" describes a terrifying forest fire raging in the mountains near the community of Sierra Madre, California. As the fire advances, spires of smoke fill the air, and trees are turned into skeletons in one minute. Heavy rains then cause floods and mudslides in the area. As the author observes all that happens in nature, she reflects that nature is both peaceful and dangerous. She appreciates both aspects.

Set a Purpose for Reading When you read, it is often helpful to **set a purpose for reading,** or determine what you'd like to get out of a piece of writing. To get an idea of that purpose, try asking yourself questions that begin with *who, what, when, where, why,* and *how.*

Fill out the following diagram to help you set a purpose for reading "Forest Fire."

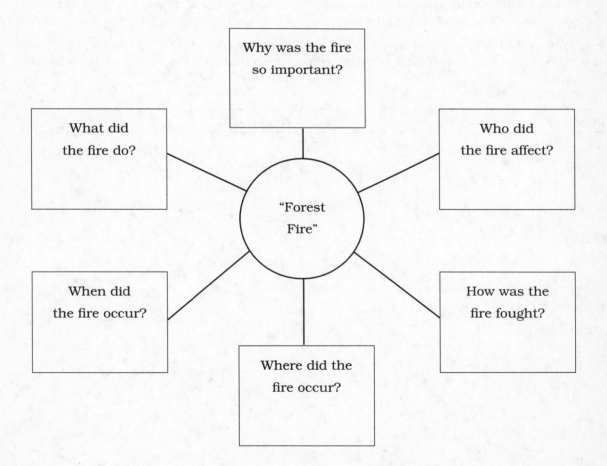

"The Trouble with Television" by Robert MacNeil
"The American Dream" by Martin Luther King, Jr.

Summary "The Trouble With Television" sharply criticizes television, calling it a medium that discourages concentration. Catering to viewers with short attention spans, television often presents incomplete bits of information as well as overly simple solutions to complex problems. In "The American Dream," Martin Luther King, Jr. urges Americans to help make the dream of equality of people of all races a reality. Quoting the Declaration of Independence, which proclaims that "all men are created equal," King states that "if America is to remain a first-class nation, she can no longer have second-class citizens." In addition, King argues that in today's world community, America must adopt a truly world perspective and help spread the American dream to other nations. America should aid countries whose citizens are plagued by poverty, disease, or starvation.

Identify Persuasive Techniques Persuasive techniques are the means by which writers or speakers try to convince you to think or act or in a certain way. One common persuasive technique is the use of emotional language. For example, in the following sentence from Martin Luther King's essay, words with positive associations, like *Founding Fathers, noble,* and *dream,* cast King's views on equality in a favorable light, while words with negative associations, like *schizophrenic, tragically,* and *against,* stress his opinion about the danger to America if equality is not achieved.

> Ever since the Founding Fathers of our nation dreamed this noble dream, America has been something of a schizophrenic personality, tragically divided against herself.

As you read King's essay, or listen to the audiocassette recording of it, use the chart below to jot down words with positive and negative associations that he uses to make his ideas more persuasive.

Positive	Negative

The Diary of Anne Frank, Act I by Frances Goodrich
and Albert Hackett

Summary: Mr. Frank returns to Amsterdam to bid good-by to Miep in the cramped attic above his old business. There, with the help of Miep and Mr. Kraler, he and seven other Jews had hidden for two years from the Nazis. As he holds his daughter's diary, her offstage voice takes us into the past. Fear and lack of privacy create strains for two families in hiding, the Franks and the Van Daans. The arrival of an eighth refugee, Mr. Dussel, adds more conflict. When Peter Van Daan falls with a crash while a thief is robbing the offices below, the families fear that their secret location may be discovered.

Summarize Whenever you read a lengthy literary work such as a play, you will usually find it helpful to summarize passages as you read. Summarizing will help you better understand and remember what you are reading. When you **summarize**, you state briefly in your own words the main ideas and details the passages contain. Your statements of the main ideas and details are called summaries. To make each summary, ask yourself these questions:

- What main point or points does this passage make?
- What key details help make the main point or points?

Read Scene 1 of Act 1 of *The Diary of Anne Frank,* or listen to the audiocassette recording of it. Then answer the following questions on the lines provided.

1. What main points does Scene 1 make?

_____

_____

_____

2. What key details help make these main points?

_____

_____

_____

3. Incorporate your answers to 1 and 2 in a statement that summarizes Scene 1.

_____

_____

_____

The Diary of Anne Frank, Act II by Frances Goodrich
and Albert Hackett

Summary: The Franks, the Van Daans and Mr. Dussel have been in hiding for a year and a half. They are buoyed by news of the long-awaited Allied invasion, but tension is high. Imaginative and optimistic, Anne has formed a friendship with Peter. But food is scarce, fear is ever-present, and tempers are short. One day, the group's fears come true—the thief who heard Peter's crash has exposed them. As Nazis come to take them away, Anne's final diary entry is heard, ending the flashback and returning the action to 1945. Mr. Frank again talks with Miep, revealing that all the others perished in Nazi death camps. The play ends as he holds Anne's diary and her voice says, "In spite of everything, I still believe that people are really good at heart."

Picturing When you read a play, you need to picture what the performance would be like. To help you envision the performance, read the **stage directions**, the instructions about staging that usually appear in italics, parentheses, or brackets. Pay special attention to details about the scenery, lighting, and costumes; to what characters say and how they say it; to information about the characters' physical appearance and movements; and to any sound effects.

Reread the stage directions at the beginning of scenes in *The Diary of Anne Frank*. Then, in the space below, make a quick drawing or diagram of what you picture as the main setting of the play.

"The Secret Heart" by Robert P. Tristram Coffin

Summary The speaker in "The Secret Heart" lovingly remembers how, when he was nearly asleep each night, his father would check on him. First, his father would strike a match in the dark room so that he could see his son's face. Then his father would curve his fingers around the match, enabling the boy to see a glow between his father's hands. By framing the burning match this way, the father's hands made a shape that suggested a heart, "the secret heart." It was just a fleeting glimpse, because the match burned out quickly, but it was enough of a glimpse for the child to see love "too tender for the day to trace" on his father's face. It is this vision of his loving father's face, glowing in the match light, that the speaker remembers best.

Use Your Senses To appreciate a poem completely, you need to **use your senses**. What does that mean? As you read the poem, concentrate on specific words and phrases that appeal to your senses of sight, hearing, taste, smell, and touch. Do not merely read a phrase such as "With his great hands full of fire." Close your eyes and concentrate on the image. Try to see the flame of the fire. Try to feel its heat and smell its aroma.

For each passage below, identify the sense or senses—sight, hearing, taste, smell, or touch—that the words appeal to. Some passages may appeal to more than one sense. The first item has been done for you.

Passage	Senses
1. In the stillest hour of night The boy awakened to a light.	hearing, sight
2. The man had struck a match to see If his son slept peacefully.	
3. He held his palms each side the spark His love had kindled in the dark.	
4. A heart that gave out such a glow No son awake could ever know.	
5. One instant, it lit all about, And then the secret heart went out.	
6. But it shone long enough for one To know that hands held up the sun.	

Name _____ Date _____

"The Wreck of the Hesperus" by Henry Wadsworth Longfellow
"The Centaur" by May Swenson

Summary These poems tell the stories of two very different kinds of rides. "The Wreck of the Hesperus" is about a ship that is destroyed by a fierce snow and sleet storm at sea. Early in the storm, the ship's skipper brags he can weather any gale. Having brought along his daughter for the voyage, he ties her to a mast on deck so she won't be washed overboard. The ferocious winds of the storm freeze the skipper to death, wash the crew overboard, and cause the ship to break up on a reef. A fisherman finds the daughter's frozen corpse, still tied to the mast. "The Centaur" is about a young girl who goes horseback riding on an imaginary horse. She becomes both horse and rider in her imagination. Referring to her two feet as hoofs, she gallops home as the wind rushes through her mane.

Read Lines According to Punctuation In a way, punctuation marks are like traffic signs. They tell you when to slow down, stop, and continue as you read. In a poem, it is not always obvious from the line structure where you should pause or stop. You do not necessarily stop at the end of each line. If you **read the lines according to punctuation**, you will know exactly how to read each passage. Stop at each period. Pause at a comma, colon, semicolon, or dash. Read with emphasis at an exclamation point.

Read each of the two poems. Find places where punctuation helps you understand how to read the passage. Record each example in its proper column in the chart. One example is provided.

Punctuation Signal	Passage
Stop at a period	_____
	_____
	_____
	_____
Pause at a comma, semicolon, or dash	_____
	_____
	_____
	_____
Read with emphasis at an exclamation point	"And tonight no moon we see!"
	_____
	_____
	_____
	_____
Ask a question at a question mark	_____
	_____
	_____
	_____

"Harlem Night Song" by Langston Hughes
"Blow, Blow, Thou Winter Wind" by William Shakespeare
"love is a place" by E. E. Cummings
"January" by John Updike

Summary Each of these poems expresses a connection between the physical world and human feelings. In "Harlem Night Song," being in love makes the speaker joyous, proclaiming the beauty of the night with its shining moon, blue night sky, and dewy stars. The speaker in "Blow, Blow, Thou Winter Wind" finds the biting cold wind less destructive than do many people. The cruelty of nature is less harsh than human cruelty. Bitter as the wind is, it is not as sharp as the sting of a "friend remembered not." In "love is a place," love is the central place through which everything else moves. Love can provide "brightness of peace" for all other smaller worlds. "January" depicts winter, when daylight between the morning and evening darkness is brief, below-freezing temperatures burst bottles, bare tree branches look like patterned lace, and the radiator "purrs all day."

Identify the Speaker The **speaker** in a poem is the person talking to the reader. In some poems, the speaker represents the poet. In other poems, the speaker is a character that the poet has imagined. Regardless, in all poems, you can learn about the speaker from the things that are said and by the way they are said. Each detail is a clue to the speaker's personality.

Read each statement below made by a speaker in one of the poems. Explain what the comment seems to tell you about the speaker's personality. One example has been done for you.

1. "Thou art not so unkind /As man's ingratitude." ("Blow, Blow, Thou Winter Wind")

    What it indicates about the speaker:

    The speaker is a bitter person who doesn't seem to think highly of his fellow human beings.

2. "Come, / Let us roam the night together / Singing." ("Harlem Night Song")

    What it indicates about the speaker:

    _____

    _____

3. "I love you." ("Harlem Night Song")

    What it indicates about the speaker:

    _____

    _____

4. "Most friendship is feigning, most loving mere folly." ("Blow, Blow, Thou Winter Wind")

    What it indicates about the speaker:

    _____

    _____

5. "... through this place of / love move / (with brightness of peace) / all places" ("love is a place")

    What it indicates about the speaker:

    _____

    _____

"Ode to Enchanted Light" by Pablo Neruda
Two Haiku by Bashō and Moritake
"She Dwelt Among the Untrodden Ways" by William Wordsworth
"Harriet Beecher Stowe" by Paul Laurence Dunbar
"John Brown's Body" by Stephen Vincent Benét
"400-Meter Free Style" by Maxine Kumin

Summary Each poem in this group is an example of a different poetic form. In "Ode to Enchanted Light," the speaker admires the light that falls in patterns on the branches and leaves of trees. Peaceful and happy, the speaker praises the rich beauty of the world. The haiku by Bashō and Moritake present images of nature. In Bashō's poem, the lightning flashes at night while a night-heron calls sharply. Moritake's haiku paints a delicate picture of a butterfly alighting on a branch. In the elegy "She Dwelt Among the Untrodden Ways" mourns the death of a woman who lived a simple life and was unknown to most people but was greatly missed by the poet. In Paul Dunbar's sonnet "Harriet Beecher Stowe," the speaker praises Stowe's courage in supporting the cause of freedom for African American slaves before the Civil War. In the passage from the epic "John Brown's Body," the speaker calls on the "American muse," or the national spirit, to inspire him. America is so vast and various, however, that the speaker finds it hard to sum up the American spirit in words. The shape of the concrete poem "400-Meter Free Style" suggest the laps of a swimmer's competing in a race.

Paraphrase Lines When you **paraphrase lines** of a poem, you restate passages in your own words. Paraphrasing helps you determine just how well you understand the ideas expressed in the original text. As you paraphrase, be careful not to change the meaning of the original lines. Merely state the meaning in your own words.

Read each passage below from each of the four poems. Restate the same idea in your own words on the lines provided.

Original Text   **Paraphrase**

1. The world is a glass overflowing with water.   _____

   (from "Ode to Enchanted Light")   _____

2. And slashing through the darkness, /   _____

   A night-heron's screech.   _____

   (from Haiku)   _____

3. But she is in her grave, and, oh   _____

   The difference to me!   _____

   (from "She Dwelt Among . . .")   _____

4. . . . At one stroke she gave   _____

   A race to freedom and herself to fame.   _____

   (from "Harriet Beecher Stowe")   _____

5. . . . the swimmer catapults and cracks/   _____

   six / feet away onto that perfect glass. . .   _____

   (from "400-Meter Free Style")   _____

"Silver" by Walter de la Mare
"Forgotten Language" by Shel Silverstein
"Drum Song" by Wendy Rose
"If I can stop one Heart from breaking" by Emily Dickinson

Summary These poems speak of the importance of all living things. The moon in "Silver" bathes everything — birds, mice, trees, and dogs—in its luminous light. By making even the tiniest creatures appear as if they are made of silver, the moon gives all of them great worth. "Forgotten Language" attributes human characteristics to flowers, insects, and weather by giving them the ability to speak a language that the poem's speaker once knew. "Drum Song" seems to beat a tribute to the typical rhythmic patterns of behavior in the lives of turtles, woodpeckers, snowhares, and people. For example, the woodpecker is cited for perching on a vertical branch of a tree. "If I can stop one Heart from breaking" speaks of the need to live a useful life. Doing something good—no matter how small, such as putting a bird back into its nest—makes life worthwhile.

Make Inferences When you **make inferences** in a poem, you reach conclusions—based on evidence in the poem—about things that the poet does not state directly. For example, in "Forgotten Language," the speaker never says that he is now an adult. However, you might make that inference because the speaker repeats several times that "Once" he did this and "Once" he did that. Those clues imply that he is now grown up and no longer does the things he once did as a child.

For each of the four poems, make an inference about the speaker or something he or she says. Explain the reasons that lead you to make each inference.

"Silver"

Inference   Reason

_____   _____

_____   _____

"Forgotten Language"

Inference   Reason

_____   _____

_____   _____

"Drum Song"

Inference   Reason

_____   _____

_____   _____

"If I can stop one Heart from breaking"

Inference   Reason

_____   _____

_____   _____

"New World" by N. Scott Momaday
"Lyric 17" by José Garcia Villa
"For My Sister Molly Who in the Fifties" by Alice Walker

Summary These poems use imagery to create vivid word pictures. "New World" presents a majestic, rugged landscape. The speaker leads the reader in the course of a day from open sky to forested mountains, grassy plains, and moonlit rivers. "Lyric 17" describes the attributes of a poem. A poem, for example, must be "musical as a sea-gull" and "slender as a bell. " The speaker in "For My Sister Molly Who in the Fifties" demonstrates Molly's warm personality by sharing her antics as well as her concern for other people. Molly would create a rooster from food on her plate, cook and clean, teach the children how to speak properly, and tell the children stories that would make them laugh.

Use Your Senses To appreciate poetry fully, you need to **use your senses**. As you read, think about specific words and phrases and how they appeal to your senses of sight, hearing, smell, taste, and touch. Don't merely read a phrase such as "the earth glitters with leaves." Close your eyes and concentrate on the words. Try to see the leaves glitter and hear them rustle.

For each passage below, identify the sense or senses—sight, hearing, smell, taste, or touch—that the words appeal to. The first item has been done for you.

Passage	Senses
1. Meadows / recede / through planes / of heat	sight, touch
2. Grasses / shimmer / and shine	
3. The gray / foxes / stiffen / in cold	
4. Rivers / follow / the moon	
5. Then musical as a sea-gull	
6. And hold secret a bird's flowering	
7. The luminance of dove and deer	
8. Once made a fairy rooster from / mashed potatoes	
9. Green onions were his tail	
10. Waking up the story buds / Like fruit	

"The Dark Hills" by Edwin Arlington Robinson
"Incident in a Rose Garden" by Donald Justice

Summary These two poems deal with death, but in different ways. In "The Dark Hills" the darkening day reminds the speaker of past wars and the bones of warriors buried in the ground. The coming dusk makes not only the hills, but also all wars, seem to come to an end. The setting in "Incident in a Rose Garden" is a surprising one for death—a rose garden. Here Death, in the form of a person, arrives dressed all in black with his white teeth shining. The gardener is frightened and runs to his master to say he is quitting. The master goes to the garden to confront Death. Death politely explains his presence in the garden to the very person he is seeking, the master himself.

Respond When poets communicate their work, they do not want you merely to read or listen. They also want you to respond. When you respond to a poem, you consider how it relates to your own life and experiences. You think about whether or not you agree with the poet's ideas. You ask yourself questions about the poem, and then attempt to answer those questions.

Complete the outline below with your responses to each poem. You may not have a response for every line in the outline.

I. "The Dark Hills"

   A. How it relates to my life:

   _____

   B. How I feel about the poet's ideas:

   _____

   C. Questions it inspires me to ask:

   _____

II. "Incident in a Rose Garden"

   A. How it relates to my life:

   _____

   B. How I feel about the poet's ideas:

   _____

   C. Questions it inspires me to ask:

   _____

"Chicoria" by José Griego y Maestas and Rudolfo A. Anaya
"Brer Possum's Dilemma" by Jackie Torrence
"Why the Waves Have Whitecaps" by Zora Neale Hurston
"Coyote Steals the Sun and Moon" retold by Richard Erdoes

Summary In each of these selections, a character tries to control a situation. In "Chicoria," a poor New Mexican poet overcomes the rudeness of not being invited to sit at a rich landowner's table for dinner by using his wit to teach a lesson in manners. In "Brer Possum's Dilemma," the snake outsmarts the gentle possum, and the possum gets bitten. In "Why the Waves Have Whitecaps," Mrs. Water, tired of Mrs. Wind boasting about her children, drowns the children. When Mrs. Wind calls for them, their feathers come to the top of the water, making whitecaps. In "Coyote Steals the Sun and Moon," the coyote and the eagle, seeking light for hunting, find the sun and the moon in boxes and steal them. When Coyote opens the box, the sun and the moon drift far away, bringing winter to the land.

Recognize the Storyteller's Purpose When you **recognize the storyteller's purpose**, you understand why the story was told. Some tales are told in order to entertain or amuse the audience. Others are told to inform or educate listeners. Still others are told to persuade the audience to accept an opinion, or to teach listeners a lesson about life or about how to behave. Many times, a storyteller may have more than one purpose for telling a single story.

As you read each of the four selections, identify the different purposes that each storyteller has for sharing the tale. Then list details from the tale that help you recognize each purpose. For item 5 below, add any additional purpose you discover.

1. Storyteller's purpose: <u>to entertain</u>

   Details that help me recognize the purpose:_____
   _____

2. Storyteller's purpose: <u>to teach</u>

   Details that help me recognize the purpose:_____
   _____

3. Storyteller's purpose: <u>to model behavior</u>

   Details that help me recognize the purpose:_____
   _____

4. Storyteller's purpose: <u>to explain</u>

   Details that help me recognize the purpose:_____

5. An additional storyteller's purpose that I found:_____
   _____

   Details that help me recognize the purpose:_____
   _____

"John Henry" by Traditional Song
"Paul Bunyan of the North Woods" by Carl Sandburg
"Pecos Bill: The Cyclone" by Harold Felton
"Davy Crockett's Dream" by Davy Crockett

Summary Each of these selections is a tall tale. "John Henry" tells the story of John Henry, the legendary "steel-driving man." While excavating the Chesapeake and Ohio Railroad's Big Ben Tunnel, John Henry wins a tunnel-drilling competition against a steam-driven drill, but dies as a result of the strain. "Paul Bunyan of the North Woods" introduces the giant lumberjack Paul Bunyan. Everything surrounding Paul is oversized, including his one-acre camp "cookstove." In "Pecos Bill: The Cyclone," the wild cowboy Pecos Bill rides a vicious cyclone until he tames it. In "Davy Crockett's Dream,"Davy Crockett tells about a dream he has in which a person named Oak Wing uses a long pole to ram him deeper into a log. Later, Crockett asks Oak Wing for an apology in Oak Wing's next dream.

Predict As you read a tall tale, you may be able to guess, or **predict**, things that will happen to the characters. To make a good prediction, pay close attention to story details. Think about the type of person each character is, and how that character has behaved in the past. Think about everything that has happened in the story so far. By doing so, you will better be able to predict what characters may do next or what may happen to them.

As you read each of the three tall tales listed below, fill in the blanks. Make a prediction about a future event. Tell why you think each event will occur. Then, record what actually happened.

1. "John Henry"

a. My prediction: _____

b. Why it may happen: _____

c. What actually happens: _____

2. "Paul Bunyan of the North Woods"

a. My prediction: _____

b. Why it may happen: _____

c. What actually happens: _____

3. "Pecos Bill: The Cyclone"

a. My prediction: _____

b. Why it may happen: _____

c. What actually happens: _____

(Acknowledgments continued from page ii)

Random House, Inc.
From *I Know Why the Caged Bird Sings* by Maya Angelou, copyright © 1969 and renewed 1997 by Maya Angelou. From *The Diary of Anne Frank* by Frances Goodrich and Albert Hackett, copyright © 1956 by Albert Hackett, Frances Goodrich Hackett and Otto Frank.

Russell & Volkening, Inc.
"Harriet Tubman: Guide to Freedom" from *Harriet Tubman: Conductor on the Underground Railroad* by Ann Petry. Copyright © 1955 by Ann Petry, renewed 1983 by Ann Petry.

Scribner, a division of Simon & Schuster, Inc.
"The Secret Heart" from *The Collected Poems of Robert P. Tristram Coffin* by Robert P. Tristram Coffin. Copyright © 1939 by Macmillan Publishing Company, copyright renewed © 1967 by Margaret Coffin Halvosa.

Simon & Schuster Books for Young Readers, an imprint of Simon & Schuster Children's Publishing Division
"A Glow in the Dark" from *Woodsong* by Gary Paulsen. Text copyright © 1990 Gary Paulsen.

Viking Penguin, Inc., a division of Penguin Putnam, Inc.
From *Travels With Charley* by John Steinbeck. Copyright © 1961, 1962 by The Curtis Publishing Co., © 1962 by John Steinbeck, renewed © 1990 by Elaine Steinbeck, Thom Steinbeck, and John Steinbeck IV.

The Estate of Yoshiko Uchida c/o The Bancroft Library
"Tears of Autumn" from *The Forbidden Stitch* by Yoshiko Uchida. Copyright © 1989 by Yoshiko Uchida.

Note: Every effort has been made to locate the copyright owner of material reprinted in this book. Omissions brought to our attention will be corrected in subsequent editions.